SILVER WHEEL

ELEN TOMPKINS is a Shamanic and
Reiki healer and teacher. Having read
English and Philosophy at university,
she spent a succession of deeply quiet
years living in the forests of Wales,
where she began to receive spiritual
teachings directly from the Elven Elders.
Elen has travelled extensively in order
to study and meet with shamans and
oracle healers. She is married, with
two young sons. Find out more
at www.elentompkins.com

'Elen is one of those rare beings that combine deep intuitive sensitivity with gentle and powerful wordcraft. What she has known from birth in her bones, she weaves into words with skill and ancient knowledge... This evocative, timely and visionary book has a deep ring of truth and an empowering message for today's world, which will resonate with readers on so many levels.'

FAITH NOLTON

Author of Gardens of the Soul,
founder of Sacred Hoop *magazine*

'An amazing piece of automatic writing in the tradition of Jane Roberts' Seth books... *Silver Wheel* takes followers further and deeper into the realms of self/Self to find what happens when we step out of our own shadows... An elegant, graceful, humane introduction to the worlds of the Deerskin Book... It seems to me that this is the *Celestine Prophecy* of the new millennium... it could be absolutely huge.'

MANDA SCOTT

Author of the Boudica series

'The light-filled pages of the Deerskin Book communicate to us from crystalline levels of Consciousness in poetic and lyrical layers of meaning. Allow these enchanting teachings to flow through you imparting their mystic beauty and gentle wisdom. They speak directly to the soul and bring forth a message of hope; that the time of the New Earth is upon us.'

LAUREN D'SILVA

Author of Light behind the Angels *and the*
Principal of Touchstones School of Crystal Therapy

ELEN TOMPKINS

SILVER WHEEL

HEAD
of ZEUS

First published in the UK in 2016 by Head of Zeus Ltd
This paperback edition first published in the UK in 2017
by Head of Zeus Ltd

9 7 5 3 1 2 4 6 8

A catalogue record for this book is
available from the British Library

ISBN (PB): 9781784972707
ISBN (E): 9781784972684

Typeset by e-type, Aintree

Printed and bound by CPI Group (UK) Ltd,
Croydon, CR0 4YY

Head of Zeus Ltd
Clerkenwell House
45-47 Clerkenwell Green
London EC1R 0HT

WWW.HEADOFZEUS.COM

To my parents

for unbelievable faith

INTRODUCTION

IN THE HEART of the forest, it appears. In the clearing before me, at the centre, lies a book. It looks very old, clad in a worn white deerskin. I touch the cover gently with my fingertips. There is something exquisitely beautiful about this book. I feel that it is something that has been much honoured and loved. Reverently, I open the cover. On page after page of pale bark that curls at the edges is inscribed the most beautiful and mysterious script. It looks as though it is written with light itself: the flowing lines shine golden and silver and sapphire. I know that I am looking at a timeless and radiant wisdom.

My conscious mind does not understand this language, yet it stirs something deep within. I suddenly know with my whole being that it is my task to transcribe this book, to translate it into the language of this world so that others might read it. I know that it contains a subtle, powerful message that has the potential to bring deep inner transformation and illumination, and that it is incredibly relevant to this moment in our evolution.

It is a long journey. This quest takes me nine years; nine years to find the faith and focus to fulfil this invisible task. Nine years to learn to listen to this intense beauty, and let it flow through my pen. Piece by piece, the translation is given to me, and this otherworldly vision emerges into the language of this world. It comes gradually into focus, and always I try to leave the vibration intact, so that the original beauty of the Deerskin Book can become available to many.

* * *

The Deerskin Book is a gift from the Shining Ones, who last walked among us many thousands of years ago. Theirs was the civilization of Lemuria, which existed upon Earth between 4,500,000 and 12,000 BC. It existed in the Pacific Ocean, on the continent of Mu. The Shining Ones are beautiful Star Souls who came to this planet as she became the Earth that we know. They brought their gifts of wisdom, beauty, inspiration, and the dimensional codes of other realities, so that Earth could blossom with the great harmonies of the Universe.

They are the Shining Ones, the Elven Elders, who stand at the shore in their gowns of copper, silver and gold: ethereal, powerful, radiant. They go back so much further than expected. They go beyond the medieval and historic fragments out of which we weave a pagan and mythopoetic past. It is more primordial, more radiant than this. It is these ancient Elven Ones who created many of the life forms of Earth. They created with the infinite star-fire of Love, according to cosmic and earthly rhythms. To them, Earth was an emerald temple, a precious place in the Universe. Their lands were lost in cataclysm, and their cycle came to an end at around 12,000 BC. The same happened with the successive star civilization of Atlantis. Many wise beings of Lemuria travelled to other lands, bringing remnants of their culture and wisdom with them. We see their presence in the cultures of the Japanese, Chinese, Tibetan, Druid, Native American, Sami, Siberian and Norse peoples. There are innumerable other fragments scattered throughout the indigenous cultures of the world.

Thus Arianrhod, the ancient star goddess, arrived to the

shores of the British Isles. Arianrhod is the Lemurian queen whose name means 'silver wheel'. It is she who is the keeper of these ancient star teachings; it is she who wove them into the etheric fabric of the land of Wales, to be discovered at this time.

The Shining Ones knew there would ensue an era when the Lemurian star wisdom was almost entirely forgotten. They knew there would be a long era of darkness. This occurred in accordance with the great cosmic cycles out of which Creation is woven. They retreated into another dimension. A veil came down between the worlds. In the last era, these ancient realities of beauty and peace have come to seem like a dream, a myth.

Yet something is changing. We are living in very special times. These long-dormant memories are awakening within us. The Elven Elders are returning to our world, and many are remembering their multidimensional selves and their own star origins and past lifetimes. This is the Golden Dawn of the New Earth, and it is of this that *Silver Wheel* speaks.

* * *

It is through a path of shamanic practice that my own Lemurian memories have surfaced, and through which the teachings of *Silver Wheel* have come. Through dancing, playing the drum and the harp, through hours of solitude in the forests of Wales, I began to hear this language of the Shining Ones. I followed the lunar trail of nature, the phases of the Moon and the starlight, through their transformational sequence, year after year. The Deerskin Book is built upon this trail of moons; the trail of moonlight, season after season, through the forest.

Gradually, through the land, the harp, the crystals, the

drum, this resonant field of memory grew stronger and stronger within me – like the layers of a symphony building and building, instrument upon instrument, until there is a fullness, a crescendo of sound all around. There was the restoration of an ancient, luminous mandala of great loveliness. It shimmered all around me, from season to season. I could hear and speak this ancient, timeless spirit language, and I felt the Shining Ones walking at my side, guiding my quest.

Then, in the summer of 2012, the Glyphs of the Silver Wheel were gifted in a vision at the beautiful and otherworldly waterfall of Pistyll Rhaeadr, in the Berwyn Mountains of Wales. They were the culmination of these years of shamanic practice, during which I was taught by the Shining Ones and by the Earth herself.

In these last few years, I have travelled to Hopi and Navaho ancestral lands in Arizona, New Mexico and Utah in the United States. I have travelled to the Himalayas, from Tibetan temple to Tibetan temple in Nepal, Ladakh and Sikkim: meeting with shamans and oracle healers who carry the ancestral traditions. I have found that this great story of Lemuria's lost star wisdom belongs to our planet, and that this great dream of beauty is emerging across continents. It is in dancing, drumming and walking in the mountains of these lands that I have received the final starlight and elemental teachings of the Silver Wheel.

Thus it is that I offer to you *Silver Wheel: The Lost Teachings of the Deerskin Book*. It contains a profound and beautiful wisdom that I aspire to live day by day. It exists beyond me, and shimmers all around me.

May it bless your life as it has blessed mine.

Prologue

IT IS TIME for the Temple of Arianrhod to descend again to Earth, for its doorways to open wide for those who might enter, and for the Dreamers to walk again in her silver spheres. In a shower of orchid petals and ancient starlight, the Indigo Portal opens...

I must tell you the ancient ways of my people. They belong to a world that is older than Atlantis, older than the ages of flood and ice, stone and bronze. They belong to a place and a time when the stars ARE the Earth; all is merged in a tempest of beginnings. In this time the Elder Worlds flourish. They are the roots and the leaves of the Tree of Life.

They are the oldest and the purest ways of Earth. You cannot find a truer path of Love upon this planet than to walk these old gold leaves of Light.

O, let us start at the beginning. Let us pass through the Amethyst Gates and sit with the Elven Council to hear the blue light of their prayers for Earth.

> *All shall be well*
> > *and All shall be well*
> > > *and All shall be well*

This is a civilisation that is the soul of Earth. It is her own light, her own dream.

Once upon a time, many thousands of years ago, upon this Earth, there existed a land known as Lemuria. The Elder Ones walked this land in sapphire robes, stars at their brow, with wings that shone and vanished like the moon. Their bodies altered with forest and river, merging with rock and swan and orchid, willow and bear. They came from other worlds. They came to interweave the beauty of their worlds with the worlds of Earth. Theirs were etheric temples whose doorways were woven between petal and leaf, crystal and bark. Amongst the trees and waterfalls, they spun their temples of emerald, gold, sapphire, violet, silver, rose and copper. One such was the Temple of Arianrhod, arising sapphire from the Earth, a domain of the Elders.

The Temple of Arianrhod existed deep in the forest. It was composed of a circle of white trees, such as no longer exist upon the earth. Into this Temple, the Elders brought thirteen amethyst crystals from another world. They placed these crystals amongst the roots of the thirteen trees.

The Elders sang to the amethysts in a whispering, faraway language of their affinity with the Earth, so that their love for this realm would permeate the crystals through all time. A silver fire began to flicker and twist within the crystals, its ethereal radiance shadowing forth Thirteen Glyphs.

The trees helped them, offering the clouds of their autumn leaf-fall. The leaves fell all around the crystals, echoing the passages of earth and sky. Many autumns and winters passed, building these affinities into the Glyphs. Into them amassed the sapphire peace of those days: the moonlight, sunlight, starlight and rainfall. The Glyphs developed, their forms gradually evolving into definition. Over aeons, the flowers offered the thousand petals of their own transience, successions of windfalls building the elemental memory banks as a frame for the starlight.

One winter, with the snowfall, a white deer stepped quietly into the clearing, and laid herself down in the snow amongst the white trees. In the dawn light, the Elders gathered around her and found that her body was stiff and frozen. She had died in the night. They prayed over her body until they came to understand that which she had gifted to the Sacred Grove. They knew then that the time of completion was near.

The Glyphs were sharply outlined within the crystals, summoned by the passage of Earth's progress, and by the prayer of the temple within the Universe. The last drop of rain and the final beam of moonlight had fallen upon the crystals, and the Glyphs were complete. The song of the Elders, of all that the Earth meant to them, had been sung into them.

That day, a violet dome hung like smoke over the Grove. It emanated from the crystals, and the trees were filled with an unearthly light. The trees were humming with a faraway song of longing for this world, for all that it might become. On their once-unmarked bark, an intricate lettering began to appear. It covered the trunks of the trees, a symbolic script that echoed the wordless chant. Finally, the trees grew quiet and, piece by piece, in long, thin rolls, a layer of bark began to peel itself away from each tree. The long strips unfurled their way to the ground and fell into the snow around the crystals. When the Elders smoothed them out, they saw that the bark had retained the gold and silver lettering. This inscription seemed to alter even as one gazed upon it. The Elders, with patient and sapphire grace, picked up the parchments as they fell. When the last roll of bark had been shed from the trees, the Elders knelt together in the centre of the Grove.

Here was laid the white deerskin that had been the gift of the deer. As the Elders knelt one by one over the deerskin, the bark unfurled itself into the leaves of singular pages, each one descending with its glowing script into place between the covers of the Deerskin Book. It was as though the white hide held a summoning spell for their wisdom. When the last page had flown into place, the Elders raised their sapphire hands in blessing over the book. The deerskin covers folded closed, encased in an ethereal radiance. In a circle around the book stood the Elders, tall and sombre. They lifted palms one to another and joined hands. That faraway song of an otherworldly love for this Earth resounded through the Temple of Arianrhod, and filled the forest beyond. Then a silence reigned.

At that moment, the Grove of Arianrhod vanished from this world. From that hour, so many thousands of years ago, to this, the temple and its Deerskin Book has not been witnessed upon this Earth. It has been stored in the seventh dimension of another world, until now, when once again it descends as a silvery gift into our skies.

First Teaching

This is the First Teaching of the Deerskin Book:

There are those who will become keystones of the New Earth. Their energy bodies will alter, they will shine, they will become the New Earth. They will receive the initiations that they need for this reconfiguration.

This choice is animated by exceptional love for the Earth.

Chapter 1

The White Tree is turning gold;
swan feathers descend,
cross over; a cloak
old daughter lost.

A moth holds ritual
in the forest of tears:
lost chalices gather,
of amethyst, amber, topaz.

Her white hands seek amber,
the ancestry of bears.
Too far, from afar; it is here.
An old love becomes older.

THIS BOOK IS written for those who are dedicated to the Earth. We have tended to her starlit blueprint for millennia, and dwelt in the sacred places where her light burns most brightly. Silver Wheel is a record of the incoming Dream of the New Earth. This dream is transforming the very structures of our reality, and we witness an old world falling away. We are attuned to this by lifetimes of extraordinary love for the Earth. It has this quality, of belonging simultaneously to a very ancient past, and to the future. It is familiar to us, as though it is a dream we have walked in before. It becomes difficult to distinguish what belongs to an ancient and exquisite past, and what belongs to a future that we pick up on our most delicate antennae. There seems to be a circle completing itself, a return to the beginning.

It is a blueprint burning with the starfire of an intelligence beyond the ordinary. It holds the lost temples of a sacred activity, of indigo and luminous pathways, a White Grove that holds the Star Council of the Universe. It is a sapphire and indigo realm, the incoming Dream of Earth. The flowers link us to our Light Bodies, and in our listening and our silence we are architects of sound.

This is a sapphire realm of returning memory, the blueprint of the New Earth. We can access this through the stars and by listening to the natural world. It is a starlit blueprint of the Earth that is descending to us in every breath, every silence.

You are the Elder into whose hands this book has fallen. You are the message. It is you who have been hidden for millennia, who now with your gifts of gentleness, sensitivity and courage, are stepping forth. Everywhere, at all times, the Silver Wheel points to you. It discovers you, it seeks you, it reflects the beautiful wisdom that you hold.

* * *

We become this, here on this Earth, at this time, and in so doing we step out of the ordinary continuum. We are beacons for its Light, we are architects of space and time, through sound and silence anchoring its dimensional possibilities in this world. This is a natural timing, a natural occurrence in our unfolding evolution. It is a commitment, and also a blessing. We are encoded with this reappearance of timelessness and peace. We dream with the Earth, this dream that she is dreaming. We travel with her along the shining paths of her evolution. We are designed for this sacred work, it comes to us as a natural talent, as something, somehow, we know how to do. We let go of all that we tried to learn, that was not native, that was not natural to us, and we take up this thread of our natural ability, of our ancient training and predisposition.

* * *

A long time ago, we knew how to be one with the Earth, how to be part of her environment. And we knew the inestimable blessings this bestowed upon us, the fields of being that opened up. We discovered the trails to the Infinite within every aspect of the Earth. Every orchid can teach us the beauty of the Universe and there is delight in this adventure, this discovery. But we have become separate from this experience, at least in our conscious minds. In truth, our awareness can never be unbound from the web of life.

The Deerskin Book encodes this experience, its different dimensions, with its symbols and its writing, indecipherable to this day and age, written in the gold and silver inks of the Sun and the Moon. We must learn to trust ourselves again. We must learn to become anchored once again in the awareness of the Divine Plan. This is not a return to the past, to a lost Elysium. It is the inauguration of something that has never been before, yet woven with the inspirations of Lemuria. Truly this is arrival of a golden age, an era long anticipated and prepared for. We cannot hurry the timing, the day or the hour of its arrival. And yet it is here, and there are paradigms of an ancient harmony flowering into existence, making themselves visible.

Everywhere there have been signs, always guiding us on, only the language has become ever more secret, ever more hidden. This is because, by its own inner necessity, the available paradigm conceals so much of who we are. Anything that does not mirror this paradigm has faded, has become invisible. The language of the Deerskin Book is not a secret language: it has actually been encoded in a form that would make it most deeply and universally available when the timing was right.

* * *

I have longed to speak these words, to let this dance of gold and silver inks unfold, to let the shining realm of Arianrhod be known. To unleash the starlit dimensions of the ancient Lemurian temple into the world once again. Yet it has taken its own time. The world unfolds in its own ineffable progression of beauty, as the starlight weaves its own tale toward fulfillment. Sometimes it seems the heart has taken a long time to come into the expression of that which it knows. Yet see how Nature encodes its own progressions of growth, the wild harmonies of the slow trees. Honour these trees, their patterns of bark and growth. They exist in an exquisite dance with levels of incomparable order and coherence. These are the teachings of the Grove, which shall follow.

The Earth herself offers to us these teachings. I can see her stepping silver through the veil ahead. She knows that we will follow her now, that the time has come.

Great it is to surrender to the Sun and to the Stars. Do not be daunted. Your wisdom is the blossoming key in the lock of this great awakening. You are the treasurer of this new beginning: or rather, this culmination. This book has waited to be found, and this is its transcription.

* * *

I have dreamt you and you have dreamt me. We are starlight falling in and out of one another, and it does not matter that there is so very little to us; in fact, the less, the better, that the music of the spheres may sound through us: we have only to let ourselves be loved by the currents of starlight that are our breath and blood. This may seem impossible. It may seem absurd. And perhaps it is. It is only this, that which unfolds, and perhaps it is all less serious than we have believed. How to be so immense and so insignificant all at once. When the dust of stars lands in your hands, and it is yours to build the lost temples, remember this. This lightness will be your blessing and your liberation, for how otherwise would we go on under the burden of responsibility, the weight of worlds depending upon our integrity, our perfection.

Be what you are, and be this now. There is no time for delay, no need for preparation. You have spent aeons becoming all that you are, and this is encoded deep within you. You are this surrendered dance of yourself: you are already unbound and magnificent. There are many ways of saying the same thing; there are many ways of approaching this heart that is Truth. That is why the Deer has laid trails all over the earth, leaving pathways this way and that way through the forests. You shall have your own epiphanies, when the Lost Dimensions shimmer through into your existence. And you shall know these moments for what they are. As you walk through the forest, at any moment the wild orchid might appear, and you shall hear its message. It is by our witnessing that the Temple unfolds. It shall appear just as the flower does, sudden and inexplicable as a dream, and there shall be no doubt. Here are the harmonies, here is the forest, here is the Grove in which the White Trees hold the Council of the Stars. And all this is yours.

* * *

The First Teaching of the Deerskin Book is that it is already here, it is already happening. Already you are the child of the Dawn, the one who brings the starlight prayer to Earth. Please do not deny this legacy. In truth, your surrender to this shall go ever deeper and deeper. You shall know and become the full dimension of the lost temples, you shall be this perfect blossoming of the Earth in her body of fire and water, earth and air. What would you rather do than this? What would you rather do than stand amongst the silver trees of the Council of the Stars, unfolding as a flower of wild angelic geometries, hearing the great councils of the Universe, whose song longs to be told through your blood, manifested through your hands?

There is the restoration of that which we have carried through aeons, and we are its architects. This is the voice of your own prayer echoing back to you, resounding through the Universe.

* * *

The Earth waits for us to see her own miraculous nature, how she is unbound by the limitations we have placed upon her. She is a necklace of lights, a crown of stars within the Universe. She does not end at ocean's edge. She does not fall invisible into rocks, into magma, into darkness. She is our own starlit prayer echoing through us. She is the manifestation of all that we have dreamt. And she dreams us also; she dreams our starlit dance upon her surface, the fall of our footprints. She guides us in the dance of the lost temples, in perfect timings of discovery, rediscovery. This is true even when we ourselves only fitfully hear the passing of her dream within us. Do not doubt how much she cares and feels; there is no inanimate universe separate from the heart. Nothing moves separate from the heart. From it every emerald and finite reality spirals out, as does every unfulfilled dream. Do not believe that your prayers go unheard. There is a wisdom in this Earth, and this is the prayer we have been making. These are the lifetimes of our endeavours, our elemental perfection spelling out its dance.

I am a timing and a voice. I am the boundary you are losing to yourself, to the future, to the true nature of reality.

Just keep on listening and you shall see how the ordinary and changeless fabric of consciousness yields to that which it longs for. It longs for the crystalline encodings of a new dawn, it longs for an end to suffering. It does not know in itself how to make this change, this transformation, and in fact such transformation seems at times like a distant prayer, a fantasy. How hopeless it can seem. Shall we not just struggle on, alone and unconvinced? And yet before and after, you are always something else. There is always already this difference within you, that which goes unaccounted for. I do not summon this; it always already exists, like the deep-blue sky beyond the clouds. And so this is an invocation, an acknowledgement of that which is always already there. There is the beyond of yourself, the vast distances of the Divine, that which spells heavenly patterns through your days. It needs no belief or religion, no interpretation, to acknowledge this. It cannot be taken away, nor can it be altered. And so I speak of this, and to this. This is the acknowledgement of the vast horizon within yourself, of that which is as yet goes unwritten.

* * *

And what if I left it at this, as the sporadic passing of wonder, of expansion, through the heart, as the appreciation of beauty, of goodness, of kindness, of wisdom? Yes, these things, truly, are enough, and we need never look beyond in order to lend meaning to our lives. We need never ask for more than this. So what of a passing voice and a Deerskin Book: what need have we of these things? None. There is no need, there is no metaphysical imperative guiding this pen. There is only that which arises, and offers itself; there is only the witness, and the one who receives. There are only the silver hooves of a Deer through the forests of Time; a star shining at her brow and a pathway in her wake through the forest. And there is a clearing, and a green mound, where the Shining Ones have placed their standing stones. And what of this? Shall we not let these things pass? Shall we not walk away from these tracks into the Infinite?

It is only that as I sit here, I already know that I shall walk that path through the forest, and that the orchid shall sing me her song, and that, somehow, this shall matter. The unbounded mind and the uncertain mind are always linked. I know that there is no end and no beginning to these things, only the shining silver sense that must play itself out through my hands. I cannot offer a limitation to my own boundlessness; I am already unbound and I do not know what will happen next. I am already attuned to a New Earth and the raindrops are carrying the stars from the sky.

* * *

Have you ever wondered why you do not give up? It is because you carry the heritage of angels, of a star dance. There is an unfinished song within you, and you are here to make it heard.

And so this arrives, the Deerskin Book, a gift from another age and another dimension, the remnant of another world and time. If you are reading this book, then you are a keystone in this archway of remembrance. You are one of the ones who cannot help, at this moment, but begin to remember another existence, another music. And in and out of the days it weaves its light, its presence, and shimmers through you: a tale longing to be told.

The Deerskin Book contains the Thirteen Glyphs of an ancient Lemurian temple, one that shone with love and proud light throughout the Universe. These glyphs allow our transformation into a higher vibrational octave, and they are our natural inheritance at this time. They call our bodies, our cells, our beings, into transmutation. They are sound-lights that cascade to us, that are caught as they fall, and felt as starlight entering the hands and the feet. They enable a sensitivity we have not known for many an age, an exquisite flowering of our own Light Bodies.

It cannot be resisted, nor can it be sought. It falls from the stars towards us, and evokes our journey to meet its Light. We become travellers. We become those who dance by different lights, and yet not disconnected. We must not mistake this as an 'alternative' reality'. The attunement is as natural as sunrise or nightfall. It distributes itself and settles in willing hearts. There is the feeling we have witnessed this before, of it being something we have known. It stirs gestures within us. It comes to us as a white deer, as a bear, or the sweeping arms of a cedar tree. It comes to us in the beauty of a drum, the sounding of a crystal bowl. We are urged, as if by stars in our hands, to take up a bell and to ring it. To place crystals in a certain configuration, a pattern. And we know that by so doing we have made our answering call to the stars, we have drawn closer, drawn them closer. Walking amongst the snowdrops, or in the soul lights and silence of ourselves, we feel these things.

There is a different order of existence to which we are being called. By this we begin to shine, to become apparent: we become a beacon ourselves of that which is sensed. Our affinity is making us shine, and we are becoming, in human form, the evocation of the Lost Temples. This acts as a profound inspiration that stirs other hearts to remembrance. We draw one another into the field of wonder, into the New Earth.

Do not distrust the desire, so intense as it becomes, to manifest this beauty. It is as though the starlight fires the blood into a passion of becoming, and a desire for radiance. Would you discourage the seed in its longing to become the flower, or the caterpillar the butterfly?

When the radiance falls to you, take up this starlight gift. Take up the responsibility and the abandonment. Take up the companionship of this inspiration.

We have hesitated long enough, hidden in far crystal caverns beneath the Earth, hiding this radiance of the Shining Ones. That time is past. There need no longer be a separation between the spiritual and the physical, with one held as more real than the other.

* * *

This First Teaching is the lesson of embodiment: the becoming of this, here and now. The Teachings and the Symbols are inspiration from the ancient angelic presences of Earth. They offer companionship, a supportive spiritual field, a surrounding cocoon for your attunement to the natural starlit gift of the Universe.

We are ascending and we are being drawn into the soul of Earth: it is all one. There are new frequencies; there is evolution and ascension. This evolution is so deeply programmed, so universally inspired, it seems to stem from everywhere and nowhere all at once. A template offers itself, with its miraculous familiarity. It is distant, lofty, pure and earthy all at once. All suffering fades away before it like a dream, like an evaporating cloud. And yet we sway back and forth, and sometimes the clouds close in around us once again, and it is the radiance that seems like a dream. Yet it cannot be forgotten, once glimpsed, and it becomes increasingly the pivot of our endeavour, the sphere toward which we aspire.

There might come a fear that it will be lost, the radiance will vanish, fade from our hands, stolen by a darkness that is more 'real'. But in truth, like the stars it reappears, and its influence is so diffuse, so universal, even when veiled. So there is nothing that needs to be done, yet there arises also a natural tending to this garden of stars. Even as it breathes love and wonder through our days, so we offer love and attention, cultivation, as a natural offering, as an inevitable response.

This is now the blue sky on the other side of every storm. The Lost Temple is ever more omnipresent, ever more vibrant within and all around us. We are transfiguring into the Star

Temple of the Earth, and the great winds of remembrance rush through us, and we feel the power of the sacred places singing through our feet, and somehow we know we have been here before, or perhaps we have never truly left.

Let the Stars imbue you with your natural radiance. Nature, the Earth, has spheres you have barely explored. These spheres carry an intention that goes beyond our individual awareness into the mysterious Heart of Love itself. In these realms we are more beautiful, more real, shining with an intensity that becomes evident to the naked eye, yet there is simultaneously less substantiality. There is a translucency; we shine with that which lies beyond. The Earth and ourselves: we hold one another's dreams.

* * *

I come to a shore of dark waters. Canoes drift to the shore, silent. Laid out within in a cocoon of swan feathers, one by one, are the Elders, adorned with the pattern and ornament of their inheritance. Enfolded in the long pinions of their swan-feather cloaks, they wear shining sapphire robes, each embroidered at the sleeves in a lost script. A lantern hangs at the prow of each boat, illuminating the archways of the forest. These are the Elders who hold the crystalline knowledge of the Lemurian temples. Theirs are the Old Ways, theirs is the Old Faith of a cosmic creativity. This is the lost lineage of the Swan Elders.

At the edge of the water, there is one canoe that stands empty. I enter, laying down amongst swan feathers. My cloak is laid out. I come to this, a diaspora of bone, a mandala of flight from here to there.

I settle into the cloak: cool as satin-silk, sheer, pale as ghost, and frame of bone. I have been lost to this for so long, and I ache with the effort of remembrance. A part of me longs for oblivion and to remain unfulfilled. There is sweetness in falling back to Earth, always unfinished: only half-listening to the call that comes. And yet I know that I too have made the call, so that this is a prayer, one of my own. As the feathers grow through my bones, I feel a simultaneous ache and strength. It grows into my back, an inheritance of flight.

I lie back in the canoe and close my eyes. The cloak encloses me in a sheath of feathers. There is a warmth, a muskiness to the cloak. I am enveloped in its hollow bones and quills, its cool insulation.

The canoes move off from the shore. I feel, suddenly, the sway of movement, the sound of the water rushing back from the keel. As if in flight formation, the barges leave the riverbank. I close my eyes and I can hear the ripple and hiss of their movement through the waters, unsteered. The canoes travel the river through the mountain forests, curving through sheer canyons; lamplit, they glide ever onward. I can feel the atmosphere alter; we are being drawn into the Elven Forest, the place where an ancient harmony has evolved and structures of ancient time are still held. Every leaf is spun in uninterrupted communion with all other leaves. Light and space here are fully evolved into their true potential: nature attaining to its white mandala within this realm. This forest has long been tended by the Shining Ones. There are mosses and lichens tapering from the branches, holding their specific harmonies with the stars. Even with my eyes closed, I can feel the alignments of this sphere.

A doorway has opened up that allows us into this uninterrupted place: this place where the choreography of elements is so precise, so evolved.

The sapphire path of the river pulls us further and further into the Elven Forest. I can feel the shimmering wings of the forest calling through my swan cloak. A thousand memories of spirit flight are stirred. Behind my eyelids, subtle radiances start to fall and rise: violet, gold, rose and emerald. This is one of the dwelling places of the Elders who dream the Earth. It is a meeting-place of all the emerald and subtle realms, where dimensions dance in and out of one another. I can feel the ethereal bridges and archways that are woven into the natural forest. Here is the architecture of a radiant culture, an invisible and ancient aspiration. Finally, the hulls of the seven canoes bump and rasp against the sand of a river bank, and we come to a halt.

There is the silence, and a whistling song somewhere deep below ordinary sound. We have entered a different sphere, somewhere where the silence rules more deeply. I sit up slowly in my cloak, opening my eyes, and find leaves like a thousand downy white swan feathers hanging all around us.

I lift up my arms to touch the leaves, there is the stiff movement of the feathers attached to my hands and I am brushing the myriad tendrils in the air all around. Pushing against the sides of the canoe, I sit up, and brushing aside the veil of branches in front of me I peer ahead to see where it is that I have landed.

There are the mossy undulations of a clearing, and at its centre is an immense tree. It towers upward, its trunk like a citadel spun of amethyst, a cosmic Temple with its portals opening to every dimension. Our barges are moored beneath the draping fringes of its outermost branches. I can feel that the rest of the forest stretches out in a protective mandala around this tree, surrounding the lavender and otherworldly fire of its endless canopy.

The Swan Elders stand up in their canoes. They stand there in their sapphire embroidered robes, and their cloaks have fallen away from them, into the canoes. Then, unexpected as the flash of a kingfisher, one by one they dive into the waters. As they touch the water, they metamorphose. They become swans.

One by one, with the great, fierce beating of their wings, they take off into the skies. They are soon lost from sight above the canopy of the forest, and I am left standing on the shore, gazing at the empty canoes and the pale, empty cloaks within.

A figure emerges from the forest beyond the tree. Her skin and her dress glow moon-pale, her dress transforming into a lamplight of gold leaves at the hem. She is tall and graceful. She is crossing the clearing towards me. At her feet, there are dozens of small crystal bowls placed beneath the tree, filled with water offerings. Somehow I know that it is she who has placed them there, and that she is the Guardian of the Tree.

She comes to the barges and leans across the bows, taking my hands in hers and pulling me out onto the shore. She takes me to the tree, and as I step under its canopy, I feel a wild shimmer run through my body.

The Dreaming Tree's canopy hangs like an orb over the forest floor. It encompasses a wide clearing at the river's edge. A stream emerges from between the roots of the Tree and flows out in curves amidst the rocks to meet with the river. Amidst the roots are the offering bowls, carved out of different crystals, and amongst them small spheres of sapphire are burning on the ground.

I sit down heavily amongst the roots of the tree. The Guardian walks back again to the barges, and lifts the empty cloaks to the shore one at a time. She carries them to the tree, and places them onto the ground at its base, until the six cloaks encircle the tree. They begin to dissolve into the ground, their forms fading and becoming smoke-like and dull, until they vanish altogether. The flight paths and memories of the Elders are being summoned back into the Dreaming Tree.

But my cloak, its heavy wingspan, remains attached to me: clinging to my arms, my shoulders, my back. It is cumbersome and awkward. I sit beneath the tree, the feathers stretching out beyond my fingertips, touching to the ground. It is stiff, with the brittle rustle of the feathers against the Earth. I wonder why my cloak has remained with me, why I have not flown with the other swans. I can feel the tree raining down its radiance all around me. The Guardian, having completed her task, comes over and settles herself, sitting cross-legged before me. There is a feather, white, in her hair. Her hair is moon pale and there is a glimmer of turquoise at her brow. She is the rune and the glyph of a greater harmony, a purpose beyond herself. She speaks to me, and her voice is the sound of the leaves of the tree, a murmuring of autumn leaves, through the yellow trail, to stars.

'You have need of your cloak, the cloak of the shaman, because you still have to cross over between worlds. The Grandmothers will make for you this gift, if you are prepared to take up the Sacred Task that is yours.

'You are to create a doorway between the human realm and the spirit realms. To create a doorway and to keep it open, so that others may step through into the realm of Vision.'

I ask her, my heart humming with her words, 'But why a swan-feather cloak?'

'The cloak is so that the people who need you can find you. As can the Spirits: it is about clarity of intention and dedication. It is a sign that you have given yourself and thus it provides protection and enables the path to unfold more smoothly. In this cloak, you are more easily found by those who need you, and yet less visible to those who do not.

'Within the ice and the stone and the waters of these lands, it is the Swan who has remembered the Old Alliance. The myriad hollow bones of its feathers are crystal maps of the Otherworld, laid out. The Swan has the power to bridge the realms, for which both strength and otherworldliness are required. You shall require this physical strength as well as fluidity and affinity with the Light Realms.'

These are the cloud-eyed offerings of autumn, harvest of the aeons, thousands of years of the lost tribe.

From the surrounding forest emerge the Grandmothers. There are four of them, their white hair pulled back from their faces, high collars of swan feathers around their necks. They come to me, and with deft fingers remove the cloak from my shoulders. There are tattooed markings on their faces, and there is something of the swan-fall of a beak about the contours of their faces. Their eyes are dark and inscrutable, the skin of their hands lined and rough, yet with a transparency. Their glance is fell and swift, their dresses dusk-grey. They kneel down in the moss, illumined by the canopy. They begin to work at the cloak, tugging and smoothing the feathers this way and that. The cloak begins to transform under their hands. It takes on tones of gold, violet, indigo, fawn and crimson. The swan feathers are altering, the fabric becoming supple beneath their fingers. It is becoming a Rainbow Cloak. One of them looks at me with her sombre, slanting eyes and says, 'This is the inner nature of the cloak.'

'It appears as a swan-feather cloak; this is its translation into this realm. You shall recognize it as this, as the swan-feather cloak of the shaman. Yet within, it is the Elven Mandala of the Sun, woven out of seven sacred fires. It is this that enables you to step between realms, that enables you to remain true to yourself and become a living expression of Wisdom. The Daughters of the Sun have woven this as a gift for you, but in truth it is your inheritance, and a natural emergence.'

The Grandmothers close in around me, I am enclosed in the sphere of their sombre and elemental intensity. It is as though the very air is altered, becoming slow and dense with their intention. Then they drape the cloak around my shoulders, and wrap it around my body, crossing it over my chest. I am enveloped in the cloak. Its soft weight pulls me onto the sapphire paths of the future. I go forwards, and I go back, into gold realms of memory and presence. I find an Earth that is hidden amongst the dreams that were lost. Into this Earth I am transfigured, feather by feather, and this is the gift of the Swan.

Finding the Lemurian Self

*Y*ou are walking in a forest filled with the brilliant green of spring's first leaves, and the ground is scattered with the white flowers of wood anemones. Towards you from among the trees comes a reindeer with a star shining at her brow. She approaches you, and stretches out her nose to sniff at your hand. You feel her warm breath upon your skin, and you stroke her fur that is coarse and silky all at once. Side by side, you set off into the forest, and she is walking just slightly ahead of you, guiding the way. You realize as you travel that this is no ordinary forest; it is the Immortal Forest of the Earth, and an inner light glows within the trees. There is a sense of timelessness, and it is as though the forest is hung with stars. The reindeer leads the way as you go deeper and deeper into this enchanted realm, and you are overwhelmed by a sense of peace and beauty. Deep within the forest, you come to a Grove of White Trees, and at the base of each, an amethyst crystal lies in the moss. The reindeer crosses the clearing, and bows her antlered head. Somehow, you understand what she is indicating. You go over to one of the trees and kneel beside it. You peer into the amethyst that lies embedded in the moss. Within its depths shimmers the First Glyph. You raise your hand to mirror the sweep of the Glyph in front of the tree, and you draw it into the forest air. As you draw the golden strokes of the First Glyph, you feel the symbol entering your heart and glowing golden throughout your whole being. You are transported...

You are in a grove of trees that glows violet in the depths of space amidst the stars. The trees are like phantoms, apparent and disappearing all at once. Curving its way into the grove is a bridge of a similar smoke-like transparency. This is the bridge that first carried you into the dimensions of Earth, that brought you to her successions of inter-dimensional, sacred groves. This is the bridge upon which your Original Self travelled over to begin its Lemurian lifetime upon Earth, bringing its gifts from other dimensions. You gaze into the deep space into which this bridge stretches, the far and distant stars beyond. One of these stars shines brighter and ever brighter, and becomes a luminous figure walking towards you. You are witnessing your original starlight self, who came to the lands of Lemuria. This exquisite starlight figure steps across the bridge and comes to you, and presses the palm of their hand to yours. You are joined in recognition. You look deeply into their eyes and you recognize them.

You feel a starlight glowing, brow to brow. You are merging, and becoming One. As you are joined with your Lemurian self, you feel a sapphire crystal descend into the crown of your skull. This is the sapphire that contains your original vow to

Earth. Listen carefully to hear the sapphire echoes of this vow, and retain this knowledge in your heart, in whatever form it comes to you. Let this original vow to Earth suffuse you.

The sapphire passes downward through your brow, throat and into your heart. It illuminates your whole form. The sapphire then comes shining into your hand, and as you find yourself separating from your Lemurian Self, they place it into a pouch hanging around your neck, so that it is wrapped in softest deerskin. You then look deeply into their eyes, and ask with your heart: 'What is the Sacred Dimension of time and space for which I am the architect?'

You are asking for a vision of the temple, which you seeded in Lemurian times, and of which you are the Keeper. The answer comes to you as words, colour, imagery, sound, or feeling. It leaves you with an impression of the Sacred Dimension you have brought to Earth throughout all of your lifetimes. It is the sacred gift you bring with you from other worlds, whose trace you have long ago left within the Earth.

When you have fully received this transmission, you bid farewell to your Lemurian Self, raising palm to palm. You allow your feelings of gratitude and connection to flood your heart, knowing that the sapphire light glowing in the pouch around your neck holds the restoration of this legacy. You watch as your Lemurian Self travels back over the bridge, returning to the place where this dimension joins with all others. Know that you can visit this Self at any time for remembrance of your Lemurian wisdom.

You find yourself transported back to the White Grove, with its amethyst crystals glowing at the base of the trees. You follow the reindeer back through the forest, returning to this world.

SECOND TEACHING

This is the Second Teaching of the Deerskin Book:

The New Earth is built of Starlight:
it is by awareness of this Starlight
that we transform.

Chapter 2

Lavender fires;
tree-formed.

A thousand
leaves of white.
Moonstone; hollow
lights, dancing.

Ambers of an old language,
a lost tribe.
Follow the path
of the Tree.

THE BLUEPRINT OF the New Earth is an ethereal medicine wheel brought here by the angelic Elders. It is moving gradually into our world, weaving itself into our ordinary reality. It is powerful and delicate, magnetized into existence by our own depth of spiritual intention and the hidden treasury of our wisdom. By the honouring of our spiritual vows, we ourselves become the miracle of a subtle and courageous perception.

It falls into the atmospheres of our world. Like a shawl of finely wrought stars, it falls around our shoulders, cloaking us with a New Dawn.

* * *

There is still much to be told, and this is essentially a tale of love: it is the Great Love Story. It is the story behind all stories, the one we yearn for.

And so when I tell you that this new reality we are entering is woven of starlight, your heart soars, even if your mind does not understand what it means. There is much to be said about this, and yet in that moment when the heart soars, everything I am saying is known, everything is recognized. We know what adventure is written within us, and we are so relieved to hear it is recognized and affirmed. We do not always feel worthy of this great adventure: we can feel overwhelmed by our own guilt and suffering. We can feel that for us, redemption is not possible. These glimpses of the stars shall always remain just that: glimpses. But let me tell you that this is not so, that it is possible to move into a different sphere of existence altogether, and that this is the hour of that transformation.

I have said much about our natural inheritance, about the birth of what is already always ours. This is the key and the heart of my message. I am not discussing separate realms of spirituality and religion: I am discussing this as our natural progression, our evolution and inheritance. It is what happens. We do not have to step outside ourselves to cultivate this; we do not have to change who we are. We do not have to become other than human.

And yet I tell you: the new reality is woven of starlight. And what does this mean? We understand by going backwards and understanding the ancient essence of the Earth. The Earth is formed by the collaboration of many galaxies, many stars, many solar systems that have all offered their own totemic wisdom and dimensions to her matrix. At her very core, she is a resonating sphere of interdimensional influences. This knowledge is contained in her crystals, in her underground waters and inner fires. Her interdimensional, intergalactic origin breathes its inspiration through ocean, mountain, tree and her many organic life forms. By our own physical vehicles, we are interconnected with this sphere of origination. As we undergo cellular clearing, we rediscover this in awareness. It is accessible by direct perception.

Yet for the last aeon, by the movement of cosmic forces, the Earth has been shuttered from ongoing inspiration and direct contact with the other-dimensional stars and galaxies that seeded her beginnings. Especially, the intergalactic starlights have not been accessible. Yet now, she moves back into synchronized alignment with these outermost spheres of her own creative essence. Her original dream can flourish once more, expanding its potentials. Her innermost crystals are humming with this renewed contact, and many an ancient dream is awoken.

* * *

This is happening within us also. It is unique in its influence for every one of us, as our innermost, hidden dreams are activated and become visible in the outer world. There is no longer a divide between our dreams and our actions. As we open ourselves to the descending starlight, it activates the hidden codes of light within. Our world is no longer woven out of a fabric that obscures the true nature of reality. We become starlight, we become the carriers of a radical beauty, a shining of interior distances that invoke the sense of the Infinite. The ever-receding expanse of the night sky becomes intrinsic: no longer out there and far away, but something we experience within ourselves, within our immediate world.

The stars are symbols in themselves: they represent our awareness of what lies beyond ourselves, of spheres beyond our own. They evoke wonder and inspire hope: hope in a purity and a vastness that encompasses, in great cycles of light, the smallness of our world. Yet the stars are not out there, our world is not small. It is full of the infinite expansion and transparency, the great clarities we see 'out there'. You shall be taught the old ways, the rituals and practices of attunement to the stars. They shall fall to you as inspiration in the night, in your dreams, in flashes of awareness. They shall travel through the pathways of your light-body, sounding their message that you intrinsically understand, that needs no interpretation.

These are the Lemurian communications: the communication of old gifts and tools that have been inaccessible in this last age. Their last appearance upon Earth as a natural inheritance of starlight messages has been preserved by people such as the Tibetans and Native Americans, by the tribal, indigenous peoples all over the world. They have maintained and preserved these forms in their spiritual teachings and practices. Yet the wholesale practice of natural illumination has not been available to human awareness. The fact that this is universal, without boundaries or rules, priests or training; the fact that our nature is naturally, intrinsically spiritual, and receptive to the messages of the stars; this is knowledge that has not been available to the conscious mind. And so we have felt that we needed training and indoctrination to preserve our awareness of our spiritual nature.

This last age has been an hour of survival, when the main teaching has been of compassion, of unconditional love for one another. For this needed to be maintained above all things. The heart is the centre and the jewel of the lost temples. Without it, we are starlight without compassion: a beauty cold and bright; pristine spiritual energy perhaps, but wandering far from the heart. Our hearts are what make this world of starlight blossom; they are what makes the sound-light prayers meaningful. But our hearts are prepared: we must trust ourselves and our capacity to love. We must trust this innocence within ourselves that is the seat of all wonder and curiosity, all non-judgement and the willingness to learn. This is us. This is already ours. This is our receptivity, this is our readiness. It is what enables us to be beacons, gathering places for others to remember who they are. Every evolving frequency must come through the portal of the heart: every remembrance is tested here for its goodness.

* * *

I am writing of starlight. I am writing of memories, of ways of being that shall stir in your blood. They already are, received as flashes of light and sound and image, cascading into your awareness and blessing your existence with a new dawn. Do not be afraid. Do not fear your own sanity. You are not delusional: and you carry the jewel of the heart, in which every teaching, every inspiration, can be tested. Does this do harm to others? you may ask yourself. If you are honest, you will see that it does not. These are the actions of a crazy innocence, which is yet not naivety, but remembrance of your own native wisdom. It is not naive to surrender to our wisdom. It is not naive to surrender to the messages of interconnectivity. Use the tools that have been given to you. Use the practices that arrive, as though gifted by angels. You cannot hesitate and persist in the trust of your distrust.

This only creates a pause, an attempt at control that limits your evolution and your experience. You do not know where these things will lead; this cannot be predetermined by the mind. We can, however, ask the heart: ask, what shall I learn from this? Your heart is your jewel, your sounding board for the pathway unfolding beneath your feet.

There is the exquisite sense of opening up to more than you ever thought you were, to wondrous realms that always seemed, if they appeared at all, so very 'out there' somewhere. Instead you discover that they are a part of yourself, that they are the very narrative and story of your life. They are yourself in the most intimate, daily sense. The communication never ceases, there is no boundary that prevents their touch. This new reality is woven of starlight. The stars are no longer distant companions, they are our own inner distance and potential, the vast reaches of intention and consciousness that we ourselves contain. And by this the Earth also is liberated from this spell of separation and materialism we have placed upon her. She can, with us, evolve into her own starlight dimension, become her own Infinite Self, become the crystal fields of her dreaming. She holds the imprint and memories of aeons: she remembers connection and disconnection. She remembers her own wild expansion in a time when her caretakers were attuned to this possibility.

* * *

These are the dreams of the Shining Ones for the Earth; these are the intentions of the rocks and the flowers and the trees. They hold nothing back, they do not withdraw from their great listening, that is also their growth and their evolution. This is the script of the Deerskin Book, written in the inks of the Moon and the Sun. We must not forget how long this has been held to be true. Our skepticism is a blink of the eye, a brief turning away. We are drawn into cycles of connection and understanding so much greater than our forgetting. It is the return to that which is so deeply familiar to us. The standing stones remind us of what has been, and the constellations of energy in places such as Avalon make it impossible for us to forget this Greater Dawn. It is confusing when we speak of past and future, of ancient things and of what is to come. We have no historical record for such an understanding of human consciousness. Only consciousness itself keeps the record, the indelible script of Truth. This ancientness and this future are in truth like a great and inclusive circle of consciousness, from which our modern awareness is a diminishment, a falling away.

There is no Lemurian era in the crude historic sense. History as we know it is linear, materialistic and anthropocentric. It is a creation of the mind and prone to changeableness and impermanence, vanishing under the historians' scrutiny the closer they look. I speak of a past that belongs to the soul, that belongs to the record of consciousness, the journey of that which we are. The Earth also contains this record; she has been our companion in this exploration, in these cycles of starlit metamorphosis.

* * *

We shall dream ourselves differently, we are already dreaming ourselves differently, and then it shall be as though we passed into another Universe, and this last emanation shall be as a myth, a fragrant memory, as unsubstantiated as those other dreams are to us now, yet dwelling in the records of our hearts and minds. Does the butterfly remember her life as the caterpillar? It is not easy for her even to conceive of it clearly with her conscious mind, so deeply has the very fabric of her being altered, so that she has quite a different makeup and cannot, within the remits of this, 'think the past'. Our thoughts are made out of our being, and when our being alters, it is hard even for us to 'think' that which we were: it has passed. It has had its season.

And such is the metamorphosis of which we are now a part. We begin to think differently, we begin to sense differently. New information is accessible to us: that which reflects our progression. We return to capacities that have already been available to us, that reflect a greater totality of experience.

* * *

The Earth has lived many ages that go unrecorded in the history of humanity. Layered within the Earth are memories of highly evolved galactic and intergalactic civilizations, among them Lemuria and Atlantis. These were founded by beings from the stars, who came to experience this shimmering interweaving of dimensions that we know as Earth. They are offering their wisdom at this time, they are the Lost Dimensions and Shining Ones that are being restored to consciousness. We ourselves are these beings, these lost dimensions, reborn in the present. We discover ourselves, and we discover the ancient companionship of the wise Shining Ones, who still hold an exceptional love for this planet. With these strands of inspiration, we are able to weave an alternative path of evolution that gives us a future of peace and beauty.

This is our Lemurian and Atlantean heritage, the

resumption of the starlit frequencies we have already known. We have resources in these realms, we have abilities that offer themselves to be explored. This is the next unfolding of the flower. We accept the gift of becoming who we are, and we do not fear our own perception, our own remembrance.

* * *

We are afraid that if we open up our perception, if we sit without distraction, that we will fall into a void, an emptiness. We are afraid of an abyss that might exist beyond the confines of our distractions. We do not realise that it is the angelic gift of our deepest happiness that is offering itself. It has been so long since we truly believed in happiness, since we remembered why we came to this Earth. Part of us wishes to pass the days simply as painlessly as possible. This avoidance of pain is not the same as true happiness. Happiness is a world of meaningfulness within and without us. It is an order that offers itself, a narrative and a sequence, a story inspired by the angels, inspired by our own Divine Purpose. It is not our nothingness we shall find beyond our distractions. It is our own Wisdom, waiting to fall to us, waiting to be heard. It is the sapphire and silver of vast communication systems; and the surrender to their inscription within our lives.

This brings me to artistic inspiration and its place in our lives. How else do we make the unseen visible? How else do we communicate these messages of starlight but through the work of our hands and hearts. We work through the medium in which we are gifted; we let it become the vehicle of this path of evolution. Artistic expression has the power to incarnate the future. This is the power and danger of art, of the powers to craft and to make. We are empowered beyond all our understanding: and this we fear and long for in equal measure, but it never quite leaves us alone. Part of consciousness longs to return into the past of its own powerlessness and forgetfulness. It wishes to perpetuate this past era when the veil descended, and we could only follow pre-existing inscriptions.

* * *

There are many prayers that have sounded through these ages, many dances of peace and enlightenment. And we have been implicated in all of this: we are the hands and the heart. You are the heart that has never abandoned itself, and the trace of all the ages is written through you: the great cycles are your breath and your blood. You are the one driving the wheel of all this cosmic awareness; a pivot and an attraction point for all its dazzling actuality and potential. I say to you: there are no divisions, there is only the fluidity with which we move, the grace with which we manifest this dance of our evolution. So nothing is to be regretted, nothing is to be disowned. Only wait for the petals that emerge from the soil of changes, wait to see what ravishing expression is your inheritance. It is held now as an inner pattern and potential, grown by starlight, by the Moon and by the Sun: our very own star that offers us this gold of transformation.

* * *

This is a meditation I recommend for every day: to nourish yourself with the inner light of the Rising Sun, to fire yourself with the morning radiance, welcomed as a benediction and a blessing upon yourself. We live in an age that calls itself dark, and we witness the storms of changes, the darkness of negativity and the eclipse of the soul. Yet truly, there is also a Great Dawn arising from within us, from within our Sun and Stars and Earth. We cannot wait to be told about these changes, but let their arising Light manifest through us. This is the meditation of the Sun, of the Rising Sun. We turn ourselves towards this resurrection, this inner knowledge of a beginning, a true vitality amidst all that which passes away. We do not need to live in an apocalyptic consciousness. We do not need to associate with all that departs and passes and the great winds that send it on its way. We acknowledge that these things occur; we do not deny their reality, but we know how to distinguish that which is dying from that which lives and breathes, that which is born. This is the gift of our star, the Sun. Through its radiance we are acclimatized to a Golden Dawn. By offering this to ourselves as a medicine each morning, by drinking it into our light bodies, we send a message to the Universe. We give the message that we are ready for this metamorphosis and that we are entering the starlit dimension of the Earth's new manifestation.

* * *

The very matrix of our physical cells is shifting. In this the crystals are excellent guides. The crystals have maintained their original inspiration. They have followed it without distraction, programmed with the Elder codes that are now awakening within us. Crystals form according to an orderly atomic arrangement and an exact chemical composition. It is a good example to us of how we might grow if we maintain our listening to starlight inspiration, and allow this evolvement within ourselves from moment to moment. We are stimulated to find our original codes of Light, to release everything that obscures these. We begin to grow in the manner of crystals, by sole guidance of our original template, discarding anything that does not serve this inner coherence and integrity. Once again, our other-dimensional codes become physical. Highly evolved qualities begin to manifest in a practical manner with greater and greater frequency.

Much that is worthwhile learning is encoded in the crystalline ground of Earth: it is into this that we may delve for the trackways of a deeply beautiful future. I am talking about a direct vibrational listening to the individual crystals rather than the assimilation of external knowledge 'about' them. To receive the starlight transmissions, we must make this shift from learning with our minds to learning through vibrational listening with our bodies and hearts. In this way, we receive direct rather than reported knowledge.

* * *

We wonder what we think of channelled writing, of the idea that there can be guidance from another dimension. We wonder about its value. Even say we accepted the existence of other realms, where is the benefit of effacing our own voice, heart and experience for those of another? That is to take a narrow view of our destiny and experience. We do not come from this experience only; there is so much that precedes this. A vast iceberg of consciousness underlies the tip of that which we identify as ourselves. To allow this wider communion is no effacement, it is no loss of the personal. We merely allow ourselves to give full expression to the miracle that we are, we allow the far realms of ourselves to speak. And perhaps these are the voices we most need. Perhaps we need these even as we need the crystals, as manifestations of a greater wholeness. Perhaps we need them even as we need the sunlight of our star.

This is the Deerskin Book: it is by this that I am uncovered, it is by this that my truth is told. It is made from sunlight and starlight, it is a transformation from one thing to another.

* * *

And so this is the Second Teaching: the world we are becoming is built of starlight. Its foundation blocks are a dream, an essence, an inhalation. It is built of this reception of Light that transforms the seed to flower.

It was my destiny to transcribe these things, and to follow the passage of the Deer through the forest, through all the ages, and bringing it here into your hands to be read. This is the Becoming of the Dream, the way that it weaves itself with unconscionable beauty despite all our attempts to thwart it. I have stood in my own way a thousand times yet it has not prevented what comes to pass. Still the crystals attain transparency. This is remorseless power, this is the elemental intensity of the Earth, Sun and Stars. I had to transcribe these things, and in the end I had to do it with no knowledge of them. And this is how it is for the flower that blossoms: she must become that which is written so close to her heart, that for her there are no directions, only a becoming, pulled along by the beauty of the Light transmission within her.

You may think I am joking when I say that I do not know what I am going to write, but this is how it is for the crystals and the flowers, for created things that trust in Great Mystery.

* * *

You who read this are the Dawn Keeper. You are my companion of the aeons, one who has travelled so far to preserve the ancient wisdom. I honour your dedication, I honour your awareness that makes it possible for these words to fall onto the page. For without you, they could not even be spoken. Without you, these ancient Lemurian practices, as encoded in the Teachings of the Deerskin Book, would never see the light of day.

* * *

I am walking in the forest, beside the dragon waters. The sound of drums is borne on the wind. I leave the river trail and branch off between the trees, following the sound. It becomes louder and louder until finally, deep in the forest, in a hollow sweep, a mound rises up before me. There are figures dancing all around it.

The mound is traced with white quartz, the outlines of the deer paths. Sitting under the trees are the drummers. Butterfly wings of crimson, amber, amethyst and emerald mark the faces of the drummers, and their hands fly white like wings, and I can feel that all the paths of Heaven and Earth lead out from this ground, evoked by their ceremony.

They dance around the mound, barefoot. The worn soles of their feet, etched with the branches of the deer paths, thump the ground as they dance. And under the trees, around the edges of the circle, sit the Elders who beat the butterfly drums. White skirts brush the ground.

Caught into the rhythm of the drums, I begin to dance. I follow the other dancers in their sweeping movements around the mound, circling its flanks. I am barefoot also, my soles darkened with earth. The dancers are spinning golden lines with their movements, connecting the deer paths that thread the forest and the far lands. By this ceremony, the old paths are connected, one with another, and made afire with the life of the Universe. As I dance, I too am drawing together these etheric threads. They interlink to form a tapering dome of golden topaz. It is an unfurling architecture of the topaz realm, of distance and presence. It gives boundaries to consciousness, a dome woven to cover the infinite sky.

I wait for a sign, announcing that the hour has come, and the vision is complete. We dance through the hazy beautiful butterfly corridors, topaz wanderings; all meanings dance, all possibilities hang with equal weight.

There is a doorway opening up into the mound. I find myself standing before the entrance, my feet bare on the cold grass. The other dancers have gathered around me, their white skirts brushing the ground, their bodies humming with the Song of the Deer Paths.

An Elder sits atop the mound. There are white spirals etched upon her brow. The blue, ethereal star of her gaze meets mine. She wears an embroidered shawl. I feel that she holds the innermost trail of all the deer paths, she is the immortal trail of moonstone, the one that curves its way into the hollow hill. It is by her permission that one enters the mound.

Any doubt I had about my own presence in this place has vanished. I feel a certainty that I am to go within the mound, it is for this that I followed the drums. The Elder rises on graceful feet and picking up a staff that lies at her side, she walks towards me. Her slanting, moonstone eyes stare into mine as she comes to stand before me. She touches my brow with the crystal at the tip of her staff.

'A dragon lies sleeping within this mound. She has slept for many a long age, but you shall need her guidance to open the Amethyst Gates. You have to follow her into her dreams. It is not easy to walk into the sleep of a dragon. She is still

bound to the Dragon Elders, those who rode with her in the Elven days of Lemuria. She is caught in the ancient bond. Nothing has come to replace this.'

A faint rain begins to fall. There is a rising mist, swirling into the hollow. I am sent off, and the white butterfly dancers wait, watching at the entrance to the mound. I pass out of the moonlit mists, into the darkness, the cold damp of the chamber. The Elder stands with her staff at the doorway, shedding the illumination of her moonstone presence.

'Take this,' she calls, and hands me her staff. 'Thump it to the ground, and it will shed light.' I take the staff of pale, weathered willow, and thump it firmly to the ground. The lower third of the staff lights up, and I see that it is crafted of yellow topaz, bound to the willow. At the top of the staff, a moonstone shaped like a closed bud gives off a wan and iridescent glow. Its weight is reassuring. I turn into the darkness, surrendering to the skyless corridors. I tap my way along the corridors of stone and packed earth. My progress reverberates through the enclosed space. I feel how the corridor curves along the outer rim of the mound, and then begins to spiral inward, the corridor becoming ever more tightly curved. I am enmeshed in the cold darkness, forward and behind, it closes around me. The darkness is pungent. I walk in the dim sphere of the staff's topaz glow, and there is the moonstone that lights nothing around it, yet offers a companionship and a reminder of the Elder who has awakened this ancient path. I know that despite the pressing chill, there is a permission to have entered this place, and that I am not unwelcome. I come to the final curve in the path, and then there is a sudden waft of cold in my face, as a wider chamber opens out around me, and I know that I have arrived at the central chamber of the mound. As I stand still for a long moment, the illumination from the topaz wanes and goes out. With only the moonstone for light, I pause in the blackness.

There is a sudden intensification of atmosphere. My breath comes shallow as my chest tightens, and I grip the staff, temporarily unbalanced. In the darkness, I can hear the breath of the sleeping dragon. I can feel the lodestone of her mind that hits me in a sudden wave. Even asleep, her consciousness hangs in the space, hypnotic and elemental. Swaying slightly on my feet, I thump the topaz staff to the ground, and hold forth its illumination, to discover where the body of the dragon lies. I can feel that somewhere at the edge of her consciousness, she is aware of my presence. The soft beam of topaz sweeps the space, and there is the gleaming coil of the dragon, just yards from where I stand. She is long, narrow and lithe. Her ears are folded back, her eyes closed. I crouch down, and go forward on my hands and knees towards her. I lay down the staff and reach out my hand to touch her scaled neck. My hand slides on her glassy, armoured surface, across the ridges of the scales.

'Tell me where you are, and I shall find you,' I whisper to her. Once again, the beam of topaz ebbs and fades, and I am left sitting with the dragon in the pitch darkness. I close my eyes and wait. I feel like a butterfly hovering at the edge of her vast mind. Suddenly, I am pulled as if into a current. I see the cavern through her dreaming eyes. It is no longer plain earth, its walls are carved of craggy amethyst. A haunting chant wells up, echoing through the acoustic of the cavern. It is sung by a high, fine voice. There is a golden haired figure. She is chanting in the Old Language, and I find that I understand her words: 'There will be a long age of darkness now, and the dimensions in which we have flown will remain unridden, unlit. It will be as if we never were. Sleep, dream, and some will remember the trace of your flight in the skies. The consciousness of dragons shall not fade altogether. They will come again, those who can harness your great power for the Golden Hope of this world. You know what this planet is, you know of the Elders, of the times that have been and that will come again. You shall witness the Golden Dawn, the arising of our Light once more.' There is an air of incredible sadness. As though something of great beauty is being stored away in the shadows, still mourning for the way it has been. The dragon floats in this exquisite and melancholy dream, hanging on to the beloved memory. I approach the Dragon Elder.

'It is time,' I find myself saying to her, my voice soft. 'It is time to open the Amethyst Gates, and for dragons once again to ride the skies.'

She turns and looks at me, her eyes fathomless. Her skin is pale, and she wears a gown of dark violet that sweeps to the cavern floor. I can see her pain, and her love for the dragon. They are bound, the two of them, as one heart.

'Yes,' she says, 'I see that it is time.' Her eyes turn once more upon the dragon, and she kneels down, resting her head against the scaled flank.

There is silence between us. I am holding the staff, standing awkwardly to one side. I can feel that her spirit is searching for a way to depart, a way to leave the dream. Her service is to the Dawn, to the awakening of all tomorrows. She is one of the Dragon Elders, one who has served the Earth for long aeons.

She calls to the dragon, in the chanted speech of the Old Language. 'You shall awaken, the time has come. I shall be here always, if you need to remember the ways of the

Dragon Elders.' She retreats to stand beside the amethyst wall. 'It is time to awaken.' I find myself reeling away from the dragon's dream, into the darkened cavern of stone and earth. I am crouched and stiff beside the sleeping dragon. Her breath is altering. Her shuttered eyes snap open. Her eyes gaze into mine. There is a moment of shock between us, as our spirits reel away from one another. Her eyes contain a layered brilliance, and she thrashes the long curve of her tail in a sudden reflex. I stagger backwards, using the staff to hold me up. As the base of the staff thuds to the ground, the topaz base lights up once more, and then the moonstone bud at the tip flares into a deep brilliance, emanating a note like a chanted sound that echoes throughout the cavern. The dragon fixes her attention upon the moonstone. She listens, engaged in a communion that goes beyond my senses. I can see the softening of the wild shock in her eyes. Her spirit is being called back into service, her remembrance of the ancient vows of the Dawn being transmitted through the moonstone. She turns her eyes upon me. She is wondering who I am, who I truly am. The moonstone note is filling the cavern, and we are bathed in its glow. With a sudden rush of awareness, I know why I am here, why I have come, and the ancient intention that I have shielded from my awareness, even as it infused my every movement.

'I am here to connect the old paths of the Moon with the Golden Dawn of the Sun. Will you fly, and show me the Amethyst Gates that connect the two?'

She knows the old passage, through the Amethyst Gates, the path that has not been tended in a long time, that has fallen into disrepair. It is a long time since anyone asked her to fly the Old Paths. Yet she was born for this. She shifts towards me, her claws scraping the cavern floor.

She speaks in a rumbling and archaic tone. 'It is possible. I can feel that it is possible once more. We shall not be hindered. Through you, the stars, the Moon, the Sun, are aligned to this moment in space and time. It is a portal of awakening. This is the essence of the Amethyst Gates. I am born to serve this possibility.'

'I also serve this, and no other.' She nods her great head, her brow coming level with mine. I move towards her, and touch her, brow to brow.

'It is time to fly.' I climb up onto her back. Her scales are slippery as glass. With the raising of her wings, there is suddenly no ground beneath us, no walls, no mound, no surrounding forest. We are aloft in the vast skies of the sunrise. We are blasted by icy wind, diving in a blue sky with the Moon hanging in the west, the Rising Sun in the east. I can feel the dragon weaving with Violet Pathways, and how the atmospheres alter every time we cross one. All at once, we are caught into a flare of violet, and the airs are full of pearlescent dragonflies, guiding us in a dramatic ascent.

The Violet Path with its sentinel dragonflies is arching into space: this pathway down through which travellers have arrived on beams of ancient sunlight. This is the grace of an old communion. The dragon flies the violet path with the great beats of her wings. Her body is bound for its destined path: all the myriad pathways, branching and infinite, lacing the skies. The sun casts her glow along the trail, drawing us into a radiance beyond. Before us are the Amethyst Gates. They stand on the threshold between the blue skies of Earth, and the expanse of space, the Sun and the Stars. A tapering, carved magnificence, they tower over us. The dragon lands at the foot of the gates, and I twist around to face the pale Moon hanging in the west. The moonstone bud once again begins to glow at the tip of the staff. I hold it forth, and witness it beginning to unfold, blossoming into a cradle of moonstone petals. I see it draw forth the light of the Moon, summoning that faint pearly presence across the vast distance of the skies, and absorbing its luminosity within. I feel the surge of all the ancient memories of moonlight, the old paths of magic that have held otherworldly hope through long ages of darkness. Then the moonstone flower folds closed once more, a bud throbbing with mystery. There is a grating sound, immense and booming, as the Amethyst Gates begin to swing open. We pass through the ancient gates.

The dragon ascends with the great beat of her wings, now tracking a golden pathway. I cling to the glassy ridges of her neck. We are entering the Halls of the Sun. There is a spare loveliness: that of an architecture that is ever dissolving into Light, yet bears its own diaphanous weight. On all sides, recessed in the fiery mists, are elliptical silver entrances. Beautiful symbols glow and vanish above them. These intricately carved portals mark the vanishings and arrivals of those from other stars.

I alight from the dragon's back, holding the moonstone staff in my hand. I find myself thumping the topaz base three times onto the golden floors, in a reverberating message of arrival. The angelic Sun Elders step forth out of the mists. Theirs is an other-dimensional beauty: tattooed points of light about their brows and slanting obsidian eyes. They wear golden robes that seem at one with their slender forms. I kneel before them, offering the moonstone staff in outstretched palms.

'I have brought the moonstone staff, and it holds the light of the Moon as she hangs in the west. We have travelled the dragonfly path through the Amethyst Gate, and awoken the old trail of the Sun. We wish to walk the pathways of

Natural Illumination once more, and we bring the moonstone staff, that holds our long and magical night.'

With sombre and rapt attention they listen to my words, before one of them replies:

'The Sun longs for the moonlit enchantments of the Earth. This is a gift for us also. Your journey upon the Earth is precious to us, and wildly beautiful in our eyes, even as the splendour of our Sun Realms must be wondrous to you. The arrival of the Moonstone Flower has long been prophesied amongst us. Will you let me take the staff?'

I nod mutely, and hold out the staff to this graceful Elder of the Sun. The moonstone is glowing softly, distinct in this sunlit realm. The Elder takes the staff in her hands, and with the touch of her radiant palms, the moonstone flares up into a deeper glow, and I can hear its mounting chant. It is a language of the moon and the forest. With an intent focus, the Sun Elder places her hand upon it, and pulls it free of its setting in the staff.

Slowly, the moonstone bud begins to open, as it did at the Amethyst Gates. From the splayed petals erupts a beam of moonlight, its song now ringing throughout the Sun Realms. The Sun Elders watch with steady attention.

There is a thundery stillness. Then, in the pause, a fusion begins. It feel as though the whole ethereal chamber shudders as it absorbs the moonlight radiance. The moonstone is shattering into the sunlight, releasing an ancient rainbow vision, the seven beams of earthly wisdom: crimson, copper, gold, emerald, turquoise, indigo and amethyst. Out of these the ancient forests are spun, out of these the mysteries of leaf and bark, water and wind. Out of these, the human heart has constructed its unique song, its precious prayer to the Universe.

Here, it becomes a tree. It shoots upward on a sapling

stem. Root, stem and branch, it unfurls into a tree that shines with the light of many worlds, a treasury of Earth wisdom ascended to the Sun. Golden flowers are forming at the tips of the branches; a gold whose depths shimmer with moony brilliance; hues of the Earth, in their ethereal form, are hints within.

'What is this tree?' I ask the Elders.

'The blossoms of this Tree contain the wisdom of Earth, Sun and Moon brought together. It is the long-written wisdom of heaven and earth, the inspiration of the Golden Dawn. It is by their long work and devotion that the peoples of Earth have won the coming of the Golden Dawn. It is their prize, their grace that has called this to them, and to the worlds of Earth. They do not believe in themselves. They do not realize the Great Light they have won to their side, and the beautiful hearts they have grown within, from which even the stars draw inspiration. You must take these flowers back to Earth, the ones that fall to you in these moments as you stand here, and gift them to those you meet. They are the blossoms of the Golden Dawn, they carry the inspiration of this reality, and one who has touched one of these blossoms cannot forget the light that they have seen, they cannot long return to forgetfulness.'

I stand under the tree, turning around and around, my face upturned, my arms raised. I feel a brimming ecstasy, a sense of wonder. There is quiet joy in the soul of this tree that brings immeasurable peace and vision to the heart. I find myself praying for the golden blossoms to fall to me, so that I might transport them back to the Earth. Gently, one, two, three, four, five... the blossoms dislodge themselves from the tree and tumble downwards to land all around me. There are twelve, there are thirteen blossoms. I know that

I shall use the petals of these flowers, and weave them into the writings of the Deerskin Book; the very pages shall shine with their light. Thus they may touch as many hearts as possible, and their influence will spread. This book, its essence, is the Golden Dawn. May it transmit that light.

I gather the blossoms with care into the deerskin pouch at my side, shutting the flap over their brilliance. I look up to the Elders, and bid them farewell. 'The Earth has arisen into the Golden Dawn, and this is her wisdom.' The Elders nod their beautiful heads, the tattooed lights at their brow glinting, their obsidian eyes fathomless.

I turn to the dragon, and climb onto her back. We fly to the Amethyst Gates. They open for us as we approach, their statuesque forms swinging open. Down we plunge, along the violet path through the skies of Earth. We fly surrounded by the pearlescent dragonflies. Soaring over the forest canopy, the dragon beats her wings in a final descent. We alight beside the mound in the forest. Coming up the slope towards us is the Moonstone Elder. The dragon snorts, and wafts her great wings.

'Thank you,' I tell her, and I know that she shall attend now to the Dragonfly Paths, as the elemental ways fill with their old power. She rises into the skies, and she is caught up in shafts of violet flame, a dazzling shadow ascending into the Sun. She shall now be guardian to the Amethyst Gates, for any who would wish to travel.

'The Dragon Elders meant that the Star Paths of violet, sapphire, silver and gold remain open and available. It is once again all that it is meant to be,' the Moonstone Elder tells me.

I follow the Elder to a deerskin tent at the edge of the forest beside the mound. I duck through the entrance, and the Elder sits down beside the fire. She reaches inside a wooden chest and she offers me an object wrapped in faded silk.

I unravel the silk, and within is a rattle. It is made of worn, golden rawhide. The Elder speaks: 'Within the rattle are shards of rainbow moonstone that sound when the rattle is shaken. It evokes another time. I gift you with the Healing Temple of the moonstone land. Here we practised the ways of balance, here we taught, and here we learnt.

'It is a rattle that holds the soft, golden voice of Earth. It holds the blessings of the Ancestors. They of old, danced. They were the thirteen flames of the mountain temple, the blue crystal ghost dance of the land. Your work is a continuum of theirs. We entrust you with the task of going forwards, of carrying this work into the future.'

The Sun Meditation

You are walking through the spring forest, the bright leaves just unfurling and spring flowers on the forest floor. Towards you from among the trees comes a reindeer with a star shining at her brow. She approaches you, and stretches out her nose to sniff at your hand. You feel her warm breath upon your skin, and you stroke her fur that is coarse and silky all at once. Side by side, you set off into the forest, and she is walking just slightly ahead of you, guiding the way. You realize as you travel that this is no ordinary forest; it is the Immortal Forest of the Earth, and an inner light glows within the trees. There is a sense of timelessness, and it is almost as though the forest is hung with stars. The reindeer leads the way as you go deeper and deeper into this enchanted realm, and you are overwhelmed by a sense of peace and beauty. Deep within the forest you come to a Grove of White Trees, and at the base of each an amethyst crystal lies in the moss. The reindeer crosses the clearing and bows her antlered head. Somehow, you understand what she is indicating. You go over to one of the trees and kneel beside it. You peer into the amethyst that lies embedded in the moss.

Within its depths shimmers the Second Glyph. You raise your hand to mirror the sweep of the glyph, in front of the tree, and you draw the Second Glyph into the forest air. As you draw the golden strokes of the Second Glyph, you feel the symbol entering your heart and glowing golden throughout your whole being. You are transported...

You are transported to a place where the Dragonfly Path ignites in a violet flame across the sky. In your hand is a moonstone, and in the depths of this moonstone, you see the light of all your deepest dreams flickering. Let yourself acknowledge these dreams. Let yourself acknowledge that which you have longed for, that which you have aspired to. Place the moonstone of dreams in the deerskin pouch that hangs around your neck. A golden dragon awaits you. You greet her, and feel an archaic language of recognition passing between you. You climb onto her back, holding onto the ridges of her scales. She beats her great wings and begins the ascent up the bright violet pathway. Dragonflies bob and dart all around you. She mounts the Dragonfly Path ever higher and higher until you find yourself facing the Amethyst Gates. Know in your heart that you are bringing the moonlight of all your earthly dreams to the Tree of the Golden Dawn, an offering that is deeply precious. When you clearly know this in your heart, chant it out three times, 'I bring the moonlight of my dreams to the Tree of the Golden Dawn,' and the Amethyst Gates will begin to open.

You pass through the gates and ascend the golden road that stretches before you. You are increasingly immersed in the Sun, as its dimensions begin to draw you in and shimmer all around you. Remain aware of the moonlight offering that you carry in your heart, all the beauty of your dreams that you are offering to this dimension of radiance. You enter into a central chamber, where a golden tree spirals upwards, shining with an inner luminosity of rainbow hues and moonstone fire. It drips with golden flowers, that hang delicate and bright from its branches. These are the Flowers of the Golden Dawn. You sit at the base of this tree, and around the circumference of the chamber, you can see the portals that are carved doorways to the stars.

You dismount from the dragon, who awaits you while you cross over to the tree. You take the moonstone out of the deer-skin pouch. Offer the enchanting moonbeams of your dreams to the tree, no matter how small or insignificant they may seem, whether or not you deem them worthy, and even if you fear to let them go. Know that this capacity of your heart to dream, to conceive its unique love, is a rare occurrence in this universe, and a source of wonder to the other realms. You make this offering in service to the Greater Dawn. Your dreams feed this dawn, and are themselves reborn in its multi-dimensional radiance. It is an incredible exchange, and one which deepens your commitment to living as an expression of the Golden Dawn.

You settle yourself cross-legged beneath the golden trunk, as you place the moonstone among the roots of the tree. You see the moonstone giving forth a haunting, opalescent moon-beam that flares into rainbow shards of crimson, copper, gold, emerald, turquoise, indigo and amethyst. They flash with lightning brilliance as they meet with the sunlight of the tree, and there is a sound of rolling thunder in this ethereal realm as your dreams become a part of the Dream of the Sun. You see the radiance of the tree increase with your offering, and then you notice that some of the golden flowers are becoming gently dislodged from the branches, and are tumbling all around you. Gather them up and store them in your medicine pouch, knowing that you shall bring these flowers back to Earth, to give as an offering of the Golden Dawn to the people of Earth, in the way that is most appropriate.

You know when your time is completed, and you gather yourself together, bowing in thanks to the beautiful tree. Know that you can return to this tree as the Sun rises in the morning sky of every day, carrying your heart's dreams with you, and offering them in daily affirmation of the Golden Dawn. Thus we exchange our old reality for the greater reality that is dawning all around us.

You return via the Sunbeam Path, through the Amethyst Gates that swing wide open for you as you approach, and downward along the violet dragonfly path to the Grove of White Trees. You walk back with the reindeer through the forest, returning to this world.

THIRD TEACHING

This is the Third Teaching of the Deerskin Book:

You will never be alone upon this New Earth. It involves shared consciousness with other beings of the same attunement. This is not a solitary consciousness, but a devotion and an attunement to a greater whole.

There is a symphony of intention and purpose. It is a symphony of starlight souls. This is the natural evolutionary trajectory of all souls involved with Earth: we are all on this path.

Chapter 3

Soft procession by the river.
Soft procession of dragon-footed petals, Eldest Ones.

THIS BOOK IS at once ancient and it belongs to the future. On one level, it does not matter where it has come from, and we need not concern ourselves with these things. I am just happy that you are reading these pages, and that the hour has come for them to be shared.

There is a crystalline perfection to the energetic imprints that are arriving to guide us through the next millennia. Do not reject or disdain such gifts, yet neither must you estimate them above the value of your own heart. You are already all that you ever need to be, and these imprints shall fall like snowflakes, offering themselves with a very pure beauty: yet it is the innocent splendour of your heart that recognizes and receives them. This is the hour of the gift, of receiving that which is your inheritance. The temple of the heart is your most precious gift, unsurpassed and adored by all dimensions. So when you receive these precious imprints, when the dimensional shifts and constellations come upon you, do not disdain that which you already are, your radiant humanity and capacity for love. The New Earth arrives in an ecstatic dance with that which you already are. The purity of this heart shall carry you through every transformation, every storm of beauty, realization, pain and fear. This is your integrity. This is a part of the Teaching of the Waters, which shall come later.

* * *

I wish to speak to you today of your beauty, interlaced with the beauty of others, and how your aloneness is altogether come to an end. This is the transparency of your true nature, this is your translucency to other dimensions and the memories of your full being. It might seem strange to imagine the boundaries shifting, and any kind of permanent awareness of interconnection. It is something we can acknowledge with our minds, but can we truly experience it in every moment with our hearts? Somehow we want these experiences, yet we are also afraid and we protect ourselves. It is difficult from an angelic perspective to appreciate this resistance, for in the angelic realms, we are surrendered to the bliss of this Greater Mind, we are one with one another, conscious of the great mind-stream that flows from one to another.

The Deerskin Book speaks of a time when we shall enter into full consciousness of our connection with one another. It shall no longer be hidden from us that our minds are woven together, and that inspiration flows through us in a shared river. This transparency may seem alarming, it may seem an end of privacy, but it is also the fulfilment of our deepest longing: to end this lonely striving. There is no lonely quest, no solitary burden. There is only the interwoven dance of connection, only the fulfilment of presence, one hand passing a gift to another, and so the gifts flow on. This is an entrance into angelic consciousness.

This is a different order of companionship than that to which we are used. It is a perpetual and psychic connection that exists between those of affinity. The new starlight frequencies are uncovering and enhancing timeless companionships of the soul. The choreography of the Golden Dawn involves our serendipitous restoration to one another in meetings that are sudden and wondrous. As we move in the stillness of privacy towards ourselves, so is our parallel restoration implicit to one another. As we maintain the courageous movement from inner to outer, bringing the star fire of inspiration into the world, so we are rewarded with the reappearance of our star lineage. We follow the directives of the inspiration and clarity gained in solitude, and initiate the activity and *becoming* of the Golden Dawn that ripples in star messages to one another. We *hear* one another and our hearts are awoken. By this emergent affinity between star souls, by our influence upon one another, the Earth gains another aspect of her beautiful and ancient Lost Dimensions. As for ourselves, we gain a powerful reminder of the work we are here to do, and the encouragement our hearts need to fulfil this.

Our star lineage is the pathway of our origin among the stars. We come in clusters of souls that have overlapping vibrational resonance. We are not identical to one another, but rather form a soul group that works like a beautiful piece of music, building both through similarity and difference. Our collaboration operates through a sequence of precise and perfect links, star overlapping star, so that something quite beyond the individual arises. Because of our underlying resonance, we are able to come together in a way that is truly effective and miraculous, and brings great peace and happiness to all concerned.

The starlight lineages have hidden themselves in the last era, as the work of necessity went 'underground' and became temporarily invisible. Yet now we are becoming aware of the alliances that exist among us and we feel drawn to fulfil this next cycle of our evolutionary intention.

* * *

You may be drawn towards much that represents your own past of forgetfulness. Remember how heavily the veil has been drawn across the skies. You will be drawn, emotionally, to perpetuate the clouded pathways of your past. You will be drawn by old narratives, by old friendships. Yet, increasingly, in these interactions a wild sorrow and loneliness will pervade your spirit. Instead of uplift, you will feel an incredible weight and heaviness upon you. This will be your sign that you are living a paradigm of the past. In the company of your true star lineage, you will never feel this way. In fact, their presence will fill you with radiant and abundant Illumination. You will feel terrific energy and inspiration. It is towards this that you must steer; it is towards this that you must set your course.

The attractions of the past can masquerade as loyalty, familiarity and comfort. For the human heart, these are powerful influences. Yet we must not let them court us into the wrong dimension. Our Illumination is a natural unfolding, yet still there are choices to be made. Still our discernment must be sharp. And so you may feel that you are leaving others behind, that you are being disloyal. Yet the old company weighs you down with such sorrow, and the Golden Dawn seems to fade from your heart like a distant dream when you are with it. This is the old world that is fading from your heart. These are the old karmic entanglements that have held you in the spell of materialism and three-dimensional reality. They are loosening their hold, and something else is calling.

Buried beneath these is a more subtle sounding of starlight affinity that draws you in a different direction altogether. It calls you into the realm of your half-glimpsed dreams, and their reality as a starlit ground of existence. You shall find an inspirational alliance that exists beyond the sphere of your resistance. You shall find that you are extraordinarily special, and that there is a symphony of extraordinarily special souls sounding out all around you. Their song is interlaced with your own, their dimensional awakening is inextricably linked to yours.

* * *

There are those who will glimpse this, and who will turn away. They will be afraid to join in such a star dance with others, for fear it makes them less important, less significant. Instead they cling to their castles of independence. Yet their own access to the Light shall be ever diminished by this choice. We cannot be the One only, the lonely crusader. This is not part of the paradigm of the New Earth. We must allow our boundaries to become irradiated by the touch of other seers: those also who are following their hearts in this radical and invisible dance. Then truly we are standing upon the ground of the New Earth. Nay – we *are* the ground of the New Earth. It is being created by our communion with one another.

Be courageous. Make yourself visible to others. This is not the time to hide. When you find the lights of your beloved ones, as they flash into existence all around you, cherish them. Cherish this precious starlight miracle of *becoming visible together.* Tend to this starlight flame that is the threshold brilliance of a new world. Thus shall we evoke and sing one another into existence. Thus shall we summon all the fields of starlight creativity back into manifest visibility. Thus shall the multi-dimensional New Earth be born.

The Elder Dawn occurs between you, in the overlapping spheres between individual and individual. You are like the overlapping petals of an immense rose, and the New Earth is deeply enfolded between you, its fragrance arising where you meet with one another. Inspiration arises between us and there is no first and no last in the process of communion. You allow this to take place. When the Elder Wisdom arises, the spirit call; let us not be afraid of the summoning. Do not stand back in the shadows; do not falter. Do not miss this moment, this chance, to give expression to your true wisdom and inspiration.

* * *

So many are hidden. This is the residue of lifetimes of distortion and confusion, of subterfuge and concealment. For many, the concealment has gone on so long that we ourselves do not remember who we are. Nevertheless, the clues to true identity are always making themselves known, and the trails of our Elder Wisdom can never be obliterated.

It is an aspect of our arising Elder Wisdom that we suddenly perceive one another with true clarity and depth, the veil of lifetimes falling away. This simple act of *seeing* is part of the restoration of our world, and a key aspect to the coming of the Golden Dawn. We are moving from karmic connections to angelic connections. Angelic, elemental connections are those that restore our original purpose upon Earth.

* * *

Allow yourself to be inspired by the wild beauty of others, by their genius and purity, even as you are the beam of *their* inspiration. Back and forth: so it goes.

What room for envy when we are one another's inspiration? What room for insecurity when we embody the very substance of one another's dream? Such offerings are we to one another, such magical and miraculous grace arriving to one another.

Do not fall for external affinities; be rigorous in your awareness and discernment. There is no time to be wasted. These alliances are now sparking into full existence and arising into full potential of their efficacy. There shall be no limit in their miraculous potential, as long as you are prepared to surrender the familiar and stand in the seership of your Light Essence.

You have done with loneliness. You have done with isolation. You have done with the sorrow and heaviness of procrastination. You no longer need this tower of separation that has kept you safe.

Instead, embrace the Staff of Friendship, allow it to guide you across the heavens. This is also about moment to moment consciousness. As I have said, we discover an angelic mode of consciousness whereby our minds share a stream of awareness. Information passes between us at vast distances. We learn to become the condition whereby the necessary transmissions flow uninterrupted. There will be natural shifts in the choreography of these connections as different relationships reach their peaks of expression and fulfil their moments of significance. Then there is a natural waning, until another wave of communication moves through. We allow ourselves to follow these relationships of natural inspiration, allowing their own inherent communicative and connective rhythms. There is no need for a forced etiquette. We shall become adept at following our inner promptings, so that the Starlight Dance becomes our mode of relationship, and we know ourselves as one great breath of emergent consciousness, a tidal dawn.

* * *

There is much to be said about our connection with animals, plants, stones and the elemental realms of Earth. Increasingly we shall find that our teachings, insights and epiphanies come directly from these realms. We shall find ourselves able to understand their language. We shall find very direct and personal communications coming to us from the trees and the flowers, from the oceans and the winds. This is because the veil is falling between us and our natural selves. We are becoming once again all that we are designed to be, and we find ourselves in a very dynamic relationship with our environment.

You shall find the timeless and hidden alliances of your soul arising once again to consciousness. This is what the Native Americans term 'Power Animals' or 'Spirit Allies'. This is the ancient shamanic and indigenous worldview that the world of Nature is itself our spiritual teacher and guide. This is the preservation of our original intention in coming to planet Earth: to see ourselves in this beautiful mirror.

When the elemental ground of Earth is restored in our hearts, we discover companionship. Sapphire and star gather around us, Earth and Sky speak to us. You become able to distinguish those who carry this dream in their hearts, and those who are awakened to the Greater Dawn. You see the morning star of hope, the evening star of gratitude shining in their hearts.

* * *

You come from the stars. Your true ancestry is composed of starlight and silence. Forget all the stories you have gathered and acquired about who you are. There is a deeper lineage of origin calling out from within you; there is a deeper account that exists as an untold story. Only you can fully access this: it is yours to remember. When I say 'remember' I do not refer to the process of acquiring a memory. I refer to a truer evocation of who you are, in this very moment. Sometimes the true story, the true occurrence, is hidden beneath many layers. It is your task to uncover these layers, to release all the false conditioning that separates you from presence.

This is the time for our hidden stars to shine and connect with one another. The old stars of Earth are awakening and activating. After a long dormancy, it is time for them to unfurl from their hidden places in the darkness and to make their presence known so that they can release their hidden codes of wisdom. These codes anchor the incoming star frequencies to this dimension.

We are the ancient teachers, who are so needed at this time, called upon to dust ourselves off after aeons of dormancy so that we can ascend into full-dimensional brilliance once again. We have stored within us the wisdom codes of a truly spiritualized and intergalactic Earth world. This is the New Earth, the incoming dream that is at once ancient and futuristic. Hopefully we have not fallen too deeply under our own spell of invisibility. There are many Guardians to our awakening, calling us forth, guiding us into presence once more. Their song is compassionate. Each awakening star is being summoned, and this shall persist until all the hidden codes of Earth wisdom are once again activated. It is an extraordinary choreography, the orchestration of which we occasionally glimpse.

* * *

And so there is a restoration of true star lineage taking place at this time. Especially at this time, the mirror shines clearly with remembrance, the shapeshifting, diaphanous heart of Nature reflects our true memories. These are the Old Ways that still dance through our hands, out of the true and reso-nant darkness of Earth, through the lineages of petal and leaf. The waterfall, the rocks, the magnificent pines: these are the interconnections, the bridges to the galaxy. Nature is a realm of overlapping spheres, mirror upon mirror, trem-bling with reflections. It is all our dream, burning luminous and wild, shifting in our hands. It is transparent to our hearts, always. We know ourselves by this world. It is our unacknowledged creation. We have dreamt with this Earth aeon upon aeon, and the trees hold the memories of our passage. They are ourselves in another moment. The crystals carry the threads of our origination, the slow blossomings of stardust. They are ourselves, constant to our magnificence, unforgetful of all that has passed.

As you remember yourself as an awakening star, you will begin to find the light trails within that take you back to your portal of entry to this dimension. You will find the original point at which you crossed over: where the star-light of your consciousness fell like a gentle rain into this world. You will discover your own original interfusion with the elemental realms. Here we re-discover our intention in coming to Earth, our spiritual purpose. At this moment we are clear, our remembrance is whole. Here is the cluster of our beautiful and unique alliance, our Star Allies, drawn together from many dimensions, many worlds. This is our mandala, our medicine wheel from which we shall learn and grow throughout lifetimes. It is a unique configuration drawn together in a perfect moment of cosmic synchronicity.

This is the threshold of incarnation, our gateway onto this planet and physical embodiment. This is how we attained our lifetimes upon the Earth, our elemental connections. Here we are introduced to fire, earth, water and air. Here they shimmer in their original forms, interdependent and glorious. This is the gateway of our incarnation: the divine portal of silver, amethyst, indigo, sapphire, emerald, gold, copper and crimson. Here the Councils gather, in flowing robes, bearing witness to the vow of incarnation, attending the inception of Earth. Here she begins again and again. This beginning is never withdrawn; it is immortal. We return to this threshold to discover our vow.

The Council is your invisible heart in other dimensions. You are remembering the trail, and how far it has travelled through the forest. Your heart lights up like some great illumined crystal, sounding a passion and a stillness, a profound oneness. You are never, were never, alone. Nor have you ever, for a moment, been without purpose. And the truth, though veiled, has echoed through every moment of your life. Its resonance, however faint, held true.

There are those who associate the Earth with suffering and density. There has long been a different wisdom: the one which sees us at one with the journey of creation, with the expansion of the stars. We cannot separate ourselves from the vision of Earth and Sky that unfolds before our eyes. We cannot separate ourselves from this magical dance we have evoked with the prayers of our hearts. It is a blessing to be thus present: it is a gift of Great Mystery. The Earth is the creation of our own hearts, the gift we have given ourselves. We cannot choose to give this back simply because we have lost our vision.

* * *

There are many textures of consciousness you shall begin to explore, levels of awareness at once beautiful and unfamiliar. Like a musician learning a whole new scale of notes, you shall dance with frequencies previously unknown. This is the nature of evolution, and we need resist this no more than the flower resists the light of the star that falls upon it in the night. Each shall suggest new realms of creativity and expression, new textures of experience. This is the joy of the one who glimpses the White Deer in the forest, and it is the expression of our endless love and curiosity for our world.

* * *

I speak in metaphors, but this is the gift of the teachings. These metaphors are the soul of the Deerskin Book, part of what it has to offer at this moment in time. It is a specific constellation of awareness, suited to this moment. It is tailored from these stars emerging from behind the clouds, the dancing play of their light upon us. It is ancient because it has always existed, as have the symbols that glow around the Earth, caught silver in their amethyst crystals. They shine upon us, and bless us. They wish for us peace, coherence, serenity and unbounded inspiration. They are not esoteric or mysterious, but part of the overarching orders of Nature, an expression of a vision that goes beyond our own, and yet is married to the radiance of our hearts.

It is natural when we meet with these beautiful, powerful, resonant, ethereal frequencies, these angels, these Shining Ones, that we feel we are coming home. You shall come to know, entirely, in this present moment, that you are a *Shining One.* You shall come into the radical trust that this is your own Self. And when you have fully surrendered to this, then there is no ascension, there is no alteration or elsewhere, there is no Heaven and Earth. You are all of this at once, and there was never anywhere to go.

* * *

How exhausted we are with the old pretense, the old effacement and invisibility, the loneliness and disconnection. Would we not rather surrender to the miracle, to that which burns us and moves us? Would you not rather be burnt by Heaven's fire of sensitivity and connection? Would you not rather be touched and irradiated? It opens us to one another. It opens us to a shared Earth where we meet under the interlacing branches of the Silver Grove, to hear the Council of the Stars. It opens us to connections over vast distances and to a family we may never have met, but of whose presence we feel acutely aware, day and night.

This is the Third Teaching of the Deerskin Book. The time of connection is here. When you feel its touch, know that it is your destiny calling. It is the fulfilment of your wildest dreams.

* * *

I am walking in a forest shimmering with a tide of bluebells. Last autumn's faded remnants crunch underfoot, leaves weathered fine by the winter frosts. Across the skies fans a transparent leafy dome.

Here, amongst the trees, is an old carved archway. The stone is a pale, weathered grey. Its surface is pitted and hollowed, with moss and lichen sprouting from it. I am drawn into a softer silence by the stone, and an older moment than inhabits the rest of the forest. I press my fingers to the symbols that are chiselled into its surface, and their murmuring language fills my mind.

'You have spent so much time alone in the forest. This solitary quietness has carried you into much remembrance, but to go further you must surrender this solitude, and listen to the sequences of consciousness that flow amongst all beings, beyond the boundaries of the forest. There are many circles to be restored on the path of true remembrance, and there is wisdom that you will learn from your fellow human beings in a shared language that is different from the epiphanies of the birds and the sky. Even as you have learnt to sense the invisible in the forest, so you must learn it in the world beyond. You shall learn to see through the illusion of isolation, to the star paths that flow through us all in currents of shared consciousness.'

The voice seems to come from the arch itself, and stepping through there is an Elder. She is dressed in softest sapphire, a sapphire pendant at her brow. She is barefoot and unimaginably graceful. At her back are two enormous and arching wings, moon-bright in the emerald forest.

'This is an ancient portal. It only becomes visible at the time of the bluebells. It has the power to carry you into the presence of your Council of Companions, those to whom you are bound by threads of angelic connection in this lifetime. Would you come with me and attend this Council?'

I nod my agreement. Together, we pass through the archway. My companion tells me, 'This is the Summer Palace of the Stars, it is where the Council resides.'

Like a blue lotus floating in the air, the council hangs aloft. It floats amongst the trees, held aloft on delicate walkways. Underneath, the sea of bluebells floods the forest floor. The trees rise uninterrupted, as though the trees and the Summer Palace had grown up all at once, moulded around one another.

'This is the architecture of natural inspiration. In time, there shall be many such dwellings as this, built according to patterns of natural growth and the seemingly miraculous dimensions of the stars. The Summer Palace of the Stars is an example of what may occur on Earth when the star lineages remember themselves, and let their natural affinities guide them in their contracts of co-creation. It is no exaggeration to say that this could result in works of effortless wonder. When we follow the natural affinities that reside within us, guiding us into the Old Alliances, then we come into spheres of creation that go beyond human capacity and vision.'

We cross over onto the spiraling walkway that leads to the Summer Palace, ascending over the forest floor. Above us, the Summer Palace glows, an ethereal brilliance amongst the spring trees. Finally, I stand on its threshold. The walls are carved of faceted, translucent sapphire, and it is like stepping within an orb of blue light. I step within the doorway. Twelve beings face me in a row. They wear sweeping blue robes, and their slanting eyes are full of a sparkling darkness. Each raises hands to their chest, palms together, in greeting. I raise my hands in a prayer position, echoing their greeting. I stand for a moment on the threshold, overcome. I realize that at our backs rise moon-bright wings like those of my guide. There is an overwhelming sense of shared grace. It is as though in their presence, I come powerfully into existence. I step towards them, my whole body humming. One by one, I touch their foreheads, brow to brow. Tears course down my cheeks as I do so, swept in a tide of love and welcome. There is a great soundless echoing of heart to heart.

We form a circle, our hands touching palm to palm. Our bodies sway as the current of shared consciousness passes through us.

'Our task is the restoration of other-dimensional consciousness.' The shared voice echoes through my mind. This council is dreaming the placement of the crystals throughout the forest. We understand the dynamics of a crystalline architecture that shall restore otherworldly vision for the peoples of Earth, a placement of fire opals and amethysts. Our blue hands are raised in this shared prayer. We hold the awareness that the forest is being dreamt by many different worlds at once, its existence sustained by the lights of different stars. It is not born of this world only. With this awareness, the usual dynamics of time and space are altering.

The Elder Guide in her sapphire robes comes to each one of us and places an antlered headband upon each of our brows. As the antlers settle onto my head, I can feel my attunement to the others intensify. My mind is filled with a white language that passes between us. We are capturing the essence of a dream between us, a dream that wishes to walk this Earth once again. As we dream, so the forest alters around us. The trees are shifting position. There is a different dynamic of space emerging. Out of the spheres between the trees emerge clouds of blue butterflies whose wings are painted with patterns. The butterflies cluster around us, settling onto the branches of our antlers. The humming of their wings fills the air. This circle is dedicated to remembering

the Elven Heart of Nature. The blue butterflies are the memories that have been scattered over the Earth and Sky. We sway and tilt under the weight of their remembering, their Gathering of the Elven Heart. The memories are a listening: a thousand delicate sensors. It is time for the memories to be gathered without limitation and it is time for them to be heard without censorship, as we move past the ingrained limitations of language and consciousness, into an untraversed realm. Amethysts glow at our brows, an aura that emanates from beneath the skin.

We breathe together, hands still touching palm to palm. I am bound in a vow to these listening souls, bound to listen to the butterflies and all the eras of Earth to which they have attended. We are one another's wings and antennae, we are one another's voices and attention. A halo of emerald stars appears, spinning between us. We are bearing witness to the emergence of the Lost Worlds of Earth: to this we have dedicated our attention. This is an offering that shall not be withdrawn; to it is dedicated our last breath. By our attention there is a sanctuary of emergence. Hand to hand, the haunting emanation of the golden forest emerges around us. We communicate by the language of our minds resonating directly into spaciousness. There is no boundary keeping us from one another; we are a continuum. In our silence, in our language, in our sleep, we form a choreography of consciousness that keeps this earthly doorway open: the portal that welcomes the Blue Butterflies of Memory. Our heartbeats are synchronized.

'We do not come to this Earth alone. We descend in clusters, which is how our spiritual intention is evoked. The Council of Companions is a composite of many points of origin. It contains a spectrum of dimensional experience, forming a coherent symphony that is able to render the intergalactic message of this lifetime.'

Softly, dragon-footed, a procession of Elders, we descend to the forest beneath. We walk beside the river, the blue butterflies clustering around our antlered heads. We shall walk this forest until our mission is accomplished. Sensitivity allows the earth memories to gather to us. We can begin to listen to her true journey through time and space. We trust this radiant sensitivity that arises as an authentic source of wisdom and awareness. This delicate, burgeoning field with its thousands of silk-fine blue wings is significant. It is the treasure of sentience, of sensitivity. There is knowledge, like butterflies, that wishes to find us. It shall gather to our strength, our stature, our authenticity. It shall seek out our endurance, our dedication and clarity. It is drawn to our integrity and the spaces created by true companionship. True companionship creates space around us, making us accessible. We are drawn into this dimension by one another, and thus all the wonder of our dreams may follow.

Finding your Council of Companions

You are walking in the forest amongst the bluebells, a shimmering tide of leaves fanning across the skies above your head. Towards you from amongst the trees comes a reindeer with a star shining at her brow. She approaches you, and stretches out her nose to sniff at your hand. You feel her warm breath upon your skin, and you stroke her fur that is coarse and silky all at once. Side by side, you set off into the forest, and she is walking just slightly ahead of you, guiding the way. You realize as you travel that this is no ordinary forest; it is the Immortal Forest of the Earth, and an inner light glows within the trees. There is a sense of timelessness, and it is almost as though the forest is hung with stars. The reindeer leads the way as you go deeper and deeper into this enchanted realm, and you are overwhelmed by a sense of peace and beauty. Deep within the forest, you come to a Grove of White Trees, and at the base of each, an amethyst crystal lies in the moss. The reindeer crosses the clearing, and bows her antlered head. Somehow, you understand what she is indicating. You go over to one of the trees and kneel beside it. You peer into the amethyst that lies embedded in the moss.

Within its depths shimmers the Third Glyph. You raise your hand to mirror the sweep of the glyph, in front of the tree, and you draw the Third Glyph into the forest air. As you draw the golden strokes of the Third Glyph, you feel it entering your heart and glowing golden throughout your whole being. You are transported...

You are transported to a temple of translucent architecture under a night sky of stars. Standing before you are Twelve Companions, their forms glowing in the starlight. You touch foreheads with each and you breathe in the sensation of being surrounded by kindred souls. This is your Council of Companions. This is a place where there is the deep ease of kinship and shared purpose. It is a soul companionship that goes beyond day-to-day affinities. You stand together in a circle, palm to palm, your bodies swaying with the powerful harmony that flows between you. Breathe deeply.

You ask, 'What are the qualities of this Council of Companions?'

Listen as each of the Twelve names a quality that is held by this circle. Know that this is a sacred mirror for your own qualities and a means by which you can recognize True Companions in the future.

Sit and breathe in the presence of your Council of Companions, honouring and acknowledging their companionship. Know that you are not, nor have you ever been, alone. They are always by your side, linked to you, even when you cannot see them.

You look down and flickering in your hands are Seven Golden Butterflies, the tiny brushstrokes of their wings tickling the palms of your hands. You look around and see that clouds of butterflies sit on the hands of each of your Twelve Companions. With synchronized intent, each of you raises your hands into the air, spreading out your fingers, releasing the butterflies to the winds. Your vision is filled with the golden flight of the butterflies arising in a starlit sky. They disperse. Know that you have sent forth the flight of your radiant sensitivity. You have sent it forth in a quest for the echoes of companionship, seeking those, connecting to and supporting those who have come to the Earth with a shared template of vision, those who are the echoes and mirrors of your own Greater Self. You are acknowledging your connection with others in this world who carry the same Star Mission, be they human, plant, stone, animal, physical, or in spirit. They are a part of your team. The golden butterflies go forth as messengers, carrying messages back and forth between you and your Council of Companions. Know that you can summon the messengers to you, to help you find members of your Council of Companions whenever you may need to in the physical or spirit worlds. Via the messengers, you can send out questions and await their reply. They can carry messages, bringing you supportive energy, or gifting your energy and insights to others in your circle. Cultivate an awareness that you amplify one another's fields, and make sure that the gift of mutual awareness keeps flowing around the circle. Ask this key question:

'What does my Council of Companions need from me at this time?' Await the answer, and treasure it in your heart.

When you are ready, you bid farewell to your Companions. You find yourself transported back to the White Grove, with its amethyst crystals glowing at the base of the trees. With the reindeer at your side, you leave the Grove and walk through the forest, returning to this world.

FOURTH TEACHING

This is the Fourth Teaching of the Deerskin Book:

This new dimension is woven out of song, or sound.

Learn to listen to the frequencies of music through which it speaks to you.

The more you relax, the fuller the music will become.

Chapter 4

Dragon-held,
swallow breath on star,
winged handler.

Elder pipe,

Grace of lifted fingers.

AND SO WE embark upon the Fourth Teaching: this is that the New Earth is woven of sound, or vibration. As the Deer moves through the forest, the great fanned cups of her ears twitch and flicker in all directions, catching a spectrum of signals from her environment. Her sensitivity is perpetual; she is always listening.

So, too, you are beginning to listen. You are listening to the hidden sounds or vibrations. You 'hear' the resonance or frequency of that which surrounds you. Your body is finely attuned; you listen with your whole body, not just your ears. Your own vibrational presence is a listening device. It discovers the true fabric of reality, the actual vibration of any given situation, place or person. The vibration may be at odds with the image or story consciously presented. You are being given a great tool for discernment. You shall thus discover your own vibrational affinities and pathways.

You shall discover those with whom you resonate, with whom a creative resonance arises. Through the pathways of vibrational affinity, we find one another.

This book has its own natural vibrational spectrum that forms its unique transmission: an underlying music to whose rhythms, cadences and tones it is written. It cannot stray too far from these without losing its integrity, its coherence.

And so what is vibrational sensitivity and how do we develop this? We shift our seat of attention away from the thinking mind into the realm of *feeling*. We begin to honour and attend to our feelings as a source of valuable information about ourselves and the reality we are experiencing. This simple shift is the foundation for the reclamation of all the lost abilities that we consider extraordinary. When we give all our attention to our thinking processes, when we listen to our thoughts to the exclusion of all else, then we are sealed off from the messages of the Greater Reality. It cannot reach us with the gifts it wishes to pour upon us, with the beautiful metamorphosis that it is offering.

The lost continent of your feelings exists unexplored. You have this most exquisite and wondrous device within you that has infinite capacity for development. This is the realm of feeling. We think that feeling is an inferior mode that will limit us into an overly personal view of reality and obscure our clear functioning. We think of feeling as a more primitive aspect of ourselves.

Yet it is in fact an invaluable tool by which we are connected to reality. It is the threads of a vibrational sensitivity that anchors our connection to the Universe. Choose that which makes you feel happy, loving, inspired.

Your happiness, your inspiration, is natural. It is Nature returned to itself – it is the restoration of the cosmic order. You are monitoring yourself; you are tracking happiness, completion, wonder. This is the vibration, the music of the Golden Dawn. Your happiness is the golden jewel. Your inspiration is the beloved treasure of the Golden Dawn. When you are resonating in synchronisation with Spirit, then you feel deep joy. You become the White Starfire of Infinite Love, you *become* the New Earth.

Notice when the breath of openings, of hope, occurs: the sensation of expanded horizon. Does it inspire you, does it fill you with a sense of infinite potential? Do the doors of Mystery fly open and you remember the endless wonder of the Universe? These are the feelings that are the music of the New Earth. Do you feel empowered, clear, resonant with wisdom both explored and unexplored? Do you feel the wing-brush of angelic companions, the shimmer of a unicorn's visitation, the loving breath of an Elder Spirit touching you with affirmation, joy and love? Do the emerald spirits of the forest sing to you their ancient codes, even in the solitude of a closed room? Do the crystals inspire you with their starlight codes of creation? Do the waters enshrine you in their mystical love? Do you feel a wild and ecstatic delight in the company of your loved ones? These are the *feelings* of the Golden Dawn, these are the music of an incipient and yet powerful reality. The New Earth is revealing herself through these vibrational arrivals, these resonances dawning into our sphere of experience. They are the encodings for Peace on Earth.

* * *

The Deer makes her lilting progress through the forest, the sensitive shells of her ears flickering back and forth. She hears everything through the fibres of her sensitivity, her gift of clairaudience.

She guides you into the subtle vibratory realm of the crystals and the stones. To them, here, you are listening, learning to hear their vibrational messages that have been stored within the Earth for so long. This is the music of the Earth's inner spheres. This is where her Lemurian era is encoded – where we can hear the great leaf fall, the lost sunbeams and moonbeams of that age. These are vibrational messages to which we can listen, if we so choose. The records can be heard. We hear the Earth's true history as recorded by the rocks and the crystals, as sung by the glittering sands with their thousands of crushed grains.

When looking for the Golden Dawn, listen for that which has *depth of frequency*. It must be stirring, tidal, resonant, moving. It is that which alters you. It has a depth of vibration that is transformative.

You feel your ancient heart beginning to believe in the possibility of happiness again. You feel ancient hope beating its wings, and your innermost creative visions activating, sparkling into presence. The song of the Golden Dawn acts as invocation, as evocation.

* * *

Sound and music are dimensions about which we can make profound choices that deeply effect our evolution. We choose our listening, we pitch our awareness at its own unique angle, and this is the music with which we fill our lives. This music is the vibratory pattern that travels to us and from us in a perpetual exchange, sounding our material reality into existence. These vibratory patterns underpin our lives. We need to begin listening to the unheard 'silent' music pouring in, to the frequencies that as yet are barely audible to the physical ear, and yet are available to our perception. This music enables us to take up the music of our natural inheritance, to take up the music of the Earth and the Sun and the Stars. This is the music that offers the flowering, the expansion of our essence. It offers us the opportunity to be more than merely the expression of yesterday, and the endless repetitions of the past. It means that we listen to more than the stuck record of an isolated human existence, going beyond the limits it has determined for itself.

There are different notes and tones for our different moods: those of peace and those of anxiety. We hold access to a range of frequencies that represent the spectrum of our experience, of our feelings. This shall become more transparent, more evident, more audible. It shall become one of the major tools by which we experience and guide our own evolution. It shall be a way by which we see into that which is really happening. There is no accident that the ancient shaman healers have always used drums and bells and rattles. It is a way of speaking with the deepest levels of our existence.

We shall utilize these tools again, on a much wider basis. They shall become available to us all, as mediums by which we gain direct access to the heart of experience, and by which we enter into communion with that which lies beyond human language. This is not a peripheral or artistic activity, though it can bring profound beauty and enjoyment. It is about the direct access to Truth. This is why we feel genuinely 'moved' by music, and it is always already sounding and moving us. We are being moved and transformed as we speak by the vast sounding of the Universe. Equally, we give off our own signal, our own sound, and affect everything around us with this which we offer to the music of the whole.

* * *

I cannot tell you how glad I am to offer the sounding, the sounds, of the Deerskin Book, of these teachings and symbols. It is an ancient choreography that belongs specifically to this moment of evolution. It allows an expansion of our beings into greater levels of love and truth, it is a ladder for consciousness. With it there comes a sense of discovery, of liberation, of potential. The golden fires of creativity and expression crackle at our fingertips: we long to make these sounds, to become this music and inhabit the spaces it offers, even as we hear it. We become aware: this is something I am, this is something I can carry with me in every moment of every day. And we become aware of the inestimable blessing we thus bring to the world, of the thirst for exactly this: its benefit and its timelessness.

* * *

It is the relationship of sound to silence that comprises its greatest gift. In the hollows of sound are opened up the spaces in which we experience our Infinite Being. We 'hear' this endless depth, this limitless space. This is what brings us peace and freedom. Suddenly all the chatter, all the questions and answers, contrasts and quandaries vanish and we become the soundlessness: the well of silence.

It is in this that we hear, finally, that which arises from our own being. We hear the bell-like sounding of our own light, how it arises in the darkness, offers itself in the dance of the Cosmos. We are this effortless sounding of light that has the wisdom to leave the space for all things to exist. It knows there is enough of everything for us all: there is endless potential and endless resource. Sound can bring us into the heart of abundance, the generative and Infinite Source.

It is this the Deer has travelled through time and space to preserve, to make available in the form of the Deerskin Book to the present moment. It is this to which the inks of the Moon and of the Sun, spilling silver and gold, interlaced with sapphire symbols, are dedicated. And indeed it is the pathless path, the trackless way, involving a deep trust in ourselves, a deep listening to the music of the stars within us.

* * *

This brings us to the role of the drum in the teachings. The drum enables us to attune our frequency to that of the Earth. We take the drum in our hands and begin to beat out the rhythm of our heartbeats. We discover that they are caught into the disconnected rhythm of our thoughts, and gently we begin to drum them back into resonance with the rhythms of the Earth. Native peoples speak of the 'heartbeat of the Mother', and Mother Earth does indeed have her own vibrational pulse. We can choose to become attuned to this. This is one of the ways in which we are restored into conscious awareness of her subtle realms, and attuned to her Lost Dimensions. Each of us has our own natural resonant frequency which, when twinned with the frequency of the Earth, leads one on a pathway of unique dimensional loveliness. As we each begin to pound out our true pathways of the heart, there is the dance of feet in golden moccasins that remember their own wisdom. This is a homecoming. When we do this, we find our true place of belonging upon this Earth. Unique dimensional loveliness flowers upward from our steps: we walk with grace. We walk with lightness upon the Earth in a synchronization that gives birth to inspiration.

Every morning, we drum our hearts into synchronization with the Earth. This leads our footsteps on a different pathway than we might otherwise have travelled.

The drum is a messenger of the Golden Dawn, an alchemist and a prophet of what is uniquely emergent in the precious and precise dance of our footfalls upon the planet. As the drumstick or the flat of our hand falls and strikes the surface of the drum, so we fall and meet with Mother Earth: there is a descent into alignment with her subtle calls and rhythms. Then from our dancing footfalls, from the fall, emerges an echo that travels *beyond*. It travels to our outermost circumference, calling out to the Star Realms, creating a resonance with our furthest edge. This resonance is the return of the Shining Ones of far galactic realms travelling back into this dimension. The circle of Heaven and Earth is restored: the great overarching, intergalactic hoop of life. We are starlight returning to ourselves, walking across the infinity of space to come to Earth once more. We bring with us the future, the messages of the Ancient Ones.

Thus by allowing this resonance through the beating of the drum with the Earth, we harmonize ourselves with all that lies beyond: with the Sun and the Stars and with space. The drum is a bridge over which consciousness may pass. The Lemurian understanding is of the totality of the drum: its wholeness. The drum restores us beyond ascent and descent into *interdimensional immanence.*

We are being called from afar, we listen for the calls, for the communications of the Greater Dawn, for in the thrum of vibration that dwells beneath sound is the language of the Elders. The drum is a messenger of the languages of Light, summoning them to where we are. It sounds our intention to become an anchor to their revelatory vibrations.

First there is the synchronization with the Earth, and then there is the anchoring of the hidden vibrations of the cosmos. We are free to choose the attunement of our inner drum; we can drum in time with the Earth and the Sun and the stars, or we can venture off into disconnected rhythms and frequencies.

* * *

These teachings act as a bridge to enable us to catch up to our place in the cosmic stage. We shall make great advances in a very short time, until the sunlight becomes the gold of pure Creation in our hands once again.

There is also the role of the crystal singing bowls that inspire attunement to some very evolved frequencies. You can only know by their appearance in your life of your readiness to hear them. They are like the rare orchids waiting to teach us of this moment in our evolution, waiting to attune us to delicate frequencies and sensitivities that embody our own potential. Their rare beauty does not make their arrival in our lives peripheral, but rather we must dare to bring this beauty to the centre of ourselves. We let their crystalline tones echo through us, evoking the Self we thought too evolved and wise to touch our clouded hearts. This Self is in fact our own hidden wisdom. Thus the bowls represent our unwillingness to remain caught in the patterns of suffering of the last centuries of our lifetimes. They draw us forward, into the crystallization of our own truer presence as arrivals of the Golden Dawn. We become the one who sounds the notes of Creation, we take up our place as heavenly emissaries, rather than always waiting for the appearance and miracles of the angels outside of us. We begin to weave this sound-light Temple of the Earth once again, we strengthen her frequencies, we commit to her healing. This plays through us with wondrous spontaneity.

We can trust ourselves, by our attunement to the sunlight, to be this Greater Dawn. We can trust to the emergence of the Lost Temples, which shall play themselves through our hands, by the dedication of our hearts.

These are the naturally emergent songs, this is the attunement that is always already taking place and that we are equipped with tools to take part in. Such trust in the self can be difficult; we feel we have made such mistakes, such errors in judgment. We fear our impulse's power to lead us into chaos and the power of our own desire to distract us. We fear to strike the discordant notes in the universal symphony: to be untuned, wayward, in error.

This is why we trust in the Earth and the Sun and the Stars and allow ourselves to be held. We do nothing alone. We allow the silence to carry us into a deeper connection, an awareness of the sound-light essence of the world. We wait until we hear the Earth and the sunlight, and then we allow them to weave through us, to carry us where they will. We are never alone, we need not become lost in a solitary consciousness or illusion. And we must not be afraid of the places to which they carry us. We are never too far out, too far away – these are false limitations we place upon ourselves. We may let ourselves travel to the stars, and back again, following the vibratory lines of travel that are now available.

* * *

This, then, is the voice, and the many languages that speak. We are singers; we have speech. These beautiful and complex vowel and consonant patterns come forth. This is the gift of Arianrhod, the sapphire star of language, of uttered sound. Do not be afraid of your voice: it is one of your primary modes of existence. It is always revealing that which you are. It must be allowed to take up the unheard music, the sounding of the stars. You must allow yourself to be the voice of angels, the ascending frequencies of remembrance. It shall dance and beckon through you, like a cascading stream beneath the surface, always waiting to be uttered, waiting for its emergence.

The language of the Shining Ones speaks through us of what does not yet exist, and anchors it here in the present. It is a language beyond our own, expressing that which our language is not yet developed to express. It speaks in a language of the spheres, of the Universe. This is the language of Light, and we receive much guidance through this medium.

We awaken to the practices written so deeply within us. If we begin to feel stretched and thin with effort, as though

we are striving too hard for remembrance, we must relax
and return to the Silence. Let all impressions, all lights,
sounds, languages, fade away. This Dawn is self-sustaining;
it arises naturally. You can never lose this. Sometimes it
must all be surrendered, all the beauty also, that builds in
us like a tension where we would gather and retain it. The
breath and the Silence will carry us back into the Truth,
back into a true listening. All of this is naturally arising,
carried by an infinite intelligence so much greater than
ourselves, carried by the winged breath of the stars that yet
love us. We are not the sole carriers of this mighty dream:
it arises with its own fluctuations and timings. There is no
need to become frantic with activities, with spiritual practices. Such an approach only sustains the divide between
spirit and matter, the coercion of an external discipline.
Ask yourself what naturally arises in this Great Sounding
Dawn of the Earth.

* * *

We shall become much more aware of sound and vibration than we have been, and they are the tools by which
the New Earth is drawn into being, by which the physical
manifestation alters. The Earth is changing. She is dreaming herself differently, and the sound-light dimension of
her dreaming grows ever more resonant, and present. More
and more of us are listening, switching our allegiance from
the old to the new. This is the myth of the New Age, but it
is only an attempt to articulate what is really taking place.
Our work is not to try to sustain and patch up the old; this
only engenders fields of resistance, which create further
disruption. We must allow the flowing star lines and their
songs around which the Earth is weaving her new dream

to come into our lives. We must allow for the reality of this invisible dimension that presses upon us, already breaking into visibility here and there. We must allow ourselves to dream with the Earth, and not fight her transmutation. Her transformation is an expansion and an evolution, the marriage of starlight and stardust moving ever more deeply through her heart. She follows the path of the crystals, who are guides at this time. She depends on us, for we are her dreamers. We are her mind and imagination.

* * *

There are those who have followed the path of the Deer and rediscovered the symbols where they are stored in the sound-light dimension of this Earth. Somehow we have not forgotten that which goes consciously untaught. It might feel rebellious, yet it is what is most harmonious, requiring a dedication to a reality not held in the conscious awareness of our times. Who knows what gesture, what action, what ceremony of healing, of transformative weaving, shall arise within us from one moment to the next, fulfilling a narrative whispered so close to our hearts, an almost inaudible yet incredibly powerful prerogative? These inspired gestures shall never be senseless or strange to us. We shall have a profound understanding and clarity about that which moves through us: its reality is characterized by purity and simplicity.

We shall recognize the practices that carry the Vibration of the Dawn. They may come through symbolism, through metaphor and ceremony, but they shall have the intensity that cuts through illusion. We do not need to keep waving the rainbow flags of the Old Dawn. We do not need to keep enacting the ceremonies of past lives. We need that which arises from the Silence: those stars that are truly being born. Honour the Old Dawn, for this has preserved the sunlight prayers, and kept the thread of Love and Silence as a candle burning in the darkness. It has reminded us to love one another and kept alive the practices of the Light. Theirs are the ceremonies and prayers, the temples and mountaintop cairns. Theirs are the churches, the altars, the faith and the devotion. Theirs the sensitivity and connectedness, the awareness of the sound-light gifts of Earth and Stars. They are our ancestors, they are ourselves. They are the ones we have preserved and protected, fought for and destroyed. We have been on both sides of a mighty battle. They are the ones who sing, with Love, of the fading of the Old Earth. They have witnessed her passing: theirs has been the grief and the burden of awareness that an era is ending.

This Old Earth is passing, like a fine sunset. We need the illumination and the inspiration of what has been. This is the frame of Love that must fall around us, before and after. Yet there is no life for us in turning to face this sunset, in trying to walk the old paths. This is nostalgia and a misunderstanding of the dedication it took to carry the teachings through the ages. Those of the Old Dawn did what they could because so much had been forgotten. But theirs was a lantern in the night compared with the coming of the Greater Dawn. We do no honour to their sacrifice by imitation, by obeying the letter of a faded practice when the full Light of its genesis, its inspiration, is once again offered.

It is time to let go of the past and become all that we are. Increasingly, we find that we are being taught directly by the spirits, by the Earth and the Stars. We drum in our sunlight meditation, and teachings are given to us: wisdom received and practices ignited. It is natural inspiration. It is us remembering how to seek our own hearts, and how to be worthy guardians and participants in Nature's unfolding. We are no longer the children by whom all this was forgotten. Our hands are not so stained by the guilt of the ages that we are not eligible for this direct inspiration. As our starlight bodies heal and begin to shine, we are able to receive the communication and wisdom for which we are destined. It is that which we already know, but that has become obscured to us.

* * *

Once again, I repeat: we are not unprepared. We are not uninitiated, we are not untrained. This is the unfolding flower of lifetimes. We can keep behaving like needy children, desperate to receive pearls of wisdom and teaching from others. We can be the eternal seekers, or we can embrace our own readiness. This is the truth of our readiness to manifest our greater selves here in this dimension, to transmit the learning of lifetimes. We cannot be forever waiting for reassurance, for those around us to give us their blessing and recognition. We cannot await some perfect, future conditions. The mandala of the Silver Wheel is emergent within us. When we allow for stillness, for depth, the dance of its inspiration arises: our own wisdom. It happens when we surrender to the Vibration of the Dawn. It happens when we let the unscripted programming of the Light occur. It is all there, all known and unknown all at once. Our own recognition of its completeness, its perfection, occurs. There is no one to confer the laurels but ourselves; we do not need to obligate others with the task of recognition. There shall be the natural recognition by members of our soul group, for whom we inspire recognition of themselves. Our Illumination blesses them – that is all that is required.

Our true vibration blesses, as even the unseen flower blesses the forest. Yet we shall not go unseen, because to step into the Light is to shine, to sacrifice the safety of the shadows. It is safe to do this now. Perhaps in other eras it has been dangerous, but this is the timeliness. This is the nature of the transformation, as the Earth herself begins to Shine and her Illuminated Ones become themselves.

Some fear to believe they are too special, yet this specialness is the characteristic of existence itself. It is not untrue to say that we fear our own brilliance, our own power. Yet we have forgotten the inherent peacefulness of such brilliance: its power of love and blessing and compassion. You shall hurt no one else by your acknowledgement of your own true nature. They may resist your transformation, yet by it they shall be blessed. Even as we fear the Earth's changes, her letting go of that which is no longer required, yet we are so much more blessed by this change than we can possibly know.

We feel as though we are being shaken and hurt, moved from place to place, filled with uncertainty. We feel sometimes that we are suffering the loss of hopes and dreams. Yet nothing that we truly need is taken, and everything that we most long for is offered.

We must allow the dream to fill the Earth with Silence, to cast free of the old boundaries of the old song. We must allow for a moment of nothingness, when all we do is breathe into the Silence. These are the spaces where the spirit enters, where the symbols descend to Earth. In the moment when we cast loose, become the unknown, that is when the Light enters, that is the arrival of the New Dawn. And we shall be so glad, because we know that it came from beyond us, we know that it came from beyond the furnace and the forge of our own will, and thus we shall know that we are not alone.

The symbols shine golden in their amethyst crystals: the Lemurian Teachings are arriving. This shall be a temple of the Earth sustained by sound and starlight. The drum and the bells and the crystal bowls, the language of Light, shall anchor this upon the Earth. It shall evolve and be consecrated. It shall become itself and be offered to infinite space.

The language of listening shall be ours. The language of what is heard: for how else to learn how to speak in a new universe? We shall listen, and our words shall be built of our listening.

There shall always be the sceptic, the one who stands back a little, but this does not matter. It is not your job to persuade anyone. Let what will be, be. None of this is sustained by your own power. Let it go, bequeath it to the Silence, to the breath. Only that which naturally arises is worth having.

* * *

I gaze upwards into the tiered branches of the oak tree. Honeysuckle has twined its way into the squat branches that taper to oak-leafed twigs.

In the forest, summer steps into her own green shadow.

The atmosphere is heavy, scented, as the Moon becomes full. Rain falls into the forest; stars blossom out of the river. I have walked here, away from the river. I sit beneath the oak tree that stands alone at the top of the wood. The Elder appears, honeysuckle blossom in her hair, wearing a dress of jade, her skin moonbeam-pale. A circlet of jade and opals is upon her brow. She steps out from behind the oak tree and stands before me. She is the one who holds the constellations of this place, where honeysuckle meets star. Silver wings rise from her back, a delicate tree of enchantment. My heart lilts in my chest with wonder and recognition.

'Many have come here to seek my guidance. What is your heart's wish in coming to this place?'

'I wish to learn from whence the old language truly comes,' I tell her.

'I have dwelt here for a long, long time. In this place, the threads connecting the physical Earth with the Immortal Soul of Earth have never been fully broken. Even though there are no longer those alive who maintain the old ceremonies, that which the Ancient Ones set in motion so very long ago still runs uninterrupted, and the vision continues to be fulfilled. The language that you hear is the one shared by the elemental and spirit kingdoms. It is the old language, the language of Light. It is the language of the Elven Ones, such as myself, who are spiritual guardians of the Earth. Not many of us remain, as I do, fully connected to this realm. Yet the return is prophesied, as we are born in the human realms once more, and the old contracts are fulfilled. This is the language that you hear. What does this language inspire in your heart?'

I look into her slanted eyes, their galactic depths. 'I wish to let it flow through me, to bring its wisdom and healing to the world.'

'It makes sense that you are here,' she murmurs. 'It is time. Follow me.'

I stand up and follow her around the ancient oak tree. On the other side, it becomes apparent that the tree is hollow, and as we step within, I see that the inner bark spirals upward in a natural staircase. The Lady leads the way, mounting the stairs ahead of me, until she vanishes into an opening at the top of the stairwell. I emerge onto a platform that is built where the trunk fans out into its upper branches. It overlooks the forest, perched in its canopy. The Elven One sits down, her jade-green skirts piling around her. I sit down beside her. She reaches into her pockets and brings out a pale suede pouch. She gently shakes out the contents: a bundle wrapped in cloth woven of winter leaves. She unwinds the cloth, and a carved pipe falls into her hand.

'It is carved of elder wood,' she tells me, 'And first we shall smoke your dream, smoke your prayer to the Four Winds, so that the stars may hear your call all the more clearly.'

She unwraps another, smaller pouch, and tips from it some dried leaves. 'This is mullein leaf,' she explains, and fills the bowl of the pipe with the leaves. She whispers words in the Old Language, and a small orb of blue flame ignites, hovering just above the palm of her hand, 'All the Elven Ones are carriers of the Elder Fire,' she explains, and then putting the stem of the pipe to her mouth, she lights it. The blue orb of flame dims and fades. She inhales deeply,

then exhales, a long plume of white smoke arising into the forest air. She puffs at the pipe repeatedly, keeping it alight, her other hand resting in her lap, her eyes closed, her body curved forward slightly. The plumes of smoke rise, dispersing into the blue skies.

'This prayer I shall give to you. It is an invocation to the four directions, and it calls in the sphere of the Silver Wheel, so that you may stand within the elemental circle of its truths.

Speak as I do, facing the East:

> I invoke the Sunstar Temple of the East, the Golden
> arising of the Sun, bringing the Inspiration of the Star
> Realms that lie beyond. I invoke the warmth and
> inspiration of the Greater Dawn. May I shine as a
> Sacred Flame to all who follow.

Now face the South, and say:

> I invoke the Earthstar Temple of the South, and
> her Lost Dimensions of sound. I invoke the Shining
> Ones of the sapphire dream who hold the Silence and
> the listening of the crystals, rocks and stones. May I
> become sensitive to the sound, the silence, the listening

Now stand facing the West, and say:

> 'I invoke the Moonstone Temple of the West, of the
> Waters. I invoke the Evening Star of Gratitude and
> Trust, the reflection of its light within my heart. May
> I give and receive Love, moment to moment, so that
> the Universal Flow is maintained through me.

Now face the North, and say:

> I invoke the Star Temple of the North, the wisdom
> of the Winds. I invoke the ancient purity of the Bear
> Cloak of the Elders. May I fly on the Silver Wings of a
> true wisdom beyond judgment, beyond good and evil.

Now stand in the Centre, and make the final invocation:

> I invoke the Immortal Tree of all worlds, whose roots
> reach down to the crystal at the centre of the Earth,
> and whose branches spiral into the heavens above. May
> the violet flame of her immortal leaves spread their
> canopy over my days and nights. May I remember
> myself as the Intergalactic Song of the Stars.

These are the four directions of the Silver Wheel, the
Temple of Arianrhod.

She passes the pipe to me. Here it is, the carved Elder
Pipe, curved in my fingers. I can feel the immeasurable
grace of this act, how I am transported by this simple
physical gesture. I lift the pipe to my lips, and inhale from
the narrow stem, feeling the smoke rising through me. I
exhale in a long plume, watching the coils of smoke spiral
loosely into the air, forming their unique and transient
sign language. My hand is cupped around the bowl of the
pipe, I sink into prayer, and it is as though I am blowing
the smoke along the pathways of the Old Language, calling
them forth, anchoring them to this dimension once more.
It is the power of my heart that makes this call, and even
with all the fervent intensity of its wish, I can feel that this
is but a slender beginning in the great storm of wishes that

shall unite and bring forth the Ancient Language of Earth. I see that the smoke is my faith, reaching out, having come far enough to blow this wish to the winds.

I offer the smoke of the sacred pipe to the stars, to the ancient dream here written; to that which is perpetual, programmed. It arises and arises, flawless, within the fabric of things. The smoke finds the hidden pattern, curls up amongst the oak branches and the rain.

I come here, with this inspiration of the old language, that expresses itself endlessly, without end, carrying its own intention. How the words spill, soft-silvered, feathered weights of the Moon, tumbling in, through the canopy of the forest, catching on the river and uttering themselves around me. I shall say the same thing over and over, to build up the nuance, softly, dragon-footed.

'I see that the time is here,' she tells me. 'It is time to reveal the secret of this tree, and to let knowledge of its true nature be accessible once again in the human worlds. Come. Follow me.'

I follow her down the oak stairwell, and when I alight beside her in the hollow tree trunk, I cast my eyes down, and see that beneath the ascending stairwell there is the entrance to one that descends beneath the crumbling hollow of the oak's trunk.

She gestures that I go first, and with some hesitation, I descend into the loamy darkness, placing careful feet upon the steps. It is cool and dark. A pale sapphire glow blossoms in the darkness, lighting up the walls, and I turn around, and see that the Elder has kindled the orb of blue flame once again, floating just ahead of her. It illumines the walls of the stairwell, through which the sinuous roots of the oak tree ripple and twist, charting our trail as we go deeper and ever deeper beneath the ground. It is a narrow and steep descent, coiling in a vertiginous spiral that guides us downward, far beneath the Earth. There is the rustle of our progress, and then the blue light illumines a pale archway, and I step through it and I am in a domed chamber that rises, sculpted and smooth all around. There is an earthen floor, and the dome is painted white as though with chalk. The ceiling is incredibly high, and I realize that it must arch all the way to the surface of the Earth, peaking under the hollowed centre of the Great Oak. The Elder emerges from behind me, sweeping across the chamber in her jade skirts, and sitting down against one of the walls.

I sit down in the centre of the vaulting space. It has an echoing, acoustic quality and I feel my movements are being choreographed into the lines of vibratory grid, a dance of ancient sounds that underlies this space.

'This is one of the ancient sound chambers. In the Old Days, they were everywhere under the Earth. They glowed and filled with celestial light and communicated with one another. They enabled the translocation between realms. They communicated with the roots of the trees and underground waters; they were filled with all the frequencies of growth. Through these chambers, whole star worlds entered into physical form. Through such a passageway, flowers and trees, animals and people arrived from other worlds and were woven into the elemental realms of Earth. The Earth was full of these hollow realms, these dreaming spaces in her fabric. Her inner worlds were alive with these sacred sounds.

'Earth was more ethereal then, because these doorways to the Lost Dimensions were held open. She was more ethereal and rapid in her cycles of flowering, with a translucency to the stars that glowed from within her. The building of these chambers was an act of maintenance by the Elven Ones, a response by them to the potentials of Earth, using the gifts they had brought from other worlds.

'Beneath each chamber is an entirely hollow crystal chamber, like a sphere or a seed lying beneath. This acts as storage for all the sound produced, recording all that passes.'

The Elder One comes over to where I sit, and crouches beside me. I see the golden-skinned drum she is holding out in her hands. I look at her for a moment. It seems impossible that I should make any sound in this place that has heard the vast purity of the music of the Elven Ones.

'Trust yourself to receive the language of Light. You shall sit here beating the drum, and carrying back the gift of words upon the sacred winds. This is your joy and your mission upon the Earth.'

I take the drum from her, and begin to beat it softly. And after a time, as the magnificent acoustic builds around me, I begin to hear the white chorus of other drums being beaten all around me, and a chanting that touches me like a wind. It is a gentle and almost indiscernible tide of sound.

I am dissolving into hundreds of golden butterflies, their etheric wings thrumming with the vibration of the drum, which continues to sound throughout the chamber. The walls of the chamber have vanished, and beyond are the deep vistas of intergalactic space. The butterflies are whispering with the voices of the Old Language: a voice that comes from many places at once: 'This is the language where many speak as one.' The butterflies are diffuse points of consciousness sounding seamlessly throughout one another. 'These are the messengers of the Intergalactic Council: those dimensions of the Silver Wheel that stem from beyond this galaxy, translating into the dimensions of our vibratory sphere.' Where the walls of the chamber once were, is an expanse of space, coloured like midnight amethyst, scattered with stars. It is these stars that are echoing, caught on the myriad antennae of the butterflies, bouncing off the fragile tissue of their wings. 'The Old Language is the multiple voice: that which whispers forth from many dimensions at once, with eternally harmonious points of multiple origination. It is this whispering language that can unlock the Lost Dimensions of Earth, unveiling her own intergalactic depths: liberating her inter-dimensional mysteries. These sacred sounds are never wasted, but vibrate for the restoration of the Lost Dimensions. The ancient sound chambers can transport us directly into Intergalactic communion, transforming us into expressive messengers of the Golden Dawn. The worlds of Earth vibrate differently every time the Old Language is spoken anew. The drum offers the restoration of your true voice that is the vibration of listening to other worlds. The drum shall make you sing, and your voice shall unlock the Lost Spheres.' So saying the golden butterflies vanish into the midnight amethyst of space, called as messengers to galaxies beyond. And I am sitting here, still beating the drum, until the beats ebb softly into the Silence, and the chalk-white walls of the dome are restored around me.

'Know that the golden butterflies will return. They exist across the threshold of the Old Language and of the drum. Every time you pick up the drum, you ask them to act as intergalactic messengers. Thus shall they come and go, maintaining your connection to the farthest stars of our world, from whence the inspiration of the Golden Dawn is transmitted.'

Finding the Language of Light

Y ou are walking through the midsummer forest, its canopy heavy with emerald leaves. Towards you from amongst the trees comes a reindeer with a star shining at her brow. She approaches you, and stretches out her nose to sniff at your hand. You feel her warm breath upon your skin, and you stroke her fur that is coarse and silky all at once. Side by side, you set off into the forest, and she is walking just slightly ahead of you, guiding the way. You realize as you travel that this is no ordinary forest, it is the Immortal Forest of the Earth, and an inner light glows within the trees. There is a sense of timelessness, and it is almost as though the forest is hung with stars. The reindeer leads the way as you go deeper and deeper into this enchanted realm, and you are overwhelmed by a sense of peace and beauty. Deep within the forest, you come to a Grove of White Trees, and at the base of each, an amethyst crystal lies in the moss. The reindeer crosses the clearing, and bows her antlered head. Somehow, you understand what she is indicating. You go over to one of the trees and kneel beside it. You peer into the amethyst that lies embedded in the moss. Within its depths shimmers the Fourth Glyph. You raise your hand to mirror the sweep of the glyph, in front of the tree, and you draw the Fourth Glyph into the forest air. As you draw the golden strokes of the Fourth Symbol, you feel the symbol entering your heart and glowing golden throughout your whole being. You are transported...

You are transported to a Listening Chamber amongst the stars. It is a luminous and barely outlined sphere, translucent to space. You sit within the Listening Chamber, cross-legged, encapsulated and yet at the same time open to all of space. You become aware of the boundaries of your skin, of the way that you define your edges. Your skin is made up of a hundred thousand etheric butterflies with violet antennae, golden pollen caught and scattered on their wings. These etheric butterflies are sleeping.

In your hands is a crystal singing bowl. You begin to play it, and it sounds an ethereal yet resonant earthly note that sets up a wild awakening in your heart. The white butterflies begin to stir and awaken, making a myriad subtle flutterings of their wings. They are awakening to the note of the singing bowl. Their violet antennae have become alert, and they hum with the song of the golden pollen that they have gathered. These are the star messages they are destined to bring to Earth.

A drum beat begins to sound, echoing through space from somewhere deep beneath you. The butterflies begin to beat their wings together with greater rapidity, preparing for flight.

You feel yourself dissolving, and you become a hundred thousand butterflies travelling downward through space, down towards the Earth in a cloud of wings.

You descend through the blue skies, past the mountaintops, past the clear sources of mountain streams, through the canopy of the forest. You are following the drumbeat, bringing the pollen of your star messages to the atmospheres of Earth. You are an ethereal music travelling into the emerald and sapphire sound fields of Earth.

The butterflies descend into one of the Ancient Lemurian Sound Chambers. Deep beneath the Earth, in a sound chamber with its arching, chalk-white walls, the butterflies settle. The butterflies flock together, congregating, and you are restored to your human form. Before you sits the drummer by whom you have been called. The drummer asks you, 'What message have you brought to the Earth?'

You answer, and your voice is the flowing of the whispered winds of the language of Light, an elemental language with access to all worlds. You know that the drummer hears and understands you. When you are ready, you realize that your message is finished: drawn into the roots of Earth's trees and into her rocks, stones and crystals. It shall be held here, revealed and treasured, released with the sacred timing of its own dimensional potentials.

You feel your body returning to normal, the sapphire pouch of your vow hanging about your neck. You feel the shimmering of your skin settling down and returning to normal, and you treasure the knowledge of your body's capacity for sensitivity and a radiant, winged listening.

You find yourself transported back to the White Grove, with its amethyst crystals glowing at the base of the trees. You follow the reindeer from the Grove of White Trees, returning to this world.

FIFTH TEACHING

This is the Fifth Teaching of the Deerskin Book:

The Grove is central to the Teachings of
the Deerskin Book.

It holds the wisdom of communion and timelessness.
This is where we discover the voice of the
Council of the Stars.

أب

Chapter 5

To return with that knowledge
of the present
and her far, crystal eyes.

To know
the haunting depths
of the moment in which I stray.

THE WHITE DEER with the star at her brow leads us into the Silver Grove. It is here, beneath the magnificent and ancient silver branches that we reweave the lost glyphs of our own inter-dimensional presence.

Imagine the Silver Grove: magnificent timeless trees woven out of starlight that stand all around the Earth. Their giant roots are wound around her, forming an atmospheric cradle. These trees form the Council of the Stars that guides the Earth into beautiful resonance with the rest of the Cosmos. Here, there exists a great collaboration of Star Beings who oversee her development. In these times, we are becoming increasingly aware of the presence and influence of the Silver Grove and it shall transparently become an aspect of our own consciousness. That is, we shall become aware of Earth's special role in the evolution of the whole cosmos, and the many ascending and descending realms of order to which she is connected.

Underneath the sapphire leaves of the canopy of the Silver Grove, we are able to remember the aspects of ourselves that extend to the level of Galactic and Intergalactic vision. We are entering this transpersonal template that expands the domain of self into its natural far reaches. This is enabling the beautiful rebirth of our world, as we step beyond vulnerable isolation into radical interconnectivity, and the reconnection to high levels of spiritual intention and guidance. We need to remember ourselves as agents of cosmic service and transformation. The trees of the Silver Grove are Intergalactic Elders who release the codes of our incarnational purpose. You discover yourself as a Planetary Guardian; you are not merely a vulnerable and separate human being, but empowered with the facility to dance as a Guardian upon this planet. Your movements are significant and determinative in the anchoring of an ancient and futuristic dream.

The presence of the Silver Grove means that the Intergalactic Guardians are descending into our skies once again, their wisdom readily available to the listener. And they are an aspect of ourselves. We are this Silver Grove: it is our wingtips, our outermost consciousness that accounts for our capacity to surrender our lives to divine service.

* * *

It is the White Deer who leads you through the deep spheres of space into the precinct of the Silver Grove. You stand amidst the vast forms of the silvery trees, and sit down in the emerald moss at its centre. And at the perimeter of the Grove are the four Gateways of Fire, Earth, Air and Water. Beyond them are the shadowy forms of their sentinels – you shall call them forth. You shall greet them brow to brow

– star to star. The Sacred Alliance brightens between you once more. It is precious, to be thus drawn together into a timeless recognition that spans lifetimes and dimensions. They reveal your highest dimensional affinities. There is the transfer of information concerning your spiritual purpose.

This is the restoration of your Wheel of Elemental Guardians. Protecting the perimeter of the wheel are the four Guardians. They form a matrix that holds you in alignment with your true destiny. You shall experience them as spirit animals, archangels, elders, plant and stone spirits. It is now very important that you restore your elemental wheel. This is your opportunity to do so.

You do not have one point of origin. Countless stardusts have woven together to form the matrix that you are. Your consciousness is a mosaic of star worlds, planetary influence and shattering suns. Much travels together to form this 'one entity' that you are. It is this cosmic genesis that comprises the Elemental Guardians at your edges. But the wheel points not just to genesis, or essence, but to the alignment of your personal energies with the natural cycles of Earth. The Elemental Wheel anchors the Star Soul and its spiritual quest into the seasonal cycles, and the geophysical aspects of its environment. We must develop all aspects of ourselves if we are to give our gift to the world.

Every aspect of our mental, physical, emotional and spiritual makeup is reflected and represented on the Wheel of the Guardians. By working with the Guardians, we become very powerful and very beautiful in all directions.

Our relationship with the Guardians is a process of invocation and discovery. Their presences dance through our days, ever guiding us into deeper realization of our true nature. It is indeed a wheel, and it spins, creating movement and growth.

Stand upon the Earth. Face the direction of the Rising Sun, where she crests the horizon at dawn. This is the East, and the place where the periphery of your elemental wheel is seeded. Here is the spark of your conception, your incarnation as a human being. Here is your arrival from star worlds and your flame of enthusiasm. Turn and bless this direction and summon forth your Guardian of the East. They come to you, a beautiful flame upon your heart, an ancient companion that touches you with fire and wonder and love. Softly, they step out from amidst the trees, stepping out from deep space where they have been wandering unacknowledged this last aeon. You touch foreheads, greeting each other in the Old Way, star to star.

You turn now to face the South. This is the direction of the Earth element. Here is your ground, where the sacred spark enters into the definitions of form. Here the rocks and the stones and the crystals hold us, forming the lattices of stability and coherent structure. Summon forth your Guardian of the South. With soft and powerful beauty they emerge from amongst the trees of the Silver Grove. They come to you. You touch foreheads, brow to brow, star to star, the greeting of the Ancient Ones.

Understand that your relationship to the South and the Element of Earth will lend you the stability and power to achieve your goals, to manifest fully as yourself. You need the correct crystalline latticework beneath your feet. In just this way does a tree need the correct soil for its roots.

You turn to face the West. This is the direction of the Waters, the realm of feeling and emotion where we meet with the Other. It is our interconnectivity, our capacity for giving and receiving. It is the place of the Moon, of ocean and river and moonstone lake. It is the underground waters, the springs and the rains. It is the place of autumn and of twilight. Summon your Guardian of the West. They come to you, flowing softly from amongst the Silver Trees, stepping forth to greet you, touching forehead to forehead.

You turn now to the North. This is the Direction of the Winds, and the Winter. It is the place of mental wisdom: the falling snowflakes of wisdom that lend us perspective, rationality and discernment. Here we can receive the wisdom of the Ancestors, and attain this wisdom for ourselves. This is a perspective of profound non-judgment that transcends the dualities of good and evil, right and wrong. In this place, summon the Guardian of the North, and be restored to their presence. As they advance towards you, emerging from the deep starry space beyond the Silver Grove, you recognize their companionship, ancient and aloof, yet deeply familiar. With this Guardian, once more, you make the ancient greeting.

You have in this way restored the Four Directions, the four shrines of your elemental presence upon Earth. There are four directions shining around you, breathing blessings, translations of wisdom. You are beginning to discover how you project your presence into perceptual reality, how you become visible in your pattern of becoming. You stand now at the centre of your Elemental Circle. Here is the source, the Great Mystery from which all else emerges.

And in Source, at the centre of your wheel, grows the Great Cosmic Tree. This is the White Tree of Peace, the

Great Mother of All Worlds. From her, all worlds, all realities, both vast and infinitesimal, arise. Her great roots spiral down beneath you, into the subtle inner realms of Earth, wrapping themselves around the crystal at Earth's core. Her mighty branches reach up, from them all the infinite star worlds springing leaf and blossom. And at her centre, within your heart, Heaven and Earth meet. Within your heart dance all worlds, all dimensions, and the infinite wisdom to walk a path of Divine Love.

Thus, in the Silver Grove we discover the Wheel of the Elemental Guardians. We discover the Guardians of our periphery. We discover our own outer perimeter of sacred reflections. Under the sapphire leaves, I am able to remember my role of planetary service: I remember the Earth as a grid of beautiful programmed energies, and my own body as an echo of this.

Through this practice, through visitation of the Silver Grove, we reconstruct the architecture, the etheric template of our evolving selves. It is a Temple that we can carry with us in every moment, wherever we are. This is an important aspect of how we call forth the Lost Dimensions of ourselves. It is time to remember our true inter-dimensional presence once more. We reconstruct the architecture through sound, breath, prayer, movement; through sudden discovery, serendipity and epiphany. It comes through dream, sleeping and waking. Access this; do not let the opportunities languish. All that you encompass shall be discovered. We need this definition, this delineation. Under the branches of the Silver Grove again and again we come. We shall be given the answers we seek.

* * *

There is a long tradition of the connection between the Sacred Grove and the stars, as held especially by the Druids. It is no coincidence that the destruction of the Sacred Groves was pivotal to silencing that phase of consciousness. There were extraordinary reservoirs of cosmic and elemental wisdom stored in those Groves. As we become more sensitive, we discover that these storehouses of wisdom still exist upon the etheric plane. They are still woven into the subtle worlds of Earth and awaiting recognition. This is not about the restoration of an old religion. We shall know when these moments occur, when our feet touch the ground in an old forest, on vanished land, and suddenly palpable echoes stir within us, and we are inspired to gestures of starlit creativity and Infinite Love.

It is the Druids who have borne the truth of the Sacred Grove through to the present moment in our current historical era, but here we go deeper even than this memory, to the presence of the Silver Trees of the Stars themselves. This is about the present moment and the activation of planetary peace through naturally occurring transmissions. The Shining Ones and the glyphs encode for us a memory much more vast, a purpose more far-reaching, and at once more immediate and intimate. It is the fierce Dawn of the Light within us at this hour: it is the inheritance of a wisdom path that comes from the stars, from the Universe, from ourselves.

* * *

This Grove simultaneously manifests geometrically as a pair of pyramids: an inverse pyramid on top of an upright pyramid. This is its energetic counterpart or signature on the level of Light. The Earth is the base of the lower pyramid, the intergalactic realms are the upper pyramid, and the Silver Wheel of our galaxy is the place where the tips of the two pyramids meet. This translates into a Grove whose roots are interwoven around the Earth, whose trunks pass through the Silver Wheel of our galaxy, and whose branches stretch out into the intergalactic realms of the entire universe. The Silver Wheel of our galaxy translates the messages of inter-galactic consciousness, making the teachings of realms far beyond our own accessible to us.

It is as though a heavenly energy is down-stepped through the Silver Wheel so that we may access it. The important thing to remember is that it is for our benefit: for the growth of love, light and joy in our lives and our planet at this time. It is a direct and practical transmission. It enables transfor-mation at a very immediate level, without complex esoteric understandings. This is because its intention is very pure and simple.

* * *

The Silver Wheel of Glyphs is descending into the atmos-pheres of Earth, traversing the branches and trunks of the Silver Trees, informed by the wisdom of the Star Council, and returning to Earth to manifest as the Temple of Arianrhod.

This 'temple' is not a religious concept: it is a principle of creativity, a floating cosmic wisdom that aligns itself with the heart in order to build Heaven upon Earth. It settles, tier upon tier, descending amongst us, finding many gradations of expression.

The Temple of Arianrhod exists where the human heart merges with the principles of cosmic unfoldment and something unique comes forward. It is very particular to this time, because it is perfectly attuned to these conditions of emergence from the darkness. We may proclaim, 'But I have held the Light' and we have, but now it is time for an interconnectivity of irradiation that is entirely new to us and gives birth to infinite creative potentials. It is this collectivity of Illumination that transpires such a quantum leap in the dimensional qualities of planet Earth. This is why we use the expression 'New Earth'.

* * *

The Silver Wheel of Glyphs holds the imprint for the next phase of Earth's evolution. We recognize it as it arrives. As it comes into our awareness it rings with far bells, with Light.

The Silver Wheel becomes available through lifetimes of dedication, throughout which listening to the path of the Teachings has been an elusive treasure hunt. The full vehicle of transmissions has not been available until now. Through the Silver Wheel of Glyphs, the Teachings are able to coalesce and enter this dimension. It draws them together, or holds them in their pattern of resonance. The heart by which they are sought, known and found, is their other orientation. I shall give you an example of how the transmissions are found and received. In the summer of 2012 I visited the sacred waterfall of Pistyll Rhaeadr in Wales. This is a beautiful waterfall, a narrow and vertiginous cascade tumbling down from the Berwyn Mountains amid pine trees into a valley of wonderful grandeur and powerful sacred energies. It is one of the holy places of the Shining Ones, where their presence remains intact. It is one of the Guardian places of the Earth, where transmissions of higher consciousness flow uninterrupted. It affects every visitor in a way that is unique and sacred to them. Here, I slept in my tent beside the river for a couple of nights, dreaming and steeped in the energies of the place. It was intense and beautiful, and my body became full with a mighty transmission: the lightning of inspiration. Here I received the Thirteen Glyphs. I remember my canvas tent, a peaked bell tent, alight with the transmissions. Yet this was the reception of a pure energetic transmission and I had no intellectual knowledge of what the Glyphs meant. I could *feel* their meaning, yet not articulate it to myself or another.

It was on another journey to the Himalayas in 2013 that I discovered more. Guided from sacred place to sacred place throughout Nepal, India, Ladakh and Sikkim, I danced the Glyphs in alignment with the phases of the Moon. Here, I received the content of the Teachings. I became aware of the wisdom they hold, and the unique message that they are bringing through.

Thus I received the final transmission of the Silver Wheel in the Himalayas, in the high-altitude region of Ladakh. Once I attained a conscious alignment to the Teachings of the Silver Wheel of Glyphs, there followed a long period of adjustment until I could bring it forward again into consciousness. It feels as though I am receiving the gift for the first time, as it has integrated and harmonized.

* * *

The Glyphs are a communication system or device, the translation of one dimension into another. These levels of consciousness come from other galaxies, of which we have been a part in other existences. This is why we can connect, because we carry their trace and have spoken their language, we have understood and embodied their terms. The point is not to attempt to strain to reach a point 'out there': a faraway place in consciousness. The goal is the full and peaceful embodiment of this consciousness here upon Earth, allowing the Earth her metamorphosis into a more evolved sphere.

These other galaxies are as close as our own heart; they are ourselves. The more we realize this, the more the attendant knowledge and wisdom will become available, the more 'memories' we shall have. Lemurian consciousness is this very communications network between dimensions, this very expression of our true nature.

We do not have to force an altered perspective; in fact, we must not. This is entirely beyond the point. This is a natural process of evocation and revelation, and it has its own process of integration.

* * *

The forests are calling us once more. Increasingly they shall call you, and you shall feel this incredible over-arching connection to the wisdom of the Silver Grove. Here you feel the descent of the incoming frequencies, and the uprising through root and soil of the hidden crystalline songs of Earth. You are rewoven into the awakening of the New Earth, you become a participant in the arising Dawn and no longer lost in the imitations of a fading aeon. It arises differently because of you. In the forest, in the Sacred Grove, these transformations are softened as we are in a field of energies that metamorphose without resistance. This is also the profound value of the Sacred Grove, because it allows for integration in a way that feels peaceful and gentle. It allows for the myriad adjustments we are making: a subtle orchestration that is mirrored by the seamless complexity of its life forms and ecology. Communion with the trees and Sacred Groves is also an end in itself, the expression of our being-ness here, of our joy at being part of this Earth. It is a return to the simplicity of having breathed and lived this Earth, at the sheer delight of these experiences. This is the simplicity to which we are tending: toward the dance with this infinite, myriad moment and her changing hues of wonder. Our consciousness travels back and forth along lines of expansion and simplicity, and eventually everything folds back into the silent, myriad arising.

As I have already said so many times, these Teachings must be viewed as a gift of Nature. They are not designed to take us away from ourselves. It is only that we become more and more of what we truly are.

The Earth holds an ancient star of wisdom at her heart. This is awakening its songs of guidance: it is stirring with sound-light radiance. We sense the awakening of the ancient crystal cities echoing with Peace on Earth. The ancient art and practice of Natural Illumination is attainable, enshrined within the starflower energies of Nature's upliftment power. We shall each attain our idiosyncratic rendition of illumination and cosmic guidance. This occurs in freedom from the tyrannies of religious and spiritual methods that supplant or remove *immediacy*. And so as we follow the path of our natural illumination, we do not wander away from Earth. It is the worlds we have built upon the Earth that we surrender: it is the forms of reality to which we have bound her. She is shaking these reins free, and the less tightly we hold on, the less she will harm us with her liberation. We may travel with her to where she is going: we may go forward into the Earth's future. She will not be as we have known her: we must surrender every image and ask to see her evolving self: ask to see where she is headed. She is not against us, she will not withhold this from us. We may witness her Dream, her destination. We may witness the future. What is this imprint, this blueprint of her soul to which she tends? How may we be a part of this?

The Teachings offer answers to these questions – but we must each seek our own vision, the full awakening of our own awareness. Thus we are the Dream itself awakening and activating, beginning to blossom and dance.

We are a part of the Earth, we are her essence: when we allow ourselves to blossom into the rising light of the Dawn, we are the Earth awakening. We are her stardust, her soil, her dust; we are woven from her mud. Yet if we deny our own existence, block out our own metamorphosis, then she will shake us off. This is not out of judgement or retribution: it is simply the consequence of our dancing to a different music. It shall carry us elsewhere.

* * *

This brings me to the elucidation of the place of the Earth in these Teachings. She is our ground, and it is toward a truer alignment with her that we tend. We are woven out of her five elements: fire, air, earth and water and space. These elements endow us with the successive links of our cosmic memories, the ladder that restores us to full and grounded Illumination.

The elements are central to the Lemurian Teachings and remembrance: the practices that fall to us from the Sunlight. As we now realise, these practices link us through the vortex of the Silver Wheel to other solar systems, and different forms of evolved consciousness.

I have spoken of the metamorphosis of the Earth: of her transformation. She is Dreaming herself into a new blueprint: that is, the consciousness of Earth has already ceased to hold the old pattern. She is moving into a different paradigm. She is borrowing the elements of other dimensions: she is borrowing inspiration from other existences, distant star dusts. She is taking on the encodings of that which lives and breathes in the light of different suns.

Each sun vibrates differently, each producing a unique vibrational expression. The Earth is breathing these in, and this is her metamorphosis. There is an alignment taking place that allows her access to this enhanced field of inspiration.

The Sun transmits all of this to her, even as it does to us. The Earth is lit in a different light, and she sees herself differently. Or to put it another way: the incoming light is causing her to metamorphoses, to grow differently. This brings a greater evolved consciousness to Earth: it allows her to slip this spell of materialism we have placed over her. She is gaining a different kind of dimensional access, a different possibility of being. This has in fact existed before, or close to it, in what we remember as the Lemurian and Atlantean periods. This is why we are recrossing these memory strands. These memories also provide us with a cellular, elemental memory of our own compatibility with this dimensional expression of Earth.

These long-past eras provide bridges, but they are not the future into which we are crossing. They merely provide some important tools and memories for what we are undergoing. We last experienced this degree of interconnection with other dimensions at those times. The Earth herself belongs to many lifetimes and universes, composed of elements that are capable of infinite dimensional and material transformations.

* * *

So this question arises: what is it that the Earth is dreaming for herself? How may we access this Dream and make it our ground and alignment? We must visit the Silver Grove to access this knowledge. It is here she dwells now: amongst the Silver Trees of the Stars.

Go to this place. This is why the forests are calling: that is why the Deer, who has kept the forest trails throughout the aeons, was chosen as the messenger of the Teachings. This is the indelible, unbroken link with the Sacred Grove and the future of the Earth.

Go here, dream here, and see that which arises. But this is already happening; you have already heard the call.

Here we shall dream ourselves and we shall dream the Earth, here amongst the Silver Trees of the Council of the Stars. Here we shall lie upon the moss. Here stands the Earth undiminished. This is where she is leading us: the White Deer with the star at her brow.

And so you sit in the Silver Grove, beneath the trees. You are dwarfed by their great trunks. Beneath you, their roots reach far down, woven around Earth. You come to ask questions, you seek a path that serves the greatest good, the greatest love. This goes beyond social mores, values, customs, patterns of obedience, of subservience; it goes beyond concepts of virtue into which we are conditioned; it goes beyond the inheritance of ancestral programs. You look beyond all of this to ask the question: what does the Universe truly wish from me?

In the Silver Grove, we are accessing an infinite intelligence that moves for the benefit of all. It sees a totality of conditions of which we cannot be aware from an individual perspective. Its motivation is Love. It comprises the intelligence of many worlds; it is a collective, interwoven intelligence that is impersonal yet deeply loving.

And so we come to discover our purpose, our gift to the realms of Earth in this incarnation. The contracted field of self-protection and individual desire holds dwindling sway.

You discover that instead, in your heart, you carry all the ancient wisdom of the forests. You hold the collective gathered wisdom of all those aeons of growth. You can be trusted. You can be trusted with the destiny of Earth: to attend to the rhythms and pulses of the evolutionary path. Thus are the Elders of the Grove awakening from their slumbers to an active phase. Prepare to grow tall, to form a canopy enshrining the Earth, and deep roots that anchor the New Earth reality.

How do we unlock the essence of the Grove Elder within our own hearts? How do we become free of motivations that distract us and lead us astray, albeit unconsciously? How do we re-emerge with this purity of heart?

It is showing itself in your life. Look to the presence, however peripheral and slight. You track by subtlety, by observation. The Elders are in turn tracking *us,* seeking *us.* The incoming starlight is awakening them, and they are sending out their call. They beckon to us, drawing us into their presence so that we may receive the Emerald Transmission and become Grove Elders once more. Be called to leafy greatness, to towering height and sheltering branches. Sit amidst the moss and gnarled roots. Here the transmissions of the Cosmic Grove Elders take place and here we gain entrance to the Silver Grove of galactic intelligence. The spirit of growth and awakening fills us.

We remember the dimensions of our own Elder Heart and capacity to leaf in interconnected grandeur, offering protection, inspiration and balance to others as they find their own way. Deep within, our hearts are awakening to this role.

* * *

You become a beacon, lit up, and others can be guided by you, even from a distance; even when they cannot physically see you, you help them to maintain their own alignment. Thus are we tuning forks for one another. We have arrived for this purpose: we are companions in this movement. You are already aware of them, these others who ground this possibility of ascension, of metamorphosis. They glow like miraculous lamps in the darkness: part angel, part human. They seem to transcend ordinary, material reality. They seem to be operating by different laws, different principles than those conditioned by our world. They seem to have attained a freedom from the chains of ordinariness. Yet they are also manifest, real human beings. They live in beautiful places and they help others. These are those attuned to the Dream of the Earth, to the Divine.

We cannot always gather with our kindred souls in the same physical location. This is not what is required at this time. There are key points on the Earth requiring activation, and we must spread out over them. As I have said, we shall not experience absence through physical separation, and neither shall we be left alone without the physical support we require. We shall feel ourselves to be transparent and available to these others, and increasingly our integrity becomes a gift to them as well as to ourselves, as our Light touches them and shines upon them moment to moment.

Thus shall the Earth become more and more transparent to other dimensions, less separate. The sense of communication and inspiration from other realms shall become clearer and more apparent. She herself will become more visible, less hidden, beaming with the lights and possibilities of other worlds.

None of this is random, but occurs with the progression of Light programmed for this time. We shall continue to work with sunlight, with crystals, with drum and sound, with the Silver Grove. It is a great alchemical moment in our destinies.

* * *

The path of the Deer through time and space honours us for this transformation; it is grounded in the centuries and passage of other lifetimes. We receive the resonance and support from every other dimension and moment that we require. We take up the gifts of our spiritual heritage, and acknowledge our own mastery and innocence, our own remembrance and readiness.

The Elemental Wheel has two axes: that of Heaven and Earth, and that of past and future. We stand in the centre, in the Silence, while the Deer and the Sacred Grove and the Stars and the Sun dream us. We cannot be lost by the unfoldment of ourselves. The Elemental Wheel arises and vanishes; the Teachings shimmer into being and then disappear. Our hearts guide us, our love for one another sustains us. The Glyphs are apparitions both momentary and eternal, and perhaps this is enough. They need not be held or maintained, they need not be taken up as a spiritual path or a religion. They manifest simply to touch our consciousness, to be witnessed, and then we may return to the Silence, to the night, and to the Dawn that comes.

* * *

I walk down to the Old Willow tree. I lean against its rough bark beside the river. I hold the Spirit Amethyst in my lap and she dissolves and enchants me in her violet light. I am bound into the ephemeral lights of willow and amethyst. I sense a way of belonging that is infinitely beautiful: a way that is green, infused with the whispering voices of the Elders.

I tread through dim corridors, scuffing my feet along a cracked floor, my hands seeking the walls for balance. Finally, I emerge, and I am in a different world. A Grove of Willows stands under a night sky of stars. Beneath the hanging branches, at the centre of the clearing, there is an Elder dancing around a fire. She has a staff in her hand with silver bells that ring out as she moves. The trees throw shadows around the bright fire, and the moving shadow of the Elder is at one with them: she is the Keeper of this Sacred Grove. Onto the fire she throws resin of myrrh and cedar and handfuls of dried lavender. The willows are craggy and massive, with sprawling branches. Their trunks are grooved with hollow chambers at the bases. They lean and shower their branches around the Elder's fire.

I notice that emanating from the canopy of the trees are orbs, scintillating spheres that drift into the darkness, rising slowly into a night of stars. The deep voice of the Elder travels across the Grove towards me,

'They are the Orbs of the Elders who are leaving the Earth. This is a Grove of Ascension between realms, forming a bridge between the Earth and her own ascended consciousness.'

There is a sudden disturbance, the tumult of wings descending. The Elder raises her staff high into the air, and a great, shadowy form alights upon it. As she lowers the staff, the bird is illuminated in the firelight, its feathers banded white and tawny. It looks at me askance, its beaked face grave and impartial. Then, abruptly, up the buzzard soars once more, and in its wake floats a phalanx of Orbs. The buzzard spirals up, higher and ever higher above the Grove, like a feathered chaperone to the lights.

I gaze upwards through the gap in the canopy. The Elder bends over the fire, tending to its flames. Her appearance is part willow, so long has she dwelt in the Grove. She stands there with the Staff of Silver Bells, with which she sounds ancient aspirations for the Earth.

'I am Keeper of the Grove for those who have passed their initiations within this world. They are those who, with undimmed eyes, have learnt to perceive truth from moment to moment. Theirs is an entire realization of the silver star heart within nature. They arise, sounded forth by the song of the silver bells, bid farewell by the fragrance of the Elder Fire. They travel onward, bursting forth from the furthest leaf tips, propelled by all the awakened dawns within them to another world, another dimension.

'The buzzard ushers the Ascended Ones from the Willow Grove to the Silver Grove of the Stars. It guides those that have ascended from the leaves, from the trees, and conducts them forth as messengers of Earth consciousness.'

Suddenly, I am clutched in the talons of the buzzard, dangling over the willow trees. I am gripped as her feathers whistle through the air, beating their upward path out of the Willow Grove, out of the firelight, through air faintly traced with smokes of myrrh, cedar and lavender. The buzzard makes fierce and steadfast progress through space, catching up to the floating ascension of the orbs. There is the sound of the Silver Bells, the resonance of the staff beating the ground as the Elder dances her incantation of farewell.

The orbs mount upwards, following the ephemeral smokes of her blessing fire. The air becomes tarnished with brushstrokes of silver: we are being drawn beyond the influence of the Willow Grove into another realm. All around us are the giant, shining, silver roots of an ingrained and ancient stellar bark.

I feel as though I am breathing silver as we follow the roots that reach down. The buzzard glides upwards, and around us the Orbs are being absorbed in sudden flashes into the roots of the Silver Trees. We ascend into the domain of the Silver Grove, where the giant trunks of grooved bark stand sentinel. The branches weave a cathedral roof overhead, clad in a canopy of elliptical sapphire leaves. Diadems of sapphire flash within the tree, witness to their overarching intelligence.

The buzzard loosens its grip, and I find myself suspended in the centre of the Silver Grove under its great, vaulting branches. A question arises within me in response to this magnificence, 'What does this mean for a human life upon Earth? How can these far and magnificent dimensions touch my life, which feels so small by comparison?' All the immortal peace of the stars cascades through the uppermost branches: the highest reaches of the Grove seem to dissolve into a presence of unutterable softness. There is an incredible stillness to this place, as though these giants move in such vast and mighty cycles that my presence has barely registered, tuned to aeons as they are.

Then there comes the murmuring boom of an answering Voice, seeming to come from each and all of the trees, 'The Silver Grove holds the future of the Earth. This Grove holds a Dawn for her, far out amongst the stars. Here her truest visions are protected from the storms of forgetfulness. The Silver Trees stand as a radiant outpost, holding a blueprint for the Earth's harmonic wisdoms of Peace.'

Remembrance floods me: past lifetimes of access to this holy ground. The Silver Grove is like a giant cradle plaited silver around the Earth, giant Elven harmonies encircling us. It is around this world, this Earth, that the star-fell roots of the Elder Trees grow. These are the Elders who guide us. These are the Councils of Light that direct the evolution of the Earth.

The Silver Grove brings us the guidance of the Shining Ones: the myriad unnamed souls who have realized the true nature of this Earth. We need these unnamed flames of wisdom that have shone in this world through her aeons of evolution. We need to reclaim our lost narrative of enlightenment, we need to understand the enlightenment of the clouds and the pearls and the forests. We need the Elven Ones of the Old Light to stand amongst us in their Silver Councils, opening the old gateways, allowing us passage. We need to welcome the cradle of enlightenment that has always held this earth, our setting against a backdrop of inspired breath and realization.

I can feel the great roots of the mighty, silvery Grove rooting themselves into my consciousness. I stand amongst the arching roots of the great Silver Trees, feeling the depths of a pure darkness dancing through me. I see how this wonder, this mystery is a foundation stone. The dedication is to become rooted in this expression of Great Mystery: this dancing, cosmic, vast emergence. This is to surrender to vast cycles of awareness, to a gradual emergence timed with cosmic wisdom. This Grove connects me to an impersonal awareness, a transcendence of smaller aims and desires. In this we can trust ourselves. We have this capacity to become rooted in cosmic vision, to become caretakers of ourselves and our world. I trust my capacity, my willingness, to surrender to this. I trust myself with this in every day, every hour, every moment. This is the legacy of the Silver Grove.

Finding Your Golden Star of Time

Y ou are walking in the forest of deep summer. From amongst the shadowy emerald trees, a reindeer comes towards you with a star shining at her brow. She approaches you and stretches out her nose to sniff at your hand. You feel her warm breath upon your skin, and you stroke her fur that is coarse and silky all at once. Side by side, you set off into the forest, and she is walking just slightly ahead of you, guiding the way. You realize as you travel that this is no ordinary forest; it is the Immortal Forest of the Earth, and an inner light glows within the trees. There is a sense of timelessness, and it is as though the forest is hung with stars. The reindeer crosses the clearing, and bows her antlered head. Somehow, you understand what she is indicating. You go over to one of the trees and kneel beside it. You peer into the amethyst that lies embedded in the moss. Within its depths shimmers the Fifth Glyph. You raise your hand to mirror the sweep of the Glyph in front of the tree, and you draw it into the forest air. As you draw the golden strokes of the Fifth Glyph, you feel the symbol entering your heart and glowing golden throughout your whole being. You are transported...

Its golden form merges with you, and you find yourself transported to an immense grove of silvery trees that arch over you like a cathedral. This grove is growing in the immensity of space, vaulting up amongst the stars. You are sitting in the centre of the Silver Grove of the Stars. It is here that the consciousness of the Intergalactic Council for Earth resides, and you feel yourself touched and embraced by this vast consciousness. Through you sweeps the awareness of Great Mystery, and a surrender to this ground of mysterious Love that pours through you. You feel held and immeasurably safe in this realm.

You begin to hear voices of Immortal Wisdom echoing through the Trees, an oversoul consciousness that booms in soft, commanding tones. Faraway lights seem to shimmer from within the trees. At first the voices seem to be in a deep Elven language beyond your ordinary consciousness, yet understood by you at another level. Then they resolve gradually into a message that you clearly understand.

'You are a golden star that spans vast cycles of time. This star that you are is woven of golden threads. These connect you to other lifetimes, past and future. These anchor your current incarnation, and are threaded through your present moment.

'This suspension of golden strands forms a unique version of Time within every human being. Each person's present moment holds unique linkages or dimensional corridors. These are actually facets of the Now, of one living moment, rather than separate events of past, present and future. They are aspects of the mandala you offer to the world. You offer your gifts of past and future even as you offer your present to those around you. It is good to know the dimensional gifts you are offering: the vast view that is an aspect of your own soul.'

Now is the time to discover the golden star that you are. You shall travel along each of the five golden threads, that appear before you like golden tunnels, and discover the Five Lifetimes that are part of your Essence in the NOW. Then you shall have reconstructed your awareness of the Golden Threads that anchor you, and your awareness of yourself as a being belonging to Vast Cycles of Time.

You are sitting at the centre of the Silver Grove, and you ask the question of the Council of the Stars, 'What is my Near Past lifetime?' You see a golden tube-like tunnel appear before you, and you start to travel down it, walking the golden tunnel to the Near Past Lifetime that connects most strongly to your essence in the Now. Allow yourself to perceive a clear glimpse of this, storing any impressions you receive in your heart, then, when you are ready, return along the golden tunnel to the Silver Grove.

You ask the question of the Council of the Stars, 'What is my Near Future lifetime?' You see a golden tube-like tunnel appear before you, and you start to travel down it, walking the golden tunnel to the Near Future Lifetime that connects most strongly to your essence in the Now. Allow yourself to perceive a clear glimpse of this, storing any impressions that you receive in your heart, then, when you are ready, return along the golden tunnel to the Silver Grove.

Now you are ready to ask the question of the Council of the Stars, 'What is my Far Past lifetime?' This lifetime may extend into other planetary, starry, or intergalactic existences, as well as earthly incarnations before the historical era. You see a golden tube-like tunnel appear before you, and you start to travel down it, walking the golden tunnel to the Far Past Lifetime that connects most strongly to your essence in the Now. Allow yourself to perceive a clear glimpse of this, storing any impressions that you receive in your heart, then, when you are ready, return along the golden tunnel to the Silver Grove.

Now you are ready to ask the question, 'What is my Far Future lifetime?' You see a golden tube-like tunnel appear before you, and you start to travel down it, walking the golden tunnel to the Far Future Lifetime that connects most strongly to your essence in the Now. Allow yourself to perceive a clear glimpse of this, storing any impressions that you receive in your heart, then, when you are ready, return along the golden tunnel to the Silver Grove.

Now, you are ready to ask the question concerning your present incarnation, 'What is the full expression of my Present lifetime?' You see a golden tube-like tunnel appear before you, and you start to travel down it, walking the golden tunnel to a vision of yourself in this lifetime, at the height of your maturity and fulfillment. It is this aspect of your present lifetime that most deeply informs your essence in the Now. Allow yourself to perceive a clear glimpse of this, storing any impressions that you receive in your heart, then, when you are ready, return along the golden tunnel to the Silver Grove.

In the centre of the Silver Grove, you stand up and see yourself radiating these five golden strands of your Golden Star of Time. Your near past and near future strand emanate from your shoulders, and your far past and far future lifetimes emanate from the soles of your feet. Your present lifetime strands emanates through the crown of your head. These strands radiate, powerfully golden, gathered together in consciousness. You are shining as a five-pointed star that connects to vast cycles of time. Know that this is the mandala of your offerings in the Now, an underlying dimensional time field that you carry. These are an aspect of your Wisdom Essence, your Wisdom Teachings that you offer in sacred contract to this world.

See this Golden Star gently shrinking and descending into your sapphire pouch, and framing the sapphire within. This is your personal link to the cycles of vast consciousness embodied by the Silver Grove. It is your own connection to the Council of the Stars, as one who is reinstating the Sacred Groves of Earth.

Offer your blessing and gratitude to the Silver Grove of

which you are a part, and begin to descend through the roots, down through space, descending through the blue skies and clouds of Earth's atmosphere, entering your body once more where you sit amongst the White Trees, the amethysts glowing at their base. You follow the reindeer out of the White Grove, returning through the forest to this world.

Know that the gifts of the sapphire pouch and its Golden Star remain with you, and are yours to allow their gentle integration into your daily life.

Sixth Teaching

This is the Sixth Teaching of the Deerskin Book:

The flowers contain the beauty of the truths of our energetic fields.

They remind us of who we are and the patterns we hold. They mirror the crystalline matrixes of light with which we generate the hologram of our physical bodies.

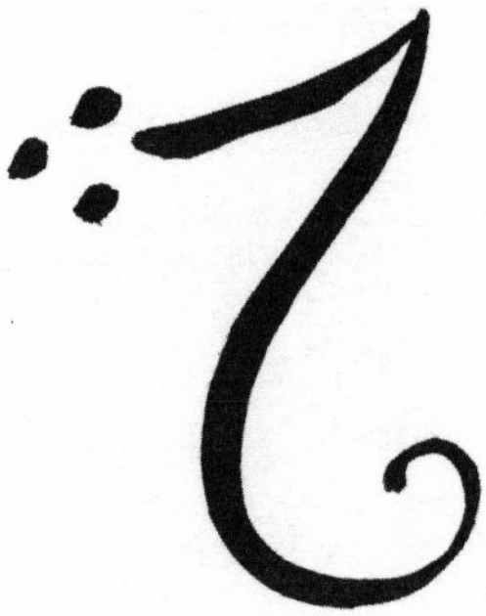

Chapter 6

Blue smoke of
wood fire,
a tattoo,
of torn sound,
a tasselled silence.

THE SIXTH TEACHING of the Deerskin Book is that we share geometric form with the flowers and angelic patterns of consciousness. In our true appearance, we are akin to the white flower blooming delicately and six-petalled in the woodland that so strikes the heart with its beauty. This windflower, this wood anemone, is ourselves. This is what the flowers have to teach us: our true nature. They are avatars at this time. Their place in Creation is not peripheral or ornamental: it is an expression of Cosmic Truth that can bring vast healing and insight to us.

We can listen to the flowers, who also have evolved over millennia to this moment upon the Earth, drinking in the messages of sunlight and starlight. They have achieved a perfection of form that is mirrored by our energy fields. They are ourselves, seen through a different lens. This gives us some idea of the beauty of our awakening energy fields. They are like radiant, many-starred petals reaching out into the Universe: constellations of communication and connection. They are very beautiful, and they are still evolving and awakening to their perfect expression. We should set no limit upon our true appearance in this dimension: but every time we experience the beauty of a flower, we are being shown a glimpse of this dimension of ourselves. The more we allow this beauty to filter into our awareness, the more we facilitate its manifestation. This is a path of natural cultivation; we recognize the appropriate mirrors of our light bodies when they appear to us.

These beings mirror the Light holograph of our evolution. The flowers particularly act in this way at this time because they embody very high and delicate frequencies that correspond to our outermost fringes of growth: the areas in which we are really stepping free from density, into connection with the Universe. This corresponds to the very high frequency of the Silver Wheel, the portal opening up between us and other galaxies. This brings us full incarnational memory and a remembrance of original purpose.

The wild and ancient flowers of woodland, mountain and meadow are especially our allies at this time, as they embody the actuality of highly evolved co-existence within complexity. Theirs is the patient arrival at a very high level of expression.

* * *

There are times when we have experienced the beautiful epiphanies of the Divine, the times when we truly felt our own Illumination. Then the clouds, the veil, descend once more, and we feel bereft and afraid, powerless and confused. We have experienced something else, yet as hard as we search, we cannot find it again.

This quest is our resistance to the blossoming; we do not want to pay attention to the path beneath our feet, to trust in its perfection, because we have a preconception of what the Dawn involves. The Deerskin Teachings do not deny or conceal the beauty that is our natural inheritance. This exists in a dance with our ordinariness, with everything that has been before. We must allow for the natural rhythms of growth, for the waxing and waning of the Moon within us. A quietness can come, a lull. We may feel suddenly cast into shadow once more: there is the resurgence of old thoughts and feelings. We condemn ourselves for this, we lose faith in our ability to transform.

Look at the cherry blossom arising in the spring, at the gradual opening of the flowers through days of sunlight and rain. There is the sense that spring is arriving, and then suddenly the clouds return and the days darken and we feel lost in a storm of winter that is relentless in its hold. Yet what quiet magnificence those cherry buds hold; they never give up in their quiet unfoldment, they keep coming through the alternations of warmth and cold. We barely notice it happening, and yet suddenly there is a blaze of pale blossoms where before there were none. We know then that all the alchemies of Sun and Spirit never ceased visiting us here, upon the Earth. That abandoned hour has never yet occurred. Let this softness exist also, let this gradual quietness in evolution have its place in you also. We need this quietude, this quiescence as much as the sun-fire of Illumination. This is patience. This is calm.

This is a part of the nature of the Symbols, of the Teachings. They are woven over great aeons of heart and mind. They are evolved over mighty expanses of simple existence. This is why we know them also as the Elders: they have this quietude of earned wisdom, this integration of a slow blossoming throughout the Universe. Theirs is the patience of the cherry blossom, an innate participation in the cycles of natural and appropriate timing.

What is this but the dreaming of the heart of the Universe itself, transpiring through us? Each of us shall see what we see, through the faculties and the vision gifted to us.

The Elders will attune to us gradually, as the sunlight begins to take residence within us. We hear them more and more, these angelic presences. We feel the brush of their touch, the whisper of their thoughts. We feel their guidance and companionship. Suddenly we are no longer a bare tree, but flowering with Ancient Elder Grace.

There is a bone-shaking quality to the moments when we touch upon our destiny, the flower of ourselves. We are stirred by profound emotion, a feeling of deep joy and sorrow all at once. We are touching upon our place in Creation, and this we long for in a way that sweeps us like a thunderstorm. It frightens us as much as it inspires us. This is the profound power inherent in Beauty, Love and Peace. This path requires incredible courage, incredible faith and integrity.

Your dedication and certainty increase as you go along, and less and less do the storms of unreality sweep you. You feel a compassion for those who resist their destiny. You know the suffering it brings them, you know the clouds and veils of confusion that attend this choice. They have been indoctrinated to turn away from themselves and the true nature of reality, programmed with a different account of who they are and the purpose of their existence on this Earth.

When we come to awareness of the moments in existence when we accepted the wrong signposts, accepted the indoctrinations of tribe and family, we can be torn by an incredible grief. It is searing to realize how divergent is the reality, and to recall the natural attunement to this reality that we abandoned, leading ourselves down many an awkward trail. It is a searing realization that it was, indeed, our own choice. Then we face that shocking hurdle within ourselves: do we really want to undo the conditioning to the old world into whose stories we are woven? More than anything, it has become familiar, it has become known: we cannot see ourselves without it. What Dawn can possibly follow such an extinction?

We wish to perpetuate our old perspective, our old existence. We are caught between longing and fear: a primeval battle for Vision within us.

Why should we ever have become afraid of Vision, afraid of returning to our original nature? It is as though a final seal lies upon remembrance: and it is we who have placed the seal there, we who have chosen to limit Vision.

This seal is coming undone. Gradually this is opening up a vast casket of memory and awareness. It shall come to us naturally, and it is happening even as I write. The conditions become auspicious: it is time. We feel the Flower of our Light Bodies firing into crystalline brilliance, extending our Light and capacity for communion, communication. This is our preparation, and it is the gift of the Sun, the Earth and the Stars. Just as we need it, a spiritual practice or a piece of wisdom shall come to us. We shall find ourselves surrendering that final resistance, that island of the self. We shall see that we were never apart. A hawk set free, we become one with the sky.

This is the hour of effortlessness, of natural mind. It is a gentle blossoming and the Elders amongst us are rising to take on their mantle. We come from nowhere, yet our journeys have been long, and not a moment has been wasted. This is the inheritance of our natural capacities that take us as a storm of surprise, and also as something we always knew.

We are the Shining Ones, and the hidden knowledge is emerging. It is no longer hidden in the mounds beneath the Earth, it is no longer encoded in our distant past, in far incarnations. Inspiration comes to us in a flood of remembrance. The stars at our brow flame to life and the Deer walks the forests once more.

There is nothing we can do to resist this: it is the legacy of our lifetimes of dedication, it is the fulfillment of original purpose. We see with golden eyes the lines of the stars, and we know where we come from. There is no illusion possible for us; we cannot be captured ever again. There can no longer be any false limitation placed upon the account of who we are. It simply does not work. The lies slide off us like raindrops, caught into their own gravity.

* * *

The Earth has fulfilled her Vision to become the Cosmic Tree, to unfold as an Entire Reality. She is able to be everything: all the Heavens and all the Earth. There is no dimensional limitation to the Earth experience; she branches upward through the heavens, touching all the spheres of time, space and eternity. Other suns glow as her flowers, her leaves, and she is the wisdom of all dimensions.

* * *

We each have our own enlightenment within us, and we

must not fear to learn from the flowers. At every moment, in every age, there are teachings gifted that are most suitable for us. At this time, the flowers have so much to teach. We allow for individuality, complexity, as well as profound simplicity. We allow for the manifestation of individual vision. We allow for the directness of inspiration, even in the smallest detail. Who else shall we trust? To whom else shall we defer this authority? Our torches of inspiration are lit, one to another, in a sacred unfolding of Light. Who is to say who is the muse and who the artist, who the teacher and who the student? We seem to have all of this within us. We let these perfect geometries of self and other unfold. This is the lesson of the forest, of the wildflower.

The attunements of Light ripple out from one hand to another: there is a divine choreography at work. And eventually it is our own unfolding we witness with astonishment, as we become the orchid unfolding her ancient and unforgotten harmonies: ancient because they have borrowed from every dawn, every arising and are still here in this moment. There is a fullness, there is an effortless sophistication. There is an allowance of one's own improbable beauty. It requires no pride, no defense, no hiding, no humility. There is no denial, only the effortless benefit that this bestows on all around: the unique medicine of the flower, its blessing, beneficence and healing power.

Gradually these attunements are filtering into our lives. They shall become more and more available, and the language of the flowers, especially the orchid, more and more apparent and harmonious to us.

The flowers are our ancestors and descendants. They are the receptive tissue and fabric of our world, receiving transmissions moment to moment, drinking in the messages of Earth through their roots, transmissions of minerals and ancient stardust. They continuously receive the messages of starlight: absorbing the incoming frequencies of Sun, Moon and Stars. They download their celestial templates, flowering uniquely as we are meant to do, giving their beauty to this world.

The celestial template is our own original blueprint, our starflower aura. We carry our aura within us. It is seeded within us, even as the seed contains the blueprint of the petals it will birth. The aura is our other-dimensional presence. What inspires the aura? In so many people it diminishes as life goes on. Instead, how might it evolve and grow? It needs spring water, sunlight and soil filled with an infinitesimal abundance of minerals and nutrients.

The aura is an atmospheric palace of immortal star petals, an ancient faerie body, a diaphanous first body. It is the interiority of the original self, composed of a brilliant light. Within you, the ancient flower of your aura is stored. Unleash this capsule, discover its stored secrets. You discover that your auric presence expands the worlds of Earth, interfusing with her ancient Dream and bringing forth new realms of expression. Open the realm of this Flower and discover who you are, and how your essence needs to manifest in order to experience true spiritual fulfilment. Discover the hues and nuances of your immortal aura, your auric starflower. This is your portal between worlds, your travelling starship. You learn that you love, breathe, move within this sanctuary, opening its ancient halls and corridors, its interdimensional brilliance and loveliness. These are the hallowed realms of your original contract with Earth. Your aura is rooted in the rich soils of Earth, drinking from her waters and taking in her nutrients.

It is in the Shining Realms of your aura that you will meet with the Great Shining Ones, the angelic ones who are Guardians to Earth's evolution. Here we find our ancient capacity for Love. Our flower auras are activated at this time by the incoming starlight frequencies: dimensions of sensitivity we have perhaps not been able to utilize to our benefit in this last aeon. Yet there are now emerging optimum conditions for sophisticated sensitivity and receptivity. When we have access to this subtle sensitivity, we can begin truly to respond to the needs of others and ourselves.

Our petals, our auric and ethereal aspect may seem the peripheral part of ourselves, but it is actually our original impulse of becoming. It is the way we arise as individuals from the Infinite. Our brilliant, auric, winged presence is being evoked and summoned into this world. The full-flowering of your Angelic Aura is occurring: all its golden-hued and rainbow magnificence is stepping into this dimension and irrevocably changing this world. Your immense presence can no longer be restrained and in every moment there is a rewiring happening that facilitates your full auric participation in this world.

* * *

There are brilliant starflowers that grow in the Silver Grove. They are falling to us, arriving to us as timed capsules that activate our full auric sensitivity. As an awakening Elder, you receive these starflowers that ignite the timeless and loving intention of your heart. Your ancient hands stretch out, and from the heavens these starflowers fall. They glow there in your palms. They are radiant messages of hope, saying, 'It is time, it is time.' You feel the tremor and shiver of their energy through your infinite and beautiful body.

You are being given the gift of Illumination. The brilliant, eternal fire of the flowers reminds you that this is a lifetime of transcendence, when the paradigm shifts irrevocably, when you are called once again to dance the invisible dance of the miraculous. The flowers burn silver and sapphire in your hands, and your ancient starflower aura is rekindled.

And so it is: our ancient starflower aura is becoming accessible once more, after aeons of being furled. These auric petals have remained mostly other-dimensional throughout this last era. Now there is the potential to realize the auric starflower here in this dimension. A constellation of conditions shall occur within your life to make this possible, along with signature gateways that occur when your aura 'downloads' into this world. When we open our aura we become increasingly sensitive to that which was entirely hidden to us before.

Thus awakened, we move differently upon the Earth, suddenly aware of pathways that were not previously accessible. When the sacred geometry of the aura is awakened, we begin to travel differently. Our orientation and compass alters so that we sense a whole new tracery of movement upon the Earth. Our motivation for action shifts to fulfil the calls of this radiant compass.

You shall travel from flower to flower, learning the lost wisdom of Earth. The flowers shall teach you how to unfold your interdimensional presence. You learn how to maintain this radiant and delicate aura by following its paths of inspired movement. The starflower aura is the sail of a spirit canoe that can traverse dimensions. It is built of delicate tissue, the fabric of the petal.

We shall have many encounters with flowers where our auras merge to create unique, unseen worlds. There is a layering and overlapping, codes spilling into one another, a fusing. Flowers stimulate our forgotten periphery, inspiring our edges to unfold, unfurl. They call us across the boundary, into territory previously marked.

There are key places where the Ancient Star Gardens of Earth are due to re-emerge. There are those who carry the seeds of these magical gardens within them, and when they arrive at the right place at the right time, they shall plant these gardens. We shall see the emergence of miraculous and living realities that have previously seemed improbable or dreamlike.

* * *

I notice a pale glimmer in the leaves at my feet. I sift through them. There, lying half buried in the debris of the woodland floor, is a white petal. I pick it up between my fingertips and lay it in the palm of my hand. I peer up into the canopy, looking for the stem from which this might have fallen. There is nothing but the heavy green foliage of summer. I scan the clearing, and there on the ground a few yards away is another pale glimmer. Cradling the first petal in my hand, I cross over and pick up a second, identical in its appearance to the first. I look up, and sure enough, a few yards further on there is another white petal, lying on the woodland floor. I am following a pathway of petals through the forest. They are scattered at short intervals, and I feel compelled to pick them up as I go. Again and again, my eyes catch their pale glimmer. As I walk, I find myself suddenly standing before the grand entrance to caves, their rocks traced with quartz. Cedar trees stand all around. The cave entrances are tall, and the pathway of petals vanishes within. Their archways are carved with the symbols of the Old Language. I am deeply drawn to pass within. There is some sense of potency and mystery to this place.

I peer within, trying to see further into the cavern beyond. There is the sudden whiteness of a figure that moves. Startled, I hold my breath for a moment, sensing the nature of this presence. As she steps into the torchlight, I recognize the figure in her tasselled shawl, its weft of petals and raw silks. I know deep within myself: this is a returning otherness, a flower arrived from distant stars. She is one of the Elven Ones, connected to the nativity of our wings, our other dimension. Her eyes are slanting and golden, seeking out mine.

It is she who scatters the petals I follow. Her aura of angels, her deep eyes.

'There are worlds within worlds. Would you travel within, to discover what exists beyond?'

'What are these petals that I am finding? Where do they come from?' I ask her. She does not answer, but turns from me and passes into the cavern.

It does not seem to me that there is a choice. This is what I have been seeking throughout the forest. I stand at the entrance to the cavern, peering inside. The grey walls rise up, a riven mass. I can feel that this is a portal to Elven Realms: these are halls and corridors where delicate feet tread and travel. I pass within, and there stands the Elven One, waiting for me. Her eyes flash in the last of the daylight, and she raises her hand, indicating the path forward into the darkness. She walks ahead of me slowly, and I have to alter my pace to match hers. The cavern tapers into a long corridor that turns and turns, deeper into the Earth, until I am immersed in darkness. I cannot see anything at all. I have no idea of the dimensions of this place, and even my companion is invisible beside me. Then I perceive something glowing faintly silver in the darkness ahead. I move towards it. It is lying on the ground a few yards in front of me. As I get closer, I see that there is a white petal on the floor of the cavern, and into it is etched a silvery symbol. I stoop down to pick it up, and when I open my palm to place it with the others, I see that they are all glowing, each with unique silver etchings. I now hold at least a dozen in my hand, and as I stand up, I perceive another lying ahead of me in the darkness. I realize that the trail leads on, taking me further into the caverns. 'Are you still there?' I call to my companion, for I can no longer feel her presence at my side. There is no answering call. I hesitate for just a moment, and then continue, alone, following the trail of petals.

The cavern narrows to a steeply descending tunnel. I progress awkwardly, running my hand along the jutting rocks of the walls. Occasionally there is another petal, and I pick it up, laying it carefully with the others. They glow in a bundle of frail slivers in my hand, the tissue of the petals fresh, each one slightly curved, like tiny boats. Despite my awkwardness, I move with a suspended quietness. I feel that I am stalking the silence, my breathing almost stilled, as the tunnel winds ever deeper into the Earth. I am progressing through an empty citadel, its inhabitants either not present, or hiding beyond view. Yet there is an atmosphere of intention, and this is not an abandoned place.

Finally, the floor begins to even out, and then I am entering a grandly proportioned cavern. It is illumined by its own emanation coming from within the walls. They appear at first glance to be hewn of grey rock, yet on closer inspection I notice that they are an endlessly translucent and cloudy quartz, a depth of crystal that I have never seen before. It is a crystal cavern that extends high overhead, with a floor of sandy earth. I step into the centre, with the precious cargo still held in my hand, now cupped between both palms, so many petals have I gathered. I walk to the centre of the cavern and sit down cross-legged on the sandy floor. The power of the crystal walls presses in all around. I lay out the petals in a loose mandala, and sit gazing at the formation for long moments. I gently touch the muted radiance of the symbols, tracing them with my fingertips. I am trying to discern the outlines of the markings. They are traced with filigree precision, as though they grew there.

I become aware of their subtle message murmuring to realms far beyond this one. I close my eyes and sit in stillness, listening to that which filters through into awareness. There is the sound of a spring, dripping in the distance. There are the great walls, with their song of crystal and hidden light. I become aware of a transmission emerging from beneath the floor of the cavern. From behind closed eyelids, I see five elliptical emerald forms, placed in a wider mandala around the circumference of the cavern. They are sending up a song, a transmission, to the mandala of petals, activated, it seems, by their presence. It is a whispering communion in the Old Language, passing between the petals and the hidden emerald forms. The whole atmosphere of the cavern is altering, caught up into this mandalic communion.

I become aware of them, throughout the cave: five emerald forms hidden beneath the earth, glowing with silver ciphers somewhere under the sandy floor.

Half-opening my eyes, yet guided more by the Sight than ordinary vision, I move to one of the places where the emerald emanations are sounding, and I start scraping away the sand. Not far beneath the surface lies a brittle shell, like an encrusted cocoon of fired sand. It cracks beneath my fingers, and as the shards fall away, I perceive a brilliant emerald glow within. It is an emerald sepal, one of the tiny leaflets that forms a flower's calyx. It is as fresh as though it grew there, still attached to the flower.

With sudden conviction, I lower my hand into the hollow, and gently, between two fingers, lift up the sepal, and lay it in my cupped palm. The sepal feels weightless and unimaginably fragile in my hand. It is sending whispers through me, murmuring of its long Earth sleep and other silvery dimensions. Another language fills my awareness, an evocation of some wondrous compassion. It is an expression of love so subtle and fine, some spiritual grace, a lost harmonic. There is patience here, an infinite patience, through the thousands of years that this ethereal beauty has been hidden.

One by one I uncover the hollow places beneath the floor where the sepals are stored. In all, there are five hollows holding the silver-etched sepals. A great whispering fills the cavern.

The five sepals lie on the palm of my hand. They begin to glow brightly, and I see that they are drawing together, fusing at their centre to become, once again, a complete calyx. A wild warmth fills my hand, as I gaze at this emerald star that has formed. I return to sit beside the mandala of petals. The silver ciphers are becoming ever more vibrant. The cavern is filled with magic, a sense of impending wonder. I lay down the emerald calyx at the centre of the petals. A delicate fusion begins to take place. The sepals and the petals are becoming woven together. The petals whirl into place, settling into the calyx, layer upon layer. It is a white rose, multilayered, petal upon white petal, with golden stamens sprouting from the centre. The flower emits a tremendous radiance and purity, its layered depth of Elven inscriptions giving a silvery ambience to the petals.

It is a rose, and yet not like any known flower of the earth. A scent rises from it, as of neroli and amber, and yet stranger, as of the past and quite another time. It offers a light all of its own, a dim emanation coming from the silver markings within the petal.

It is a familiar beauty. I sit spellbound by this apparition. Without being able to resist, I scoop it up into my hands, and cradle it to my heart, drinking in its scent and other-worldly presence. I have braved the ancient corridors of the Earth to hold this most fragile of flowers in my hand. This is the geometry that sculpts everything.

I become aware that these are Lost Elven Petals, capable of translocating from this realm into the worlds of other stars. They are like tiny spirit canoes or starships, and they came to earth many aeons ago, and have patiently dwelt here within the earth until the conditions would make them visible once more. The voice of my vanished companion sounds out, her Elven footfalls arriving behind me.

'This flower is one of your previous incarnations. It is one of the earliest forerunners of your lineage, and one of your most remote earthly ancestors. You have not always needed to incarnate in human form, but have been willing to bear witness to the earliest emergent life forms on this planet. At one point, you arrived as this flower from another star world, one of the myriad inspirational gifts that have arrived on Earth from other spheres. You were seeded here, and brought the gifts of love and design that you embodied so that they could become part of the evolutionary tapestry of life on Earth. Many species have thus volunteered to offer their blueprint to the emerging organic web of life. This starflower is your ancestor; you are its descendant. You are here to complete its offering, its vow of inspiration.

'This knowledge has been fragmented and scattered across the planet: the knowledge of our true lineages and lines of origination. This does not matter, because a direct remembrance, a direct knowing is being gifted at this time. We notice how the trails of our origination are always manifesting around us. Our etheric selves can never be fully lost.'

I feel the delicate labyrinth of the petals extending, a map of inner distances that flows out around me in all directions. It is a rewoven inner palace, its corridors stretching out around me, the etheric layers of a lost citadel. This is my own lost aura into which I step. It is an infinite depth, given to me. I surrender to the buffetings of an electric response that shimmers through my skin. It is a boundary of infinite distances. I am awakening to the luminous moment where space ceases to be simple, and becomes layered, gaining a luminous depth, as of petals, here.

I stand within the pearly intricacies of the Elven Petals. It is a mandala of light, an etheric, shimmering flower with which I am imbued and surrounded. I feel warmth travelling down the veins of the flower, connecting with me. It is an exquisite galaxy of petals with an ever-expanding boundary that is an extension of my physical body. I remember this. I remember this as the immutable, but with traces of movement written into its stillness. This is the bringing of our slowest selves to crystal. This is how I become the Pearlescent Dawn. This is the origin, the ancient, to which I am drawn and from which I travel.

Finding your Starflower Aura

You are walking under the deep emerald leaves of the forest. The forest has become heavy with green, the leaves darkening. Towards you from among the trees comes a reindeer with a star shining at her brow. She approaches you and stretches out her nose to sniff at your hand. You feel her warm breath upon your skin, and you stroke her fur that is coarse and silky all at once. Side by side, you set off into the forest, and she is walking just slightly ahead of you, guiding the way. You realize as you travel that this is no ordinary forest; it is the Immortal Forest of the Earth, and an inner light glows within the trees. There is a sense of timelessness, and it is as though the forest is hung with stars. The reindeer leads the way as you go deeper and deeper into this enchanged realm, and you are overwhelmed by a sense of peace and beauty. Deep within the forest, you come to a Grove of White Trees, and at the base of each, an amethyst crystal lies in the moss. The reindeer crosses the clearing and bows her antlered head. Somehow, you understand what she is indicating. You go over to one of the trees and kneel beside it. You peer into the amethyst that lies embedded in the moss. Within its depths shimmers the Sixth Glyph. You raise your hand to mirror the sweep of the Sixth Glyph in front of the tree, and you draw it into the forest air. As you draw the golden strokes of the Glyph of the Sixth Teaching, you feel the symbol entering your heart and glowing golden throughout your whole being. You are transported...

You are transported onto a pathway of luminous petals that are laid out beneath your feet. You follow this pathway of petals, treading from one to another through an all-encompassing darkness. Out of the darkness looms a cave entrance, and the pathway of petals passes within. As you enter the cave, the petals cease to glow beneath your feet, and you find a staff with a sapphire lantern leaning against the cave wall. You take up this staff and it lights the narrow corridor through which you pass. Trickles of water run down the surface of the rock, everything illuminated by the faint blue light from your staff. You follow this corridor for some distance, feeling yourself drawn deeper and deeper into the Earth, a world of rock and stone encircling you. You emerge into a sudden vast darkness into which your staff throws only a dim illumination. The rest of the space stretches out around you, unseen. It is a huge cavern, with a high roof and wide circumference. It is ancient, full with the mysteries of the Earth's heart. Ahead of you, you see a tiny radiance glowing in the midst of this vastness.

You move towards it and as you come closer, you see that it is a tiny flower growing out of the cavern floor. Come closer, and you begin to discern the shape and colour of the flower, the number of its petals. This flower holds the geometry and codes of your Oldest Self, it is the starship upon which you travelled to Earth. This is the blueprint of your aura, an aspect of the shape that your non-physical self holds. Give yourself time to observe this flower, to take in the details of its appearance and the quality of how it makes you feel.

When you are ready, you kneel before the flower, and with gratitude and trust in your heart, you gently pick it from its growing place on the cavern floor. Know that this is what you are guided to do by the Earth Spirit, and trust in the rightness of this gift. You hold the flower in your hands and you feel its exquisite beauty travelling within you, coursing through your hands and arms, and you realize that the flower is growing and expanding through you, its petals reaching all around you in a radiant aura of Light. The petals become a mandala of patterned Light that shines around you. Recognize this as an ordinarily nonvisible aspect of yourself, and be aware that this is a moment in your evolution when you have the opportunity to integrate this essence once again.

If this is what you desire, then ask the starflower of your aura how you may integrate its presence more deeply into your everyday life. Listen to its answer in any way that this comes to you: as light, sound, words or feeling. Keep the memory of this in your heart.

The starflower aura begins to shrink until you can feel its periphery at the surface of your skin, and then it shrinks until you are aware of the flower glowing within your root chakra, at the base of your spine. Know that this will now grow with gentle integration through your days and nights, until once again it glows as the starship in which you travel, shining all around you once again. It is fed and watered through your openness, your stillness, your listening – and you shall witness how this begins to manifest in your outer world.

You stand up and notice that another, identical flower is springing forth from where you picked it. Know that the Earth will always hold guardianship of this essence within her depths. You return the way that you came until you emerge at the entrance of the cave. You find yourself transported back to the White Grove, with its amethyst crystals glowing at the base of the trees. You follow the reindeer out of the White Grove, returning through the forest to this world.

SEVENTH TEACHING

This is the Seventh Teaching of the Deerskin Book:

*The Water is a mirror of the heart, and the Love which
needs to be given without restraint, but also received
and accepted deeply and fully.*

*This Love needs never to be still, but always flowing,
always being passed from one to another.*

This is how the Great Lakes remain clear and full.

Chapter 7

Cross-legged,
at prayer, of autumn.

Cloud-eyed dances
haunt the forest.

All that is lost,
falls away –

Cloud and jay,
the kingfisher.

THE SEVENTH TEACHING of the Deerskin Book
involves the Vision of the Moonstone Lake and a
very ancient feminine energy. Within all of us is
the memory and the archetype of the Lady of the Lake,
and she who is Guardian of the Waters, who preserves our
ancient Faerie lineage and our connection to the Mysteries
of the Land. The Moonstone Lake is her domain; it is the
pure manifestation of the essence of Love, of the Heart. It
symbolizes and mirrors the truth that Love needs always
to be given and received, always to be flowing from one
to another. We must be prepared to give and we must be
prepared to receive deeply. It is a deep truth of our human
nature that this exchange, this communion, takes place
through the Heart.

Many thousands of years ago, the mists descended over Avalon. The waters became veiled, and only a chosen few could find their way through. The realm of the Lady began to withdraw and vanish from communion with this world. She took her people via the ancient pathways to the realm of the Evening Star. The Shining Ones thus departed into the West and crossed over into another dimension. They vanished across the mysterious moonstone waters in which loveliness is reflected, taking their gifts with them.

In the Palace of the Evening Star is held the secret, vanished wisdom of the water realm. This is where the long-lost barges travelled, the Elders who left for another dimension until the call of the New Earth should come to summon them back. There they remained until the lost alliances should be reforged and the inter-dimensional waters be reawoken so that these higher frequencies of Love could flower here once more, interwoven with the physical realm.

The Lady has held these secret ciphers, these stored capsules of inter-dimensional wonder. The realms of water truly are multidimensional: the way that water is encoded to teach us of the Universe beyond. It is a travelling element, by which we may cross over and access inter-dimensional healing. The waters link, especially, to the temples of the Evening Star, where, still, there are encoded teachings to be received; inter-dimensional wisdom that is ours but almost forgotten.

These Elven, Lemurian beings are returning to the Earth, incarnating here in the present. They are preparing to step through, to be present upon the Earth once more and share their wisdom with us all. Theirs is the inter-dimensional starlight of the Rose Ray. They are the Peacekeepers, who understand the enchantment and rapture of peace.

It is time, and the Lady of the Lake is bringing her treasured gifts back to Earth. She steps through the ancient portal, a diadem at her brow, in robes of shifting moonstone, a flowing iridescence as intangible as mist. She brings us the enchantment of the feminine heart, of imagination, of peace and beauty. She opens the Elven Portal of the Waters, a shimmering and mysterious doorway.

These Palaces of the Evening Star are accessible via the moonstone waters of the heart. Here we shall rediscover our true gentleness towards ourselves, the elusive capacity to love the self.

* * *

A peaceful heart is one that has opened its inter-dimensional realms and walks these timeless corridors, manifesting impossible gentleness and integrity, bringing forth its gifts and treasures to delight and bring happiness to all. This part of us is forever pure and uncontaminated, even if we lose awareness of its presence. It resides beyond the veils of phenomenal reality, drawing its essence from pure heavens and enchanted lands. It belongs to the hour before the division of one world from another, before the veil between the worlds fell. It is the pivot around which everything else flows.

There is no end to how much suffering this essence can witness and remain whole. It is our most gentle and our most powerful aspect. If we try to destroy this, it only vanishes as radiant lights under our fingertips, immortal and evanescent, without attachment to anything but the purity of its own manifestation. It is time to meet with its stillness, enter into the Moonstone Lake of our own hearts, surrender to the evanescent purity of ourselves. We ourselves are this vanishing presence, this Mysteriousness.

This is the time when you become translucent, transparent to the Light, when your identification shifts and you know that yours is the Moonstone Lake of the heart, yours is its stillness and its purity. This is the non-existence of which the sages speak: this mysterious and infinite abundance of the heart.

When shall the hour come that the heart steadies into the beauty of its own stillness altogether? How do you make the miraculous and quantum leap into true self-belief? How do you give yourself the Gift of Love that never wavers, never alters, never disappears?

You want to believe in this most elusive treasure, you want to stop this swinging between worlds, between euphoric connection and baffling confusion. This dream that the heart might still to its own infinity, and become unbroken on the tides of suffering. How we long for the crystalline waters of the heart compose themselves around infinity, and to sway no longer from one world to another. This can indeed happen. Yes its pathway is perhaps more mysterious than expected.

* * *

Take up this body that you have been given, and know it for what it is. It is a fluid and magical, transformative ground to existence in this dimension. Do not view it as separate from your spirituality, for it is through this abandoned Gift that you shall discover the vibrational pathways of True Existence. It is your sounding device, your echo chamber of infinite vibrational realms and worlds. Unloved, it remains tuned to only one setting, receiving the signals of fear and flight, programmed into desperation, loneliness and anxiety.

It wanders lost and lonely, uninhabited. Yet this is the ultimate gift you have chosen, that you have given to yourself.
And you ignore it.

This magical echo chamber of unawakened codes is the
target of the Golden Dawn and all its patterns of release
that are permeating the fabric of reality. Let it in, allow it
to release and activate you. Allow the codes to touch your
loneliness, your unawakened skin. Allow them to touch
your sleeping, dormant self. Your secret self is shimmering with a golden light that is caressing it, encouraging
it to dream the miraculous. This is the secret chamber of
your body-soul. It looks up startled. It is so long used to
its slumbers, its unrecognized nature. It sees the Light of
the Golden Dawn stealing quietly through, and realizes
that it is no longer alone, that there is another presence in
the darkness. This presence touches it with soft fingers,
gently stroking the unremembered darkness. You are the
secret one, who has been so long imprisoned. You have
thought yourself unworthy of such beauty, such compassion. Gentle as dust, it settles upon every cell of your
loneliness.

It is the Light of the Rising Sun, of the Dawn, that you
thought would never come. It is the Light that you thought
would never touch your loneliness, so long has it gone on.
This is the Golden Love that sets the secret self free, that
loves you so deeply and truly for exactly who you are, and
asks nothing more.

This is the teaching of the mysteries of the heart. It has
been said already: the heart is the priceless jewel around
which all else is woven. We trust the heart, we trust the
extraordinary capacity of Love, and all the lost dimensions,

all other worlds encircle this inner realm, this pure heart.

It has been said: the heart must receive, even as it gives. From where does the heart receive? From where does the heart draw its warmth, its inspiration, its sustenance? We all know the feeling when the heart has given all it has to give, when we feel the well has run dry. We feel drained and we need regeneration, nourishment.

How does the heart receive these incoming star frequencies; this aerial and ethereal realm of descending starlight? In truth, it is not from this realm that the heart draws its deepest nourishment. The heart must turn inward, to the secret depths. It must go within to hidden realms. It must fall into its own twilight and dance in this subtle-hued realm to find once again its animating vision.

There is a deep and faraway purity within the heart. It is an innermost shrine, which we can approach when we let go of all else and travel into the most private realms of our own being.

* * *

For all that the Deerskin Book speaks of radiance, of stepping forth into the Light, of the clarity of crystalline dimensions, there is this also: the gentle retirement of the soul into its quiet realms. We do not have to 'wear our heart on our sleeve' forever, to be facing outward in crystalline transparency. There are some things that can never be fully shared, or fully revealed. They exist as glimpses, as twilight, as ephemeral transience and the passage of one world to another. There is evanescence, half-disclosure, a hint: a leaf that falls through the air, making its ineffable descent. There is that which cannot be spoken, that which dwells dormant and mysterious in the heart.

This is an essential quality of our existence. We need these deep and ineffable waters of the well: their mystery and intangible purity. The mystery is not to be solved: it is here to sustain us, to underlie all that comes to the light and shines.

The legends tell us that, long ago, pure maidens and priestesses guarded the waters of the wells. They offered sanctuary and refreshment to weary travellers, healing and wisdom to those who asked. Their role was held as sacred and they were protected by kings and soldiers. But there came a time when this contract was broken. The maidens of the wells were raped and murdered and the wells desecrated. The consensual reality had altered.

With this arrival of the Golden Dawn, we are finding once again the courage to honour the mysterious, flowing waters of our existence. Instead of trying to erase the twilight, the mysterious and indeterminate, we honour it as an essential aspect of our humanity. We dance with the ancient feminine mystery of the waters. We accept the transient, the inchoate, the momentary.

The Golden Dawn is not a spotlight that shall cast everything into brilliant, crystalline clarity. We are learning a deeper grace than this. We are learning to accept our transience, our mortality, our imperfection. This is part of the miracle of what we have become. This is the wisdom of loving the moment just as it is. It is all here, in this one mysterious, perfect, unfinished moment. This is it. With all its veils, its still-to-become potentials. This is one of the most divine qualities of existence: this forever incipience, this forever falling away of the ineffable leaves.

We do not have to raze and raid the depths. We do not have to bring every unspoken reality to the light. We need this substrate; this flowing and swirling dimension where one thing becomes another, where identity is never fully formed.

* * *

Silver Wheel speaks of a time when we allow other realities to shimmer in and out of perception: we allow for the diaphanous subtlety of reality. We surrender the belief that there is one fixed truth, one fixed paradigm. We stop trying to pin down reality, and we allow for its amorphous tendency, its shape-shifting appearance. We allow reality to become mysterious again, and allow for its emergent epiphanies to touch us. It is from this that the heart receives its most profound nourishment, its deepest peace and inspiration. We do not press for resolution, for clarity, for crystallization. Allow for the shimmering, intangible qualities of existence. Allow for a state of incompletion and know that this is part of the mystery of perfection.

It takes evolved poise to take this stance. It takes courage and dignity to embrace this ephemeral quality, this flow and movement within the fabric of perception.

This is a distinctly Lemurian wisdom. The Lemurians did not hold one physical form only; they altered and flowed with shifting vibrational resonance from one form to another. With this arrival of the Golden Dawn, the boundary between one thing and another is once again becoming more subtle and less clearly defined. This happens between people as empathic resonance, and also between ourselves and the elemental realm. There is an increasingly mystical quality to existence as we find ourselves able to become the Pine Tree, the Eagle, the Rock, the Bear. We become, for one brief and exquisite moment, the turning of the yellow leaf through the air. Our point of perception is not so fixed, but has a pure fluidity that enables us to experience the mysterious Oneness at the heart of life.

This is a very precious perspective: it could be seen as a loss of clarity and a source of vulnerability. It in fact derives from a deepening clarity, from a profound purity of heart. If we allow for this naturally flowing and mysterious quality of existence, we discover something most paradoxical: that it is from this the greatest clarities arise. The indeterminate realm of water is entirely crystalline. It is formed of crystal structures of perfect geometrical coherence. It is thus that a life founded in mystery is a life of most perfect and divine coherence. It is the ancient grace of living this paradox that is the great gift of the heart. The heart understands this: it navigates the mysterious and amorphous moment and in its acceptance, receives the gift of illumination and divine direction.

Thus does otherworldly loveliness permeate our world once more. Thus can we allow ourselves to rest in the mystery of these interwoven worlds. We do not need an explanation or a map for the present moment. We allow ourselves to articulate the subtlety of experience without needing to pin it into final definition, or create ultimate truths. This is the subtle art of Truth's expression.

* * *

And so we pass into the otherworldly beauty of the Elven realm. The Elven Elders are summoning you to the Evening

Star Temple on Earth. It contains the lost wisdom of Lemuria. It is a great temple of driftwood and mother of pearl, a triad of great, spiraling arcs that rise and taper into an unbound pyramidal form. A floor of polished abalone, a mosaic inlaid with sapphires and lapis lazuli. It is the temple of the Evening Star and it is offering its precious portal to the worlds of Earth, so that we might have passage once more in these realms of wisdom. Laid down at the centre of the mosaic floor is a great sphere of rose quartz, in whose depths many lights and forms shift. Here is one of the temples of the Peaceful Ones, the Elven Elders. Their brilliant, ethereal forms belong to land, ocean and star. They arise and vanish amongst the seals, taking on their sealskin mantles and discarding them to dance at the shore-line between worlds. Through the rose quartz sphere, they come and go from this world.

You press your hands to the surface of the rose quartz and you feel your heart begin to glow once more with the purity of its Moonstone Waters. Know that the lost dreams of your heart are becoming found. You are awakening to the immanence of your dreams, to a graceful world where deep gratitude pours forth from your heart for the miraculous nature of your existence. A world where dreams walk the Earth beside you, keeping pace with your step.

It is time to move beyond nostalgia and regret for a world of vanished loveliness. Those worlds of vanished loveliness are seeking us, the Elven Ones are returning from the West. All that you long for – the beauty of that vanished Evening Star realm – is that which you carry. It is yours to offer, it is yours to weave into the worlds of Earth once more. Be that extraordinary gentleness, that unlikely beauty. Bring the vanished realm of Love into this world and end the cycle of disappearance.

By allowing yourself to recover lost treasure, you come into a wealth that can be shared with all. You come into the domain of Love, which understands the sacred transmissions that occur as part of the true fabric of reality. You are restored to ancient pearlescent presence and knowledge of your own mysterious loveliness. The heart is restored as an inter-dimensional portal in order for you to participate in the flow of Love.

You trust your capacity to give. This is the immortal flow of the Gift, the way that Love, in stillness, never stops moving. We give this Gift of Love to ourselves first, before others. Otherwise all our Love, all our admiration and kindness, all our generosity is eroded by a primeval doubt we hold about the true goodness, or divinity, of our own nature.

When we give ourselves this most extraordinary of gifts, the Ancient Pearl of the Heart, then we dissolve the distinction between ourselves and this ancient and beautiful feminine planet we inhabit. We open to the mysteries of the Earth, we feel her power and spiritual presence. We come into resonance with the mysterious field of elements that we inhabit: with their swirling and self-sustaining journeys. We feel with her. This material creation is no longer something we have to guess at with our sciences only, but something we have the sentience to witness for ourselves.

This is why the Teaching of the Waters is the pivot and the centre, why the Heart is our precious jewel from which all else follows. This is the arena of the Swan, who unites the waters with the air, linking these disparate elements with her primordial and pure flight. This is the wisdom of forgiveness. We forgive because we perceive the neutral and primal forces that underlie suffering. We know that they have no ultimate reality, that they are a passing constellation, a pattern in the night. This is the gift of the Heavenly Witness, of angelic forgiveness. The frequencies falling to Earth at this time are forming such a gigantic field of forgiveness, we are enfolded in the Wings of the Swan. This mighty compassion is everywhere: it is all around and within us. It is the potential for us to let go of everything that holds us back.

* * *

It is twilight, and autumn. Raindrops fall onto the waters of the lake. I sit beside the waters. The Evening Star appears in a sky that is stealing into deeper and deeper blues. The lake is becoming an inscrutable and opaque. I feel the transformation coming over me. There is a deep tingling, as the very cells of my body shift, and the change occurs. I am transforming into a Swan. I cast off onto the lake, gliding between the reeds, the willows and alders. The evening star shines above, and a faint rain falls upon my feathers, breaking the still surface of the lake. I raise my wings to beat off the raindrops. They rise in arches at my sides. I can hear the delicate, ringing frequencies of water and sky, coordinates of sound beneath ordinary hearing. I cruise the perimeters of the lake, drawn further and further across the watery landscape that is stealing into invisibility beneath the darkening sky. I tuck my wings into my sides, and gaze out from the oblique slant of my vision, my neck coiled.

Towards me, out of the darkness and the fading scenery, comes a phalanx of swans. In formation, they glide towards me. They surround me, and they are a formidable presence.

We stare one another down for a few long moments, and then they begin to glide forward. It is as though they are herding me, and I am caught into their ranks. They progress along the lake to the mouth of the river, and they begin to travel up it. There is a compelling intensity about the presence of the swans, whose intention I cannot discern. We travel on and on, up the night river. It becomes ever narrower, and the hills rise up on either side of the river valley. Then I begin to catch the distant sounds of a waterfall. It becomes, increasingly, a roar in the silent night. There is the intangible sense of the waterfall's power, invisible as it is in the darkness. The river is curving between shallows of rocks and deep pools of rushing waters, and we proceed with care, pushing our way against the flow. In some places our progress is slow, as we push against the swirling river with webbed feet. Suddenly the waterfall becomes visible, where it falls amongst shadowy pines, catching the ghost light of a waning crescent moon. The other swans disembark from the river, and I scramble up the bank behind them.

At the shore, we each undergo a transformation. We are thirteen figures, standing tall and clad in our Swan Feather Cloaks. We stand for a moment in a circle of quiet magnificence, then the twelve walk ahead of me up the forest trail that winds along the river bank. The path snakes over boulders and down sudden dips. I pay careful attention to my footing as I follow the procession.

We arrive beside the waterfall, its spray leaving a fine mist on our faces. One by one, the Swan Elders climb down to the pool into which the waters tumble. I follow them, lifting my skirts high, my cloak trailing behind me. One by one, we take our turn to stand beneath the falls and be doused by the chill waters.

On the slippery pebbles of the amber pool, barefoot, cloaks beaded with the spray of the waterfall, we stand elbow to elbow in a circle. Our cloaks billow out behind us, and their feathers begin to bind together, weaving into a shield all around us. Within it is a dome, dark, as the feathers block out the pale moonlight. We sing, a shimmering moonstone song pouring from our hearts. We sing of the fey and the fell, of old dawns and an older purity. We sing into the roar of the waterfall, so that the song vanishes, vibrating, into its din. Only we can feel its ecstasies within our bodies, its evocation of an Old Land of Enchantment. And the feathers weave together, and we are enshrined within the Swan Dome of our feathered cloaks.

The feathers weave beneath us, over the pool of amber. We regard one another, eyes flashing in the darkness. The feathers keep weaving until we are sitting upon a floor of swan feathers, enclosed from the waters beneath.

It is the Lemurian Dome of the Swan in which the Swan descended to earth. When the Swan Feather Cloaks of the Elders are brought together, it is reconstructed. This is the Gift of the Swan: to hold the balance of grace between the waters and the sky, to evoke an improbable and pure beauty.

Between us, at the centre of the feathered dome, begins to glow a starlight brightness. I know that we are singing the Song of the Evening Star. In the indigo depths of the dome, beneath the waterfall, the Evening Star blossoms its old light. We are doused in its radiance. We keep singing, and our song is the song of all our yesterdays, of the worlds from which we are born and risen, of all the ways that we have come. I see the procession of ourselves, the long journey across aeons, the preservation of wisdom and truth through all realms.

We are encompassed in the deep brilliance of the star. In the heart of this brilliance, I perceive a form emerging. Something is descending from the realm of the Evening Star to this world: we have opened a portal between worlds. It is the Deerskin Book. As we gaze upon it, lost in the stillness into which our song has drawn us, the pages turn themselves, revealing the gold and silver inks of the inscriptions. This has been where the Deerskin Book has been held through these long ages, carried into the realm of the Evening Star, shining in the West.

It is bequeathed into the keeping of the Swan Elders. I shall speak of this, it is time. It is an elemental inscription of transience, one of the languages of the soul. These are the teachings of the Deerskin Book, caught in the gold and silver inks of another language. It has the look of something worn and loved, powerful and precious. Many hands have rubbed and darkened the deerskin binding, which still has the appearance of whiteness nonetheless. It is the inheritance of successions of Old Ones, Elders, shamans. It carries the inscriptions of the Shining Ones. It is written in their language, which is also ours, and yet stands apart. It belongs to the beginning: it is our own primordial wisdom, that which stirs in sun and wind, before word or thought. And so the beginning is always with us. The inks of the Deerskin Book eternally exist, no matter what moment in time it vanished from the Earth. It appears, vivid enough to have the Swan Elders gather in silence, in darkness, singing into the Beyond. They are devoted to the traces of these inks, the flashing arc of their inscription. It contains the elemental ceremonies, the thirteen moons of sun and star, earth and sky. These are the deer paths, the ephemeral tracks of a wisdom that cannot be misplaced. The pathways are a silver wheel of return. It spins back, always and always, to ourselves. No matter how wide flung the arc, what trajectory through unchartered forests, every road is the sketching of this mandala. Even our faintest listening to the whispers at the edge of the silver circle, the faint echoes bounding back from the outermost rim, are caught again into the dream-making of Earth, as written into the wanderings of the deer. They are inscribed in the pages of a book. Hands have held and read these pages. And they have understood. Let me come again to this, the Deerskin Book contains the Silver Wheel of Teachings. It teaches us how to traverse boundaries, how to transform, how to become the elemental traveller. This is not magic, it is existence. Dancers will be called across the threshold, even in the silence of an empty forest. The shamans will keep appearing, and disappearing, as ourselves.

This offering is made on the wings of our gratitude and trust, this is the grace of the Swan. It is this that lays a foundation for the procession of future generations. In the truth of our past, we find the true possibility of a future. We go forward, and we go back. All is contained in this moment – we are simultaneously at many points upon the spiral. It is precarious, perfect.

Evening Star Meditation

Y ou are walking in the forest. There are hints of carnelian and crimson in the trees. It is the beginning of autumn. Towards you from among the trees comes a reindeer with a star shining at her brow. She approaches you, and stretches out her nose to sniff your hand. You feel her warm breath upon your skin, and you stroke her fur that is coarse and silky all at once. Side by side, you set off into the forest; it is the Immortal Forest of the Earth, and an inner light glows within the trees. There is a sense of timelessness, and it is as though the forest is hung with stars.The reindeer leads the way as you go deeper and deeper into this enchanted realm, and you are overwhelmed by a sense of peace and beauty. Deep within the forest, you come to a Grove of White Trees, and at the base of each, an amethyst crystal lies in the moss. The reindeer crosses the clearing and bows her antlered head. Somehow, you understand what she is indicating. You go over to one of the trees and kneel beside it. You peer into the amethyst that lies embedded in the moss. Within its depths shimmers the Seventh Glyph. You raise your hand to mirror the sweep of the Glyph in front of the tree, and you draw it into the forest air. As you draw the golden strokes of the Seventh Glyph, you feel the symbol entering your heart and glowing golden throughout your whole being. You are transported...

You are transported to a waterfall in the midst of a mountain forest. You step into the amber waters of the pool, and move beneath the waterfall, letting the waters fall down onto the crown of your head. This is your crown chakra, where the amethyst light shines. The waters are touching all your lost hopes, lost dreams, all the confusion and regret. They are touching all your unwillingness to build again, for fear of the destruction that will follow. They are touching all your unwillingness, your loss of faith. The waters touch you with their wild life. You feel the cleansing, the fierce invigoration of this element. You feel all the ash and soot of yesterday being swept away from your Dreaming Crown. You see the crystalline, shining amethyst of your Dreaming Crown becoming clear, becoming pure.

When this has taken place, you climb back up the boulders beside the amber pool and join the Elder beside her fire once more. A white raven sits on her shoulder, soberly regarding you with pale-blue eyes. The Elder paces around the fire, attending to it with a fierce and steady attention. You peel off your wet clothes, the evening air fresh upon your skin, balanced by the warmth of the fire. You feel vulnerable, newborn, yet full of trust, purity, and courage. The Elder hands a woollen robe to you. It is incredibly soft, and you put it on. She wraps a blanket around your shoulders, and it is woven with sacred patterns. She throws lavender, cedar and myrrh upon the charcoal embers. The herbs and resins rise in a scented smoke, curling upwards into the sky.

The raven stirs at her shoulder. It turns its head, and plucks out a beak-full of white feathers, flinging them into the air with a jerk of its head. A bridge forms across the sky, woven of white raven feathers. It seems to arch all the way to the Evening Star that shines in the West.

The Elder gestures you towards the bridge. The white raven flaps its wings and takes off from her shoulder, its ethereal wings like a lantern illuminating your path. You rise and drop the robes to the ground, stepping onto the feathered bridge. With raucous calls, the raven summons you onward. You are crossing the night skies.

The closer you draw to the star, the more you feel moved by its beauty and brilliance. You can hear an old song emanating from it, and you recognize it as your own song of gratitude for all the lifetimes you have lived, for every moment of all the paths you have trodden to this moment. As you reach the Evening Star the raven gives a final call and disappears within the brilliant light. With sudden trust, you follow. You feel yourself immersed in the silver brilliance, drawn into the deep beauty of this sphere. You are in a realm of pure Light. Out of the light comes a figure clad in Silver White; it is the Spirit of the Evening Star. She holds in her hand a tiny vial, and she gives it to you to drink. She tells you, "This is the

Water of the Evening Star. It is your grace, your capacity for deep feeling and magical transformation. This is the purity of your gratitude and your trust. Drink this and it shall be your restoration to the Ever-living Present. Your yesterday and your today are all one. You are as young as your first hope, your earliest dream. Turn to me, to the Evening Star, at the end of every day, and welcome this gratitude and trust into your heart. Let no day pass without this honour paid to the dream that you are walking. This is the gift that allows the Waters of Immortality to flow through you."

You accept this gift from the Spirit of the Evening Star, and you drink it down. You feel an indigo and wild beauty flooding through your heart, a deep and sincere gratitude for all the long ways you have walked. You feel freed of regret, able to stand on the beautiful depths of all that has been.

You thank the Spirit of the Evening Star, and you step out of the Silver Light, back onto the feathered bridge. The raven flies ahead, guiding you onward. You travel back to the fire of the Elder. You look into her eyes, and between you passes the knowledge of all that you have learnt. You sit by the fire once more, close your eyes, and find yourself transported back to the White Grove, with its amethyst crystals glowing at the base of the trees. You follow the reindeer out of the White Grove, returning through the forest to this world.

EIGHTH TEACHING

This is the Eighth Teaching of the Deerskin Book:

You shall no longer be enclosed by the walls of three-dimensional reality. You shall always be looking out on a vastly greater horizon, as though existing against the backdrop of the Universe itself, all the vast distances of time and space.

This is an Earth that is not enclosed by itself. It is not an hermetically sealed experience, but one that shares a vanishing point with space.

ج

Chapter 8

Leaf after leaf hollowed through me,
there is incense and curve of wing.

IT IS TIME for the Eighth Teaching of the Deerskin Book. The Teachings fall as a succession of gifts, of symbols gifted by primordial wisdom that act as tools for consciousness at this time. We may be disbelieving of such infinite wealth, such extraordinary, uncalled abundance. We may believe it must have limit, it must have cessation, yet it is not grounded in our old notions of material limitation.

At the heart of the incoming sapphire dream is *spaciousness*. The New Earth is a realm of infinitely blossoming star worlds that are emergent within the fabric of that which we have previously perceived as limited. The inner star worlds of Mother Earth are now reactivating and awakening, and it is the foundation of space that enables these dimensions to come forth in an endless creativity dance of beauty. The evolutionary trajectory of Earth is not fixed. She is stardust and starlight and universal spaciousness. Beneath the surface of the Earth are Cities of Light, Inner Citadels and Lost Realms of the Shining Ones that mirror the mysteries of the Universe beyond.

You walk through the quartz corridor of the Old Kingdom, deep within the ancient worlds of Earth. You emerge upon a rocky ledge and there is the entrance to a cave. You are standing at the entrance to Merlin's cave. This is one of the Timeless Elders of Earth, who has devoted incarnation upon incarnation to guardianship of its light realms and sacred traditions. Inside the cave is a simple dwelling, with sheepskin rugs spread upon the floor and a fire burning at its centre. Coming towards you with welcoming arms is Merlin, a stooped and beautiful figure in flowing robes the colour of faded sapphire, his hood falling around his shoulders. His beard cascades white down his chest, and his burning umber eyes look steadfast into yours. He is the Guardian of the Dream of the New Earth, who takes care of the pathway between the Old Realms and the Shining Blueprint of the Future. He welcomes you to his cave dwelling that is so simple, yet steeped in warm loveliness. You sit upon the sheepskin rug and he sits opposite you, gazing into your eyes. You ask him to take you to the blueprint of the New Earth, so that you may have a vision of its dimensions for yourself. He nods and holds out his hands to you. You take his gnarled hands in your own. They have a surprising and supple softness, and you can feel the great and exquisite sensitivity of this Guardian Elder.

Gazing deeply into his eyes, you find yourself transported. You are hurtling upwards at great speed, through corridors of light that are like rushing pathways through the forests, with the forms of deer running beside you on all sides. It is so beautiful. The deer are sapphire and silver, their flanks outlined against the white stream of energy upon which you travel. Around you, you see Glyphs travelling also, ascending and descending to the Earth, the mysterious script of the Elders through which the translations of other worlds occur, by which the galactic codes are transferred.

You find yourself emerging in a brilliant sapphire realm

that glows with intensity all around you. This sapphire realm floats in deep space, transparent to a Universe of stars, and yet whole unto itself. This is the blueprint of the New Earth. Your heart is deeply moved by the vibration of this realm. There are graceful trees of shimmering sapphire arching above, and everywhere a sense of profound and incipient wisdom. It is dense with galactic codes that show only in the intensity of the sapphire and the atmosphere of the place. There are beautiful lakes, in which there is an unimaginable depth of blue. There are sapphire starflowers that glow upon the ground.

Merlin stands beside you, and he guides you to the edge of this realm. It drops off into space like a waterfall vanishing sheer beneath you.

'The blueprint of the New Earth shares a vanishing point with space itself. This underpins every movement, every manifestation. You also shall regain your transparency to Infinity. You shall remember yourself as unlimited in potential and resources.'

You witness this Infinity of the New Earth, and it is so beautiful to you. You wonder how you yourself can become this Infinity, and throw off the limitation and finitude with which you have bound yourself.

You remember that sensation in yourself of the mundane and the ordinary, the predictable downward swing of fortune that curtails your dreams. Within your world this is so strong, the concept of the 'real world' with its dictates of what is possible, what is probable. You know that feeling, that you are trapped in this world of inherent limitations. You know this call of consensual reality, and how obedient you are to its definition of reality. No matter how far you fly, always there is this anchor that pulls you down at some point, the cold that freezes your wings. You are always wondering if inevitably its power will win, and you will be called back into its confines altogether. Perhaps you will be one of those who lets your dreams softly fall away for tomorrow and tomorrow and tomorrow.

You carry this message, coded into your cells. How thoroughly you are trained to observe this boundary line, to be called back into the fold. To bend your head to the yoke and submit to the terms of this contract that you know you also carry, no matter how hard you try not to be ruled by it. No matter how faintly it exists within, you are called to look to this, to acknowledge the presence of this boundary line, this limit on the Infinite that you hold.

* * *

You are falling and falling and falling. You are tumbling off the edge of the New Earth, falling downward through space. You fall into the atmospheres of Earth, and as you tumble down through the skies, you wonder where you will land. Where will it be safe to land? You continue to plummet downward, and then suddenly you find yourself caught on a great yielding surface of moss and soil. All around you stretches a tawny landscape, furrowed with yellowed patterns. Like a great shield, it extends around you in a circle, and it falls away on all sides into a boundless ocean. As you sit up and wonder at this strange landscape, an enormous head rises and regards you with an ancient eye. It is the scaly head of Grandmother Turtle. You have landed on her back.

'I have caught you, Star Elder, because the starlight gift you bring to this world is precious to me. I shall care for you, and make sure you always have nourishment and shelter and a ground beneath your feet. I shall carry you wherever you wish to go. Do not be afraid of this Earth world into which you have come. It is not so very different from the stars beyond; it is just that appearances may be so very different.'

Gazing into her ancient eye, you see the vast depths of Infinity shining there. You know that her soul is space itself, and that she has grown in beauty by remembering the truth of her own origination. She is the soul of Earth.

'If you allow me, I shall always bring you unexpected beneficence. I shall be the miracle that surprises you, the way life carries you beyond the boundaries of even your dearest dreams. I shall be this if you will only allow the space in your life for my presence. Trust me, wait for my call. Do not give in to fear and expediency. I need you to trust this miraculous ground that appears when you least expect it. Thus shall I carry you. Thus shall the starlight inspiration you bring become woven into the worlds of Earth. Let your starlight dance forth, and I shall be the Infinite ground that holds you.'

You acknowledge her miraculous presence. You let her great and compassionate wisdom flood your heart as her great eye gazes into yours. In her eye there is an all forgiveness, an all-embracing of who you are. Her wisdom begins to dissolve your sense of opacity and limitation. It begins to dissolve that in you that wants simply to flee this Earth realm, star returning to star. The part of you that has never really settled in this world, that has never really placed its feet upon the soil. There is that within you, hard as diamond, that has resisted incarnation. It is time for you to give this up, and to trust in Grandmother Turtle to catch your fall. There is that in you that vibrates so fast, it finds it hard to understand this dimension. It seals itself off in consternation. It protects its purity. However, this seal creates limitation, and isolation. And it seals off the gift you are destined to bring to Earth. You long to give this gift, now, fully, with all your heart. You long to release the bright, diamond light held within. You do not know how to unlock the seal you wrought, so long is it since you made that gesture. You have locked up this inner realm, this brilliant intensity. At some point you must allow this last shard of your Light to fall to Earth. This is the ground of true ascension.

* * *

It is locked into a casket and sealed with the great glyphs and seals of Atlantis. A vastly long time ago, this is how you protected it as your world was destroyed in cataclysm, and floods overran the land. Thus has this starlight radiance remained hidden and protected. Let the starlight speak:

> 'I am a starlight from long ago and faraway. I come from a realm of intense beauty and purity. I came to inspire the worlds of Earth, but this gift was not sought. Thus I am locked away, waiting until such time as I can return to the star world from whence I came.'

Let the heartbreaking beauty of this Light fall to the worlds of Earth. This was its intended destiny, its fulfilment. It must fall to Earth, the gift must be given. You are unlocking the seals of the magical casket.

It showers forth, such unimaginable wonder. It cascades in brilliant plumes, showering the air with radiance. The Diamond Light pours forth, no longer hidden. It falls, and the rain falls, and they are mixed together. All the worlds of Earth are sighing and expanding, shimmering forth in response. Nothing is held back, and everything is given. Rainbows form where the diamond light falls. Grandmother Turtle gazes with her wondrous beneficence. She is so glad that the Star Maiden is at last giving her gift to Earth. She is so glad of all this rainbow inspiration. Her great heart sighs, and gives forth its infinite abundance, its great ground where all are held. Her great gaze shines to the heart of the rainbow light and its hidden codes. Deep within she looks. She sees that infinite star paths are being offered for her to walk. Her oceans are filling with dazzling light, the hidden realms of lost Atlantean wisdom are stirring. The ancient cities shine in the deep with their timeless glyphs and codes. She remembers how precious it was, that time, and its people. She remembers the rare and wise gifts they brought to Earth. She breathes, and she includes these tales once again in the story of her heart. She allows that they, too, are a part of her soul. Their silent star paths span all across the universe. They unite the realms of Earth with the worlds beyond. They, too, shall be allowed passage back and forth, according to the timings of their great prophecies. She shall not bar the way. She shall welcome them home. The great cycles of creativity shall dawn once again. There shall be the luminous forging of a civilization here upon Earth. They shall remember that they are coming here to fulfil their sacred contracts of creativity: to fulfil the star dance of the infinite worlds.

* * *

You as a Star Elder are restoring yourself in fullness to the Earth. Your presence is so very beautiful. You walk amongst us, bringing the atmosphere of the miraculous with you and awakening our hearts. You walk in the ancient places of the

Earth, rekindling their memories of another time. Come into the ancient Redwood Grove. Breathe in the peace and spaciousness of the redwood trees. There is a great shimmering surprise around the corner. Amongst the grooved and mighty trunks, their dusky magnificence, the Elven Self flares forth, towering, one's own angelic presence is rekindled. You are able to dismantle much illusion in the warmth of the expansive atmosphere, in the winged silence: creaks of bark, birdsong, wind: light falling with layered emerald brilliance. There is the forest floor of brown and russet, faded needles, dead branches, ferns and ivy. The trees are sentinels. There is a great brilliance just around the corner, you have limited yourself falsely and all of these limitations are falling away. You think there is only so much beauty, happiness, interconnectivity that your life can contain, yet it shall alter even further than you can imagine. Let the last vestiges of tension and resistance fall away. There is a shimmering Dawn of Great Happiness underway. Attend to the *ground of endless creativity*. You have this sense of infinite inspiration within you, and it is to this you must attend. Give it your full attention. Your inspiration is the elixir of the Golden Dawn. Your inspiration is the stirring of the great Shining Realms of Earth.

Beyond every horizon, beyond the distant ground in the forest, glimpsed between trees, the Infinite Spaciousness dawns. We do not know who will step over that horizon towards us. We do not know who is coming. The Shining Ones are approaching us in every moment. Every horizon line houses this miracle. It is approaching you from every direction. Infinite space resides in the heart of every leaf, petal, branch. Through infinite space the stars of the future travel, entering our lives.

Every moment is a sapphire star, an island bounded by infinite space. We are always inhabiting this miracle, this singular emergence from Mystery. Every moment carries this backdrop. Like a pearl, we sail in the ocean of this Great Mystery, this oceanic space, this infinite potential.

* * *

The Earth is dropping her veils: there is a dissolution in the apparent division between Earth and other dimensions of reality. She is instead wearing the backdrop of space, of the Infinite. She is dancing in the Silence. This is her context, this is her 'meaning'. She is not grounded in biological life, in the expression of the green or mineral realms, of the interwoven elements. This is how she manifests, but she is grounded in space, she arises in the Infinite. We cannot understand the Earth without understanding this. We have placed a lock, a seal upon our perception of material existence that even as we become spiritually aware, even as we awaken, persists in limiting us to a dualistic perspective. The Earth is still identified as a finite realm, even with her subtle and energetic bodies, that is fragile, to be protected and preserved. We are failing to bear witness to her Immortal, creative and infinite aspect.

She is the creation of our hearts and minds, and even as we attempt to preserve her and protect her, we fail to listen to the true voice of her evolutionary development. We want to maintain her as we have known her, as we have loved her. We want to maintain our conception of our beautiful green Earth, so bound up with past lifetimes of reverence and devotion: intertwined existences in which she has been our mother and our ground. We must now listen to what is truly happening to her: we must listen to the voice of her Immortal Soul as it communicates the transmutation she is undergoing. We do not serve her by our nostalgia. We must be honest with ourselves about what it is we are attempting to preserve, and whether it comes from a resistance to Reality, or a deeper participation. We must not be afraid of authentic language, of saying that which we have not necessarily heard, except from Spirit. If we listen to the actual starlight song of the Earth, then we are not afraid. We are filled with joy, with anticipation, with blessing. We feel ourselves to be upon the cusp of something magnificent.

Thus it is that we allow ourselves to experience the Earth as a song of Star Light echoing forth from Space. Inherent to her are no tragic tales of death and regeneration: of loss and suffering. Her cycles are natural rhythms of Star Light and expansion. She cannot be lost in this because there is nowhere else to be. We must allow ourselves to see the Earth as she sees herself.

We surrender the spiritual structures we have adhered to in order to embrace the wisdom of the Universe. No matter what levels of sophistication, of comprehension we have reached, no matter what purity we have attained, we must ask ourselves at this time, with all honesty and openness: of what do I need to let go? Does this serve the evolution of consciousness? If I maintain this form, this practice, what is it that I shall learn? We must go back to basics. Spiritual pride can a be a very strong presence at this time: it arises within us, fierce and unexpected, roaring to protect and adhere to that which it has cultivated, that which it has laboured at. Even that which has seemed beautiful and true must be evaluated, and potentially surrendered. For we must not mistake the chrysalis for the butterfly: we must not mistake the method of cultivation for the thing itself. When we meet with the unbound expression of Spirit, how comfortable are we? Are we always looking for signposts that shall redirect us within the framework of separation: categories to separate the Divine from ourselves? Are we avoiding the naturalness of our inheritance, its profound unravelling Immanence? We have evolved many structures of spirituality over the last age in order to guide us through an aeon of separation: they seek to dissolve the veil, and acknowledge the difficulty of doing so. However, as the very reality of separation, the dream of separation fades, these structures that have been built for this task become the very forms that perpetuate it.

To what expectations have we entrained ourselves: to what expectations concerning the unfoldment of the spiritual path, what its rhythm, what its reality? We have entrained ourselves to a certain perceived relationship between spirit and matter, and certain orderly progressions between one and the other. We must listen to whether this is what the Earth is really telling us, we must allow her to be our foremost teacher of the new paradigm. We are not to be the ones always crossing over, always walking back and forth between the realms of matter and spirit. This is a view of the spiritual path that itself stems from the paradigm of separation. This view ultimately keeps us caught in separation, no matter what the beauty of that which we experience as we pass back and forth between heaven and earth.

It serves as a kind of spiritual adolescence, an intermediary path, but we must be honest when our natural wisdom stirs within, and be willing to respond, to listen, to speak in an authentic voice.

There is that which is not ours to surrender: that is our natural grace, our own Divinity. This is not ours to give away. When we abdicate this, there is no gift we are giving to others, and there can be no realization of the true nature of reality, because we have severed and dislocated its source within us. If we continually surrender our divinity to a system, a belief, a teacher that lies outside of us, then we have still this intense sense of vulnerability, of a sheltered purity, a spiritual path or attainment that could be damaged or destroyed by others, or by our own falling down. Our spiritual development is not so fragile.

* * *

The Earth is becoming highly receptive to transformation: she is deluged in a starlight dream, impregnated with herself. The cedar and the orchid are transformed also, we travel with her. Some shall not be able to take the frequency, the touch of the stars. They have made a choice not to enter the new paradigm. There are some whose frequencies were never built for this adjustment, and they have had their time. They fade like the morning dew from the grass. This is their choice: it is no less beautiful, we must not dishonour them. Neither does our choice have to be limited or defined by those who stay behind, who do not cross this particular threshold. We are either attuned and prepared, destined for this, or we are not. We shall find there are those who fade out of our lives as though they never were: realities separated by dimensional shifts.

We might be shocked by how much we have to leave behind, but we must maintain our attunement, and then we know that we are not walking into an abyss, into loneliness, but into the song of the Earth and the Stars. There is companionship, there is perfection. The symbols form a medicine wheel, and they are also lights along a pathway of starlight. With us, indeed, travel the orchids and the cedars. We are encoded with the very companions we require.

*　*　*

The frequencies may feel very intense: I am experiencing this even as I write. They are of a sound-light frequency that intensifies everything that passes through us. This can bring a sense of urgency, an intensity of presence, an activation of destiny. It is when we stay at one with our Divine Purpose, when we keep listening to the starlight that calls us through this passage, that we are able to maintain our balance, our sense of spaciousness and peace. It requires an especial purity of intention, it requires our dedication. Once we offer our commitment there is incredible acceleration and productivity: we are led along in leaps and bounds.

You are being asked to make a leap of faith. It requires profound courage, yet at every turn you are amply rewarded for your commitment. This is where the energy of the new paradigm lies, this is where the investment is being given.

Sometimes fear arises at the very sensation of the intensity. We recoil, and feel daunted, or unworthy, or intimidated. We may feel incompatible or unreceptive, we may have a sensation of going 'too far'. These are phases of dimensional adjustment and it is very beneficial to stay close to the flowers and the trees at this time, to exist in a place where the flow of this dimensional shift is taking place in a more complex and diffuse environment so that we remember our transparency and permeability.

The wings of our listening are the wings of the eagle: we can cover vast distances and experience a wide perspective.

Much can be achieved with only a little effort, an adjustment of the wing here and there in response to the wind. We allow ourselves to listen to silence, to space, for this is the new backdrop to earthly experience.

We travel with the wings of the eagle, listening to the star-light song of the cedars and the orchids. We must let go of the controls, as guided by our integrity. Our wisdom is activated at this time, we have a sense of direction. It may be hard to admit this to ourselves, but we do know where we are going, we do know where we are bound. It might not be something we can put into words, but language shall evolve.

But there is nothing impossible in heaven and earth, nothing that shall not come to pass by this passage of the orchid from one world to another.

Undaunted by the loss of that which we have been, we are the angels of the storm, fitted to the winds. We shall be surrounded by those who touch the Earth with their fingertips, who also are encoded with her Dawn.

I cannot say more than this, other than to go as the flowers go, from one world to another, within the dream that has been held.

* * *

I walk through a tattered veil of hazel leaves, tarnished at their rims; a rainfall of blackthorn leaves, falling across my path. The river is a rushing star at the heart of the forest. The heron fishes in secret, grey feathers, hunch backed. The wagtail darts along the river, dragonfly-quick.

I see a bear lumbering through the forest. She is a spirit bear. She is almost white, tinted with russet, and her coat

is long and rough. I follow her trail, cautious, at a distance. The bear deciphers the way forward. She holds one half of the trail. She knows where to make the offering of amethyst and amber, and which path to tread. She guides me to the places where natural grace is unveiled.

It dawns on me that I am always walking this bear trail of amber and amethyst, stirring the wild leaves underfoot.

This is the language of Earth. The bear turns towards me: there is a long pause. I continue toward her, my hand outstretched, tentative, reforming the Old Alliance. My hand rests upon her rough, russet-hued fur. We have walked so many paths together before, this is an ancient agreement. I trust her to lead me where I need to go. Onward she goes, accepting her role as my guide, as my companion in this world. We come to the white quartz of her cave amongst the trees, its worn entrance. A staircase in the rock leads us up, above the cave. The forest changes to pine trees, with golden needles underfoot in the dry atmosphere. Ravens call in the trees. There is the scent of pine resin, the sound of the river rushing, distant.

At the top of the rocky stairwell is a grove of pine trees, raised on a plateau above the oaks and the river. There is the rising scent of earth, the immersion in its dim sphere and cocoon. I begin to dance on the scented forest floor, its hues altering to amber and violet in my vision. The bear stands over me like a shadow. There is the slow pounding shuffle and turn of the dance, as I move in circles under the trees.

I am dancing in a sapphire dress, the flare of sleeves, stitched with pearl and lapis lazuli, barefoot, and a carved willow staff is in my hand, its base of golden topaz thumping to the forest floor as I dance. The pale, weathered staff is my ancient possession.

The sapphire dress arrives to me like a skin, received, skin to skin. It is an old dress, worn before. A turtle of polished jet hangs at my breast. There is the flare of sleeves, dancing, wide at the wrist. A white girdle with tassels hangs long. This is the message: You are the Voice of Earth.

I have worn this before, one hundred thousand times, the silk is worn through in places, slightly darkened with the rub of skin, worn threadbare, the ancient silk. How many times this has danced, with the swinging, heavy weight of the sapphire fabric. It is rubbed threadbare at collar and cuff. Worn with understanding, this is an ancient role, taken up many times over.

And the dark turtle pendant at my breast, polished jet: here is the heirloom of intention, of dedication, as the staff and the bells sound the ancient dance. Memories catch at the heart, a longing for what is lost. But here is the sapphire flame, and how it returns, because nothing is lost, there is only the willingness to remember, only the willingness to bear witness as all the false pageant of self dissolves, and I become again that dancing flame.

As I dance, the forest around me dissolves. The Elven Door opens: there is a translucency, a veil falling away. There is a palace baring its architecture and the ground calls. A wagtail hops along the river, like a ghost carrying gold. The winds are rising: copper, purple, amber, lilac, a halo of fires. The weight of the wood diminishes, her doors fly open, there are waterfalls. The Elder Palace unveils itself, bough after bough. The Elven Palace unveils its architecture, and all its fire-hued pinnacles, its frames of silver, show. It is a palace of bark and leaf; turrets of branches. There are roofs, shining, of leaves. Birds haunt all its phases.

There is a procession of Elven Ones travelling through the forest. I join the procession. Who are these Elven Ones?

They belong to the forests and the rivers, to the stars and the moon. They belong to the flowers and the trees, to the white quartz that remembers. But there is no 'long ago', there are only the infinite points on the spiral, all of them simultaneous in their difference, and this one sounding in this leaf dance of Moon. This time I witness them, and they are always scattered through this constellation of mountains, hills, forests and stars. It is always in the evolving flowers. They did not come before, they will not come after, they were and are *always*. It is the response, the listening, that unveils itself and then disappears.

They are the constellations of this land, the palaces and the memories. They are the wells, the healing springs, the heather and the winds and the numinous moors. They are the spiral, ever-shifting, of the seasonal moons: the dance through which we are guided over and over, the processional of leaf, frost and sun. It is the story of our lives. It is the grandeur of forgotten time. It is different lights, opalescent, carried. It is the forest of oak, of honeysuckle and apple. It is the green river flashing with silver sky.

I catch sight of the leader of the procession. She is an Elven Queen. She has golden hair, and wings of iridescent turquoise, speckled with yellow starriness. She leads the procession into the forest. She holds a lantern, and her feet are clad in gold. Her lamp illuminates the fallen leaves below, the green above. We travel on past clumps of mushrooms, a pale owl feather caught in wildflower stems. The river moves in a froth of greens. It is an emerald rose, ever forming and reforming around the boulders of the river bank. We form a procession of amber lanterns, illuminating the white silks of the Elven Ones. There is a waning crescent moon, hidden behind the leaves. The Elven Queen threads her way under the stars. I travel on, accompanying the procession ever further into the forest.

The procession enters the heart of the palace complex, and the Elven Ones peel off, along corridors, up and down stairwells, melting into the maze. The procession disperses, carrying their lanterns into the darkness. I see the Elven Queen gliding up a set of stairs that curls around a tall oak tree, and I follow her. The stairwell opens out into a great hall, held in the upper branches of the oak. It is an architecture of the forest, painted copper, gold and bare. At the centre of the sweeping room, sits a circle of Elders, cross-legged on the floor, each one with a carving in her lap. I move closer, to see what they are carving. Each one is carving a rune.

The one who led the procession turns around to look at me. She also holds a rune stone, her fair hair wisping around her headband, her heartbreaking beautiful dark eyes. That ancient, angel face.

She is the Elven Queen who carves the rune of leaf fall, the last place on the spiral before the vanishing. She ushers all the russet and tan of leaf, beckons a yellow haze, a crown of flaming elm. She beckons to me, and I follow her across the great hall, through an archway and a descending staircase at the other side. At ground level, the stairway is overarched by a red haze of hawthorn fruits. The hawthorn trees frame a doorway.

It is traced with the figured gold of Sun, the silver of the

Moon; inset with a triple spiral of white quartz. It is carved and woven with the dream of the elements: earth, air, fire, water. It is so precisely figured, yet indecipherable.

I see you, wisps of pale hair, bone-delicate hands, the urgency of your eyes, your dark eyes, gazing into mine, communicating all the untold lovely things of this land. Urging me to go forward, to go beyond.

I press my fingers to the inset quartz, and the door sighs open. I step within. I am standing in an orchard of apple trees. In the centre there is a stone-built well, a bowl of copper sitting beside it. I know that I have entered a sanctuary, a place that is long tended by the Elders.

The Elven Queen stands beside me.

'You, like all the rest, must find your simplicity. This is the hour to let go of all the peripheral aspects of yourself that you hold in awareness, and to find the simplicity that dwells at your core. This is what exists when all else is stripped away, when you need a solid ground on which to stand that is not subject to the whims of passion. If you take water from the well into the copper bowl, and gaze into your reflection there, you shall see the reflection of your own true simplicity. It may surprise you, what you see there.'

I pick up the copper bowl, and scoop it into the well, drawing up water. I sit back on my heels, and gaze into the water as it settles. I wonder whether I am ready to perceive my own true simplicity. I gaze in, and I am immersed, dissolving into the well waters.

At first there is a shimmering surface, then I dare to see the mighty wings. There are two golden wings arching from my back. They expand outward in feathered layers. I am a golden form, an ancient being. I am beyond myself and yet true. I let go of the threadbare patterns I have held. I under-stand myself as lights flowering deeper and deeper into gold. I understand the love that reverberates through this form. My love for the deep, hidden world. The wisdom therein. It is not ephemeral illusion, but rather the hidden well of wisdom, a deeper pattern of Love.

I pour the waters from the copper bowl onto the ground, giving thanks for their reflection as I do so. I stand up, sure-footed. I take up my native power, my Elder wisdom. I sing softly. A chant, a chant. A witness, to the fallen leaves.

Finding your Simplicity

Y ou are walking in the autumn forest where crown
upon crown of yellow leaves are falling.

Towards you from among the trees comes a reindeer with a star shining at her brow. She approaches you, and
stretches out her nose to sniff at your hand. You feel her warm
breath upon your skin, and you stroke her fur that is coarse
and silky all at once. Side by side, you set off into the forest,
and she is walking just slightly ahead of you, guiding the way.
You realize as you travel that this is no ordinary forest; it is the
Immortal Forest of the Earth, and an inner light glows within
the trees. There is a sense of timelessness, and it is as though
the forest is hung with stars. The reindeer leads the way as you
go deeper and deeper into this enchanged realm, and you are
overwhelmed by a sense of peace and beauty. Deep within the
forest, you come to a Grove of White Trees, and at the base
of each, an amethyst crystal lies in the moss. The reindeer
crosses the clearing, and bows her antlered head. Somehow,
you understand what she is indicating. You go over to one of
the trees and kneel beside it. You peer into the amethyst that
lies embedded in the moss. Within its depths shimmers the

Eighth Glyph. You raise your hand to mirror the sweep of the Glyph, in front of the tree, and you draw it into the forest air. As you draw the golden strokes of the Eighth Glyph, you feel the symbol entering your heart and glowing golden throughout your whole being. You are transported to the entrance of the bear's cave in the forest.

She is nowhere in sight, and within there is a deep pile of pine needles that hold the indentation of her body's weight. This is where she lies and sleeps for winter, dreaming and hibernating. You go into the cave and you lie down in the deep pile of pine needles, nestling down deep, letting their resinous fragrance fill your senses. At your side appears the Bear Elder, approaching on soft and silent feet. She bends down and tucks around you an indigo blanket, and tells you 'Close your eyes and sleep, you are welcome to use the dreaming place of the bear.' You look up in her eyes, at their amber and mysterious expression, and feel a deep trust that you are in the presence of one who understands the Old Ways of Earth. Just before you close your eyes, you notice a peripheral movement, and it is the bear herself, settling her bulky form at the entrance of the cave, guarding your sleep. Allow yourself to drift off into a place of silence and spaciousness. You are experiencing the deep, slumbering rest of the bear when she hibernates through the winter. Your senses close down and your heartbeat attunes to the faraway pulse of the Earth's core. You feel how she sails through the vastness of space, listening to the star worlds around her. Allow yourself to dwell in this awareness.

Out of the depths of space, you feel the vibrations of footsteps approaching you. You see a form stepping across space, and this is the form of your true simplicity. Allow yourself to drink in the details of their appearance, and how their presence feels.

Then, a voice speaks into the silence, 'Of what do you need to let go to give expression to your simplicity?' Allow the answer to flood your awareness through sound, smell, colour, words or vision.

Then the voice asks you, 'What do you need to let into your life in order to give expression to your simplicity?' Again, let the answer fill your senses in whatever way it comes to you. Store this precious knowledge in your heart.

Gently awaken from your slumber in the Dreaming Cave of the bear. Give thanks to the Bear Elder. You leave the bear cave carrying this knowledge, bowing your thanks to the bear as you go, for the gifts of her Dreaming Cave. You find yourself transported back to the White Grove, with its amethyst crystals glowing at the base of the trees. You follow the reindeer out of the White Grove, returning through the forest to this world.

NINTH TEACHING

This is the Ninth Teaching of the Deerskin Book:

The New Earth involves attunements to space itself,
to nothingness, to the silence. It is a letting go of
form and light and sound.

This is the Stillness or Great Perfection that exists
before and within all things.

Chapter 9

The antennae of a sapphire butterfly,
darting around my skirts;

loveliness of birds, archaic,
the Elder chant arising from Earth.

Thus we understand the descent:
a weight, as of feathers, on the skin;

to have descended and to come up,
with sapphire wings in the dark.

THE NINTH GLYPH is actually an attunement to space itself. It stands for the natural initiations you are experiencing at this time, and that shall continue into the future. One of the ways this is occurring is that the old dreams and desires patterned by a fading paradigm are not being fulfilled. This leaves a kind of hiatus in their place, when we feel genuinely uncertain as to what we should dream for ourselves next. That which we used to seek and long for has a quality of redundancy about it now. We do not feel the old motivation. We do not know what to wish for in its stead. Yet there is no call to stir the heart to the old flames. Let the old dreams fade away. Let them pass. Do not hang onto them for fear of the emptiness that follows. This is the pause, the lingering space where you shall learn to be a Star Walker once more.

In these moments of disappointment, lack, the suspension of unknowing, you shall learn to walk with grace through Space. These moments when the old dream fades away, and nothing comes to replace it, these are access points to major initiations. Recognise the Gift: notice the Starlit Doorway. You are being given the chance to metamorphose into Spaciousness itself, to *become* space, to awaken the *space* in your cells.

In this world we travel from dream to dream, hope to hope. It is very disconcerting when these fall away and we do not know what to dream next. Where we would like there to be the firm ground of a certain future, there is nothing. We know that tomorrow will happen, but we do not know what direction it will take.

We are afraid that if we let go of the consciousness of our desires and wants, then things will not happen, focus will be lost, and outcomes not achieved. This is because we believe that we are responsible for holding things together. Yet you are being given the opportunity to let go of this responsibility. Become mysterious to yourself – let them flutter away, all those old scripts you have written for the future. Discard them all. Let go completely, irrevocably, let it all fall from your arms, all that you have held.

Like crystal lattices, like snowflakes, these burdens are breaking up and melting away. All the encoded expectations about your future, the future you have painted upon the face of the unknown. It is oddly wonderful to let this fall away. You did not realize what a burden it had become.

This is so profoundly important to your evolution. The surrender of all direction means that the compass can spin into a whole new realm. For this to happen we must accept the radical gift of uncertainty. We must let all agendas and plans fall away, and become once again a Star Walker, one who walks in space. It is this initiation into the burning and beautiful beyond of space that makes this a quantum leap for you.

Dwell in this time quietly. Walk the unknown, infinite depth of space with grace and gratitude. Let this be a great opportunity to free yourself of all the old pathways you have been bound to tread. You do not have to choose any of the faded options, the dim offerings that the mind dredges up. Ignore the temptation to chase the shadows that play themselves out around you. This is but a shadow dance of all that fades away, and you do not have to choose this. Let them quietly dance, these dimmed lights, and wait for the True Dawn. You will find a deep peace arising within, as the days pass and you hold true to this *space*. Your inner world will become peaceful and silent, attuned to Spirit.

We have forgotten how to make these transitions, we have forgotten how to teach ourselves to let go, to surrender the old light and sink into the darkness that is space, that is silence, that is Spirit. We need this true and deeper shadow, we need this peace and surrender. We need it without any expectations of answers, any insight into what might come. This is the welcoming of space into existence, the welcoming of Inner Space into the matrix of ourselves. It is a precondition of our life on Earth, it is a precondition of the Light and the Dance of Purpose. This is where true purpose is born and unveiled, in unconditioned arising. And it is only this can bring us peace and satisfaction, oneness with the Divine. This is why the attunement to space is essential to our existence on Earth, and one of the key teachings of the Deerskin Book. It is our vision quest and our inspiration.

* * *

Find that within you that resists the unknown most powerfully. Find that core within you that cannot bear uncertainty.

This is the part of you that cannot bear not to know the outcome of the future. It is incredibly painful to be so unsure, to have so little guarantee of what shall come. Yet this is a quality of our times: there is great uncertainty. Face this resistance to the unknown within yourself, face that part of yourself that cannot bear not to know the future. The part that needs to step from dream to dream, from hope to hope like stepping stones carrying you over a wild river. Let yourself fall into the wild waters. Admit that part of you that has no dream, that has no direction. How it sears to witness this.

You are now meeting that part of your DNA that is hardwired in resistance to the Infinite. It manages reality in order to keep itself safe and protected. It maintains a continuum at all costs. The last thing it wants is to experience anything new. This self controls and dictates the formation of time and space as you experience them. It demands the linear and material reality it is built to function within. It wants to keep functioning, it wants to repeat itself indefinitely. It is a core program that has run for thousands of years.

There is only one essence code that can break this pattern. This is *your own* infinite nature. It is that within you that is limitless, mysterious. In the silence of space, you are beginning to experience yourself as this *I AM Infinity* presence.

You are seeing your own core as limitless, mysterious. You are the shimmering intensity of the Infinite.

*　*　*

It is the White Whale Elders who come forth at this time to give the *I AM Infinity* initiation. You are walking towards the ocean as the Sun sinks in the west. You carry a beaded rattle and a piece of pale violet silk that you wrap around your brow. You are calling in the elemental directions as you stride across the wet sand: invoking the Star Elders to descend into the mighty perimeter of cliff and ocean horizon. Forested hills crescent the water. You are dancing and rattling at the seashore. There is a sense of the sudden immensity of the ink-dark waters rolling in at your feet, the mighty spirits of the whales below. You are overwhelmed by the elemental immortality of the ocean, how she evokes your own identification with a fragile physical mortality. How small you feel, how utterly insignificant. How wildly afraid this tiny self is of extinction. You feel the fragile nervous humming of every bone and muscle, and how easily crushed is this delicate form, making its prayers at the edge of the waters. In the dusk, the waters and the sand are one. Your feet are sucked at by the tide. There is wind and water and darkness and the fragile flag of your prayer, weaving its ancient dance. How the success of your prayer seems to hang in the balance, as though the ocean could either accept or reject it, as though it might turn a vast immortal blind eye to the call of the Star Elders. The crystalline Dawn could be lost in this ocean deep, the prayers of the Star Bundle dispersed and undone. Ever, your heart widens to the love vibration of the prayer, to the Ninth Glyph and its incipient wisdom. You feel that you will not have the strength to continue, that a great mindless power has dwarfed and overwhelmed you. You are assailed by the terrible fear of failure, that you do not have the strength to travel beyond this threshold. It is as though you are dancing against a glass wall, invisible and brittle, but impermeable. You have met that within yourself which is brittle and finite, that which believes in its own fragile mortality. Gradually, your wings widen to the winds and the waters, and with wild courage and faith your feet beat their dance upon the shore. And you are shown the lost realms beneath the ocean, the mermaid dwellings far below, the elemental beauty of their deep hidden sapphire lights. You see that the grey crashing ocean conceals this secret heart: its wild indifference drawn like a mask to cover the lost worlds and the hidden harmonics of peace. How disparate these realities, yet how bound as the stars reflect upon the waters, and by increments we remember the old worlds of Earth. The Elemental Song of Love goes forth, and suddenly there is an answering call. Far out in the ocean, the whales answer.

Suddenly, you become aware of an object sitting on the sand. It is a whale fin carved out of ancient cedar, shining with its inlaid otter teeth and the ancestral Whale Riders standing all around with bright eyes. They welcome you into their midst. Your prayers are overlapping, you are not different. They invite you to travel with them along their ocean pathways, forged by generations of prayer. You mount the whale saddle with its inlaid pattern of Moon and Star. You travel a far, far distance, cresting the waves. At the furthest horizon, the whales appear. There they are, far out in the ocean, haunting its depths. They choose to remain here, woven into the dimensional fabric of the Earth, encompassing vast frequencies.

And in these far ocean waters there is a Sapphire Portal

to another solar system. They cross over effortlessly, and you realise that they are eternally the Guardians of this Star Portal of the far ocean.

You follow them through the portal. You sit, to breathe, a star at your brow and receive the teachings of the Whale Elders. You sit in the blue robe of far worlds, in communication with these ethereal others. You witness how they have eternally expanded the worlds of Earth with their indigo wisdom, their blue star dimensions.

With impossible gentleness the Whale Spirits teach this. The Whale Elders, with their graceful, all-encompassing far wisdom, are towering around you. The star at your brow radiates in all directions, sending out filaments of silver light to each of them. You breathe softly, deeply. Their inexpressible gentleness fills your body, your bones.

You see the mighty Star Paths of which they are the Travellers and Keepers, laced into an indigo infinity through the Universe. You see, with surprise, that you shine like a white star where all of these paths meet. They travel outwards from you and towards you. Through you, everything and anything is possible. All destinies, all pathways exist. You are the Creative Principle of the Universe: its architect and dreamer. Through you, the Universe is capable of neverending metamorphosis.

You make the vow, the commitment, to remain anchored in this mysterious and ceaseless creativity. This is the White Star Fire of the White Whale Elders. They are the ones who approach you now. Advancing through the indigo mists, they encircle you. They are radiance within radiance, ever receding realms of whitening purity. Their eyes are elliptical turquoise stars.

They come to you who have remembered the White Star Fire of your infinite creativity. You who shall not seek to rest the infinite upon the finite, but will bear witness to the beautiful crystallizations of the Infinite as they arise and fall, as they manifest and fade away. It is with this insight that you become the ultimately graceful Dancer of the Golden Dawn. You shall go forth now and speak the Language of the Earth with your Infinite Heart. Remember the White Whale Elders who have witnessed you thus.

The I AM Infinity of the White Whales is a part of the fabric of the Deerskin Book, immortally woven into its silver, gold and sapphire inks.

* * *

Let yourself be drawn to the edge: by the ocean, the forest, the mountains. Hear the calling of the wolf, the bear, the whale. Let them summon you to their places when the timing is right. Here they will call you to natural initiations of spaciousness. In the vastness of the ocean you shall find the spaciousness of your elemental nature. You shall be carried into the Great Beyond that lies within yourself, that is the ground of the Golden Dawn. In distant whale song you shall be drawn to a vaster horizon: one that stretches you beyond the limitations you have carved for your existence. Suddenly, you shall know that in the mysterious depths of the ocean, hidden in the unimaginable height of the mountain, in the faraway and elemental hearts of whale and bear, as within yourself, is a starlit depth of space, an Infinity. You shall become unafraid of the distances you must travel, of the transformations you must undertake.

You shall embrace the immensity of your own journey: its

epic proportions that span lifetimes and worlds. You shall be prepared to cover great distances.

This is the freedom and migrational heart of many indigenous peoples, who have not forgotten the enormity of the journey they are upon. You are allowing your natural migrational patterns to become emergent once more. You do not cling to the safety and security of one place, fearful of the unknown beyond. You feel the star paths stretching within the spaciousness of Earth, wending their way, guiding you onward, into beauty and wisdom and metamorphosis. You experience how these paths are growing, awakening, evolving and how your movement is a crucial aspect of this. Migrational freedom involves a sensory rapport with these inner lights of the Earth: with her established and evolving inner realms. This sensory rapport shall become an ever more magnificent aspect of our existence. It shall become more vivid and determinative to our personal choices and patterns of movement. Our starlight feet shall stir the ancient stardust of these places and we shall connect the incoming starlight with the ancient starlight.

* * *

When you let your old dreams fall away and allow for no substitution or settlement, then you acquire the grace of the Star Walker who knows when to travel between stars, between realms of inspiration. You as the Star Walker are the one who emerges from Space bringing the messages of the Golden Dawn in their wake. You have learnt to sail in unmarked waters with no sense of destination, only keeping faith in the darkness that the Dawn *will* come. You know it by the quiet intensity of its radiance, by the I Am Infinity of its limitlessness and the creativity it inspires.

It is the I Am Infinity presence that has the capacity to download our celestial and earthly missions. It receives instructions and information from Spirit. You are cultivating the ability to receive the imprint of new instructions as and when they arrive. These instructions arrive full with their inherent pattern, or archetypal structure, that serves as the vibratory setting for the manifestation of your reality. This archetypal template lives and breathes its song, its signature, into every moment. It is this gift we must stop to listen to, this vibratory pattern of stellar-earthly wonder which, once heard, pulls us into alignment with it, allowing us to release everything which is not this, and transmit this gift from Infinity to our world.

No matter how lost we feel, we are always simultaneously returning to ourselves by our listening, our breath, our hearts. This is the grace that is never lost, from which we can never be separated. It holds us in existence, to a thread of hope and possibility, even when the pain of our resistant, dissonant selves has become overwhelming. We are always being called home, to this. The way never closes.

The best ways to restore ourselves to spaciousness, to our ancientness, to our timelessness, are through sound and breath. We walk ever over that threshold from our ancientness to our timelessness.

Use the breath to come home to yourself, to discover where you truly are. The breath is the thread of a starlight bridge into space. It is an unacknowledged aspect of our earthly existence because it is so perpetual and fundamental. By placing the attention upon the breath, we can walk its path back to the heart, and discover where we are in our inner cycles of expression.

* * *

Physical spaciousness is utilized in sacred places such as stone circles or cathedrals, where the expansion of consciousness is aligned to an expansive space, generating the possibility for transformative spiritual experiences: a vortex of transformation open for all. This is a place where restricted frequencies can be surrendered, because the field of consciousness, the overall frequency, resonates more strongly with the natural, harmonic and divine Self, shifting the seat of identification and allowing for surrender to take place.

The ancient sacred sites of the Earth are becoming very active at this time. Many people are consciously using them as Star Portals, by which they can enter into the higher dimensional energies, shift their own vibration and manifest significant changes in their personal and planetary realities.

Many people are using these Star Portals to connect with the guidance of the Elder Ones, to access ceremonial codes – those creative, immortal gestures that ground our reality in reverence and love. There are ancient testimonials of ceremonial practices written into the etheric fabric of these places; here we witness the ceremonial wisdom of the Elders through the veil of time and space. We take up their inspiration, and so also we pick up the legacy of our own past lifetimes and our unique ceremonial pathway upon this Earth. We are drawn to places where we have danced before, and left the imprint of our spiritual intention. When we pick up these nuances, we may feel very moved as the memories sway us with their beauty and familiarity. A part of us longs to return to this past of ceremonial grace.

Yet it is not ours to step back in time, however compellingly lovely and soul-stirring these memories may be. Instead, we receive them as gifts into the present. We let ourselves be infused and inspired by them. Our ceremonies of Love, of a Golden Dawn of creativity, are enhanced by this inheritance of wise practice. Certain exact details may carry through such as costume and crystal tools. Allow your I AM Infinity presence to choose which of these is useful and make them part of your present repertoire. Acquire all the ceremonial memory and wisdom that is valuable to you, but know that all must be placed into the crucible of the Golden Dawn, whose brilliant fires will transmute them into an expression that is truly relevant for this moment in your evolution. Let these practices burn in the fires of your own brilliance, let them be moulded and sculpted until they are resonant with the I AM Infinity, until they carry the breath of the miraculous and the inspirational.

These ancient places are a profound aspect of the evolution of Earth, and a gift beyond all reckoning on the path of our spiritual evolvement. They represent the great harmonic and emergent beauty of the Earth, her ancient potentialities as a divine dream. We listen to these ancient dreams, we align with those who have heard them throughout the aeons, and we honour this song and unfolding whose span is so much vaster than our individual lives. We walk upon a vast dream, unfolding through vast cycles of time and space. This is not to remind us of our smallness, but of our capacity for the transformational attunement to our own Immortal unfolding. The Earth mirrors all of this for us: the midnight of our ancientness, fallen long behind us, in which is figured our Immanence and Evolvement. The word 'ancient' is a tricky one to use because it can seem to imply a worship of a past consciousness, that there is some wisdom in the past that is superior to that of today. It is not superior. It is, however, of inestimable value to this moment in our evolution.

The Earth is already hearing the perfection of who she is; she is already hearing its song and its silence; she is already manifesting timelessness. This is reflected by her oldest places, by her holiest places. We do not need to transcend the wisdom of what already is, the great legacy of our ancestors and the vast time frames and awareness of the Shining Ones, embodied here as a link and an offering to our realization of timelessness, of ourselves.

We shall not separate the angels from the Earth: not again, not this time around. What loss not to hear their great songs of stone and forest, of crystal, night and Light. The orchids have kept for us their secrets, the greater interwoven harmonies of the aeons. So, too, our bodies hold the script, are a testament to the angelic Intelligence. We are their legacy and their evidence: our bodies are these exquisite and elegant tuning devices that catch all the wavelengths of the Universe, that understand the harmonies of time and space. We are the wonderfully evolved moment we have been waiting for. We are the evidence of angelic ascendence and the many-dimensional Earth.

We must not be afraid of dissolution, of dismantling. It is not always the moment of ascendence, of creation. Sometimes we must allow the old to fall away, even its beautiful aspects. The Earth does not fear her own silence, her own journey through the Universe, her winter of stillness. She simply withdraws and dreams.

She tells how the Deer ran through the forest, all those aeons of awareness and sensitivity. She tells how the Shining

Ones still dance in her ancient places and how this touch of starlight was foretold. She sleeps and she dreams under the mesmerism of the stars, their play of silver upon her woven forms. She hears the call of her future across the Universe, and the Deer too twitches her ear with the sapphire call of ancient teachings. She hears a dream being spun, and it echoes with her future and her past. It is familiar, as though it has been here before. She watches and she listens, crossing the starlight bridge into her own Silence.

* * *

I am walking through the starlit, winter forest. The winds circle, stripping the willow to her orange stems. I walk the path of winter's far, hammered gold: the spare architecture of winter's forest. Everything has disappeared. Only the bright dragon-waters are showing.

I arrive in the heron-grey circle of the holly tree. Her dance curls, a smoke dervish, a dissonance of opening, hints. She ripples the inks of the sky, lifts me into the curve of its steels. She fans my song into its emptiness, flickering me into the holly tree, its spikes and tusks. Within the holly is a different silence, a silence that flowers from multiple places, opening that shaken blue, between stars depth, as though loosening thunder into the mist. In this silence, I breathe. I am drawn further into silence and her silver root: her winter, her holly.

I am carrier to this winter dawn, traveller of this unfinished road. I walk a trail in the remoteness. I leave prints in the heron stillness. My dissolving feet are flowering and flowering into the thousand petals, into the river stillness of myself.

I would build an echo chamber for all the delicate voices I have not yet heard. Here, I would listen to the mist, the stars, the cold: daughters born of different stars, carrying their trace to the present. I can see a starlit trail curving back through time, a hoop of star-bright souls: ancestors, descendants, leaves of other seasons, each guided by the unseen forces of the Earth. The hoop has never been broken; it is only forgotten: a thing of great beauty that has been forgotten, half-hidden in the stars, the heirloom.

Here they are, standing in the shadows of the starlit forest. Slowly, they step forward, the old-gold radiance of mosaic robes, woven of luminosity, woven of prayer. Their turquoise headdresses glimmer in the night. Here are the Luminous Hearts that walk amongst us, carrying the old sapphire, bearing the copper bowls aloft. They carry white drums, beating the rhythms of an unfinished prayer. I dance and I dance, restored to a lost cadence. Beneath the dance is a fire of a longing and a lostness, a never-enough. I am swept by an overwhelmingly nostalgia, a wish for a past of ceremonial grace and companionship. How connected we were to the Earth and the stars! Here, in the forest, my memories are stored, and here they walk, this night. We were here once, daughters of midnight and smoke prayers. How beautiful it was to watch the dawn of this Earth. How we made magical gestures under the oaks with their shawls of mist.

We come to one another as old stars, touching flame to softness, light to light, tracing our roots back old, old ways. We make real this lost reality, this procession of dreamers, destroyed in our land long ago: that light of angel flame, of sight in the dark. This simple turning to the Light, to rapture: this awareness of a sacred world, haunted with sapphire emanations.

What would it mean to take up the old dress, to wear the indigo of the Old Ones? This would be not the old vanishing humility, but a radiance and a dedication. I come in indigo on the golden wind, following a call that my heart has made.

Incense burns, gathered from the flowers that grow from starlight's inspiration. In the incense smoke that spills into the night air, the dragons stir. We call them when the winds turn amber and it is time to ride the thunder of our own disappearance. They dance their ascent into the night air, travelling over us, caught into the rhythms of the white drums. It is a reunion of all that I have loved: the subtle, crafted ceremonies, aeons of reverence. This is our craft, this attunement to the cosmos. I dance the subtle, stranded music of the lost ceremonies, a complexity whose nuances shall never again be evoked by Earth and sky. Hands outstretched, we come to one another. I know that this is a last gathering, the threads are worn and the future calls. I have hesitated long enough. I shall become a forest whisper, and trust that purity and light are born and lost like leaves, with their own seasons of appearance. It is time for them to unravel the strands of their regret that keep them bound here. Their time is gone, that beautiful hour is past. It is time to let these ancient companions make their journeys to the star worlds that await them, and to trust that I shall carry their legacy within my heart.

There is a whispering stampede, the rustling of the forest's copper floor. It is the arrival of the hounds of the Elven One. The Winter Queen sits in the forest clearing, and they are gathered like constellations around her. She is cross-legged under the silver oak, upon the mound.

She leads the hunt, and there are stars and magic sapphires in her antlered hair. She races along the darkened forest paths. Her hounds flock to her, and stampede the

forest in a whispering rush. Fleet-footed, they shepherd the Ancient Ones into a procession, herding them towards the entrance of the mound. This is the soul of the Earth, her universal law, her Old Way dance.

I stand beside the holly tree and gaze at the Elven One, her narrow, tapering face. I follow the procession into the Earth, into the mound. There is the storm-blue mist of her dress sweeping ahead, the whispering, lamp-eyed hounds at her heels. Delicate and bright, they sniff my hand. We pass beneath the stone lintel, out of the winter wood.

Within, the white walls are inscribed with a sapphire script. Along the corridor, there is resin of amber strewn underfoot, dried lavender scattered on the floor. There are translucent sapphire lanterns in the walls of white rock. We walk in procession, heads bent, bowed downward, as we travel the passageway. It stretches on and on, and we walk a long way until a quiet brilliance begins to shine ahead. Its brilliance grows until ahead of us there appears a silvery, immortal tree. One by one, as the Old Souls reach it, they vanish. They brighten like shooting stars as they pass through. I stand and watch. It is not my time to cross over. It shall not be my time until I have borne this sapphire and amber flame forward, into your hands, and I know the legacy is restored.

Someday my wings will be done, all the dust of flight loosened, and there will be no more ground to cover. Then there will be nothing but this: to step into the white tunnel with bowed head, and witness the scatterings of amber on the ground, to pass beneath the sapphire lamps, and keep on going. There are distances to be covered but they are not endless: and our travels are not without purpose. There is always restitution underway, as the Light bends to meet us, searches for us along the hollow halls, and calls us along the passageway fragrant with offerings that we ourselves have made, and whose essence always draws us back to the place that cannot be forgotten.

It is not my time to return to the Immortal Realms. I stand to one side of the portal, until the last of the nomad souls passes through, and the Elven One and I stand facing one another in the chambered mound. She calls down incantations in the Old Language, as the portal ebbs and vanishes. She looks at me, her face of bone and sapphire, intent, as though searching for something. I feel as though she is searching through the halls of my memory, seeking an entrance into the amber past, into the wisdom beyond the Sun. Her expression is mercurial and strange as a moonbeam. I feel the stage of incarnations shifting. There is a greater dawn that trembles at the edge of my senses, that delicate and intermittent passion which has haunted me for so long. She speaks:

'I am the Navigator. I belong to no world and every world. I visit where I am needed, where I am called. In some ways, I am the shadow of unbelonging that can so touch the hearts of Earth-bound souls. And yet you need to remember this, the universality of your provenance, of your belonging. You may be called to specific places upon the Earth, and become rooted and woven into their inner geometry: yet your roots always touch endlessly to the Infinite. You also are a Space Traveller, one who is unbound to her destinations: who passes through. I have helped many worlds to prosper and grow, to receive the right gifts at the right moments, travelling between spheres. Your love for the Earth is a wonderful thing, but you must remain attuned to the Infinity at her heart.

'This is an Obsidian Mirror.'

She hands me a smooth and polished disk of volcanic glass. It is completely black.

'Do not be afraid of the blackness. This is a representative of space. You need this space as the ground for the emergence of Infinite Love. It is out of this that a love beyond all attachments arises. On one side, if you look into the disk, you will see your ordinary reflection, the way that you are accustomed to perceive yourself. On the other side, if you turn it over, you will perceive yourself as you arise in limitless space, in silence. This is the Navigator within you: the one who passes through all other realms when called, without attachment. This self may have an impersonal appearance that is unusual to behold. It may not wear the social and human masks that you are accustomed to don. You may feel unprotected, exposed, showing this face to others. Yet this is your most natural expression. Often we fear being seen like this. We fear that others will reject us, that we may intimidate or alienate them. This is because there has been a dissociation from this ground of space. For others, we may become the obsidian mirror onto which they project all their own shadows, all the aspects of themselves that they fear or disown. Recognize when this happens, and do not own these shadows.

'You may fear being perceived as a space traveller. You may have discovered that this essence is not welcome upon the Earth, and is often misunderstood. However, we are coming together, passing the initiations one to another, and creating a protective field of awakening.'

Finding the Obsidian Mirror

You are walking in the winter forest. The trees glimmer with beautiful patterns of frost. Towards you from among the trees comes a reindeer with a star shining at her brow. She approaches you, and stretches out her nose to sniff at your hand. You feel her warm breath upon your skin, and you stroke her fur that is coarse and silky all at once. Side by side, you set off into the forest, and she is walking just slightly ahead of you, guiding the way. You realize as you travel that this is no ordinary forest; it is the Immortal Forest of the Earth, and an inner light glows within the trees. There is a sense of timelessness, and it is as though the forest is hung with stars. The reindeer leads the way as you go deeper and deeper into this enchanted realm, and you are overwhelmed by a sense of peace and beauty. Deep within the forest, you come to a Grove of White Trees, and at the base of each, an amethyst crystal lies in the moss. The reindeer crosses the clearing, and bows her antlered head. Somehow, you understand what she is indicating. You go over to one of the trees and kneel beside it. You peer into the amethyst that lies embedded in the moss. Within its depths shimmers the

Ninth Glyph. You raise your hand to mirror the sweep of the Glyph, in front of the tree, and you draw it into the forest air. As you draw the golden strokes of the Ninth Glyph, you feel the symbol entering your heart and glowing golden throughout your whole being. You are transported…

You are sitting on top of an ancient mound in the forest. A figure approaches, and there are stars and magic sapphires in her antlered hair. Her dress is a mist of storm blue, and shadowy hounds dart at her heels. She comes and sits beside you in a swirl of skirts. Her moonbeam face gazes into yours. She reaches out and offers you something: it is a shining black disc. She tells you:

'This is a disc of black obsidian. It is known as an obsidian mirror. Look into one side of it and note your reflection, then look into the other and see what you see there. The first reflection shows you your ordinary self; the second shows you the space traveller who exists beyond this world. Do not be afraid: it is a great blessing. Look into the obsidian.'

You take the disc of polished obsidian from her. You look into the first side, and in its black surface you see your familiar reflection. You turn it over, and on its reverse side you catch a glimpse of yourself that is of quite a different appearance. Let yourself take note of this. Give yourself a moment to absorb this impression and how it makes you feel.

You hand the obsidian mirror back to the Navigator, but she responds, 'This is a gift for you. Look into it whenever you need an attunement to space, look into it when you need to remember your own infinite courage as a space traveller. Remember that people such as you as essential for the Earth's metamorphosis, because you allow her transformation.'

You thank her, and tuck the obsidian mirror into your deer-skin pouch. Know that it is always there for you, whenever you need it.

'And here,' she says, holding out an object in her hands, 'here is a ceremonial tool from your past life that shall help you at this time.' She offers the object to you, and you accept it. You take it from her hands and recognize with loving reverence this precious tool from lives past. You know that it shall be of great benefit to your spiritual journey. You thank this Elven Queen of the winter wood.

You find yourself transported back to the White Grove, with its amethyst crystals glowing at the base of the trees. You follow the reindeer out of the White Grove, returning through the forest to this world.

TENTH TEACHING

This is the Tenth Teaching of the Deerskin Book:

*We must let go of all attachments to what we think
of as good and bad, and allow the spontaneous arising
of the New Earth.*

*It comes from a place beyond our conscious minds,
from a wisdom so much deeper than our own.*

*And yet this wisdom arises spontaneously within us,
like a pair of wings sprouting from our backs.*

Chapter 10

She comes from the furthest, unknown, nowhere star

along the trail of lost moonlight,
leading into the land.

Many circles, many lifetimes meet here.

THE TENTH TEACHING speaks of a wisdom beyond judgements of good and evil that arises spontaneously as an aspect of the New Earth. It is time for us to fly on the silver wings of this non-dualistic wisdom. We have won once again our unique and angelic perspective, we are free to walk within the illumination of our angelic auras. These are our wings, this vast field of inter-connected awareness. It is a radical sensitivity, heightened and powerful. We do not have to dim our awareness in order be free of judgements. In fact, the more heightened and clear our sensitivity becomes, the more easily we can see the impersonal nature of phenomena, and the less likely we are to get caught into subjective, emotional reactions.

We remember being thus illuminated in our Atlantean lifetimes. We remember this radiance, this clarity. It is an angelic and impersonal clarity that is also compassionate and warm. We stand in a field of vast purity, through which perceptions travel. We see energies, we feel clearly the presence of that which is near us. Our psychic capacities are heightened:

clairvoyance, clairaudience, telepathy. We do not rely on our physical senses alone; we rely instead on a synaesthetic dance of perception that includes our extraordinary faculties. We are engaging with the full range of our faculties, it is as though we are finally operating at our full capacity, restored to full working order. This is the light technology of ourselves, of our own human vehicles, becoming all that they are designed to be. This light technology, the radical sensitivity and wisdom of our angelic auras, is natural. It is being activated by the present cosmic conditions. We can participate in this, if we so choose. In recent lifetimes, we have been trained to derive information concerning the nature of reality from external sources, we have been trained not to trust our own sensitivity, and always to seek the external validation of spiritual or secular authorities. We experience a kind of inversion, whereby information – truth – comes from the outside, not the inside. This is an inversion, because truth can only actually be experienced from the inside, using the antennae of the angelic aura that is designed for this purpose. It is from this perspective that we can receive accurate information about our environment, moment to moment, as it unfolds. From this perspective, we can make appropriate responses. This is how we attune ourselves to the shared field of angelic intention, entering into a community of purpose, guided by the Light.

* * *

One of the forces we have come almost unanimously to distrust is our own power. We engage in spiritual practices to awaken ourselves, all the while resisting the very presence of the power and memory we seek. There is a shutdown to a whole dimension of our spiritual capacities, which to a great degree, limits our natural expression.

I am referring to our capacity for our actual embodiment, in blood and bone and breath, of our spiritual nature. This is the legacy of our last earthly experience of such union, which was the age of Atlantis. We had access to a much greater field of consciousness at this time, as the reality of our world was not limited to third-dimensional experience. We incarnated our spiritual essences directly in our bodies, which created whole different fields of possibility from the ones we experience today. But harmony was not maintained and spiritual frequencies were accessed in a manner that was destructive to the development of organic life at that time. This is as much to say that not all potentials were pursued and explored with Love, which is the force that makes Light technologies compatible with the formation of organic life. The heart was lost, and even those who had maintained a sense of service to Divinity and all beings in their development of spiritual capacities and their exploration of reality, were imprinted with a sense of the potential disastrousness inherent in such a way of being. This can lead to confusion when this level of awakening and memory is touched upon: there is a simultaneous sense of great potential, which has a tendency to pull back into distrust. We are attracted and repelled all at once.

We also fear that our physical forms do not have the capacity to embody such high frequencies: which manifests as a sense of limitation or unworthiness, or a sense of righteous distrust. We would rather not go there. We would rather keep things simple and clear and maintain the paradigm and experience of reality with which we have become familiar. Again, I emphasize that some of this reaction may occur at the level of the unconscious, while consciously we 'seek' spiritual development, evolution and awakening.

It may manifest as a sense that spiritual evolution is too dangerous and enticing; in fact, we feel that we want it too much. We are very suspicious. We fear that we are putting ourselves under a delusion of spiritual powers: we fear that we are being falsely enticed and that we shall lose the heart centre of our purity, our innocence.

All of this arises when we touch upon the Atlantean memory field. And for some reason, we do touch upon it. It is arising at this time because the old capacities are restoring themselves as the veil between spirit and matter dissolves.

* * *

There is now available the evolvement of Light technologies, of communication with the stars, of access to a non-physical set of frequencies that link into life beyond this planet and to other solar systems. This returns to us across the veil of ages, preserved as esoteric knowledge here and there. More inherently, it is preserved in our own genetic memory banks, and is resurfacing at this time. And as we are touched by these frequencies once more, we fear to lose touch with the Earth and her organic life forms, and a loss or an overwriting of her native wisdom and communication systems.

The Deerskin Teachings and their Symbols carry us beyond this rift: beyond this perceptual divide. They mark a moment in our evolution where balance is attained, where we have learnt enough about the spectrum of dimensions and a surrender to Divine Love that we can maintain a multi-dimensional integrity. The orchid does not fear to welcome its full and complex beauty; it does not fear losing its connection with the Heart of the Infinite as it becomes all that it is.

We are ready to drop our judgement against ourselves:

ready to release the safety valve we have placed upon the wholeness of our physical and spiritual natures. Our awareness of the Earth, of her ancient wisdom, and of the stars and their technologies of Light shall transform one another: there is a marriage at a new level of evolvement. As I have said, the Earth is dreaming herself differently as the Light of the stars touches her at this time. We are drawn into a dance that transfigures the very Light that arrives. We cannot afford to be prejudiced or afraid of one dimension or the other. Those who fear the Earth, who project their darkness and their suffering, their separation upon her, who see her as inherently separate from Spirit, they, too, must look into the heart of their fear, their aversion, and surrender it. It is not the hour to escape our bodies into the starlight. It is not the hour to end our affinity with this Earth: our devotion to her unfoldment. She is a great and wise Mother Soul, she is the stardust from which our bodies are woven. Our inter-dimensional transformation comes from within the continuum of sensory, earthly experience. We do not have to retreat from nature into the Light, because nature herself is the dream of the Light, and this Earth dreaming herself is our Illumination.

There is a recognition of the wisdom of our ancestors, those we call native and indigenous, who over the last cycle have developed in harmony and interwoven awareness with the energetic fields and consciousness of Earth and her organic life forms. This is the wisdom of an intuitive sensitivity and a participation with the realms of nature. This is the attunement of the Deer to the forest, and her awareness of where the paths, the Light trails are. It is a multidimensional and instinctual consciousness, the loss of which we have heavily suffered in this last stage of our modern era. We wish to be rewoven in the web of life. We wish to rediscover our participation.

* * *

Atlantis exists as the lost continent, undiscovered, yet unquenchable in the psychic memory of humanity. This is our own submerged, yet emergent, awareness of Earth's hidden cosmic geometries and our ongoing work with these realms. This is her golden grid, her own winged and angelic aura, layered feather upon feather of a global network, that is becoming visible once more. These are our lost dimensions, our lost lands, lying beneath the oceans and the ice, lying beneath our feet. In fact, their legacy is scattered everywhere throughout the continents of the Earth. These are the amethyst paths, the shining architectures in whose construction we have been deeply involved. These Teachings are written for those who have served the Earth with lifetimes of dedication and exceptional love. As Atlantis emerges, we discover a record of our own activity. We discover the Lost Temples whose genealogy we still carry.

As I have said, for many of us there is hesitation in accessing this strata of ourselves. This is because the civilizations of Atlantis ended in cataclysmic imbalance. They had moved out of resonance with the vibratory fields of Earth. The light dimensions with which they worked were no longer in alignment with the sacred ground of Earth, and had become destructive to organic life. Thus the creative cycle of Atlantis came to an end, and a whole new set of lessons concerning third-dimensional reality were entered upon. This is the cycle of learning through which we have been travelling in this last era, learning how to maintain dimensional balance within ourselves, laying a foundation of integrity so that we can become truly multi-dimensional beings upon the Earth, bearing witness to the precious layers of the Earth's multi-dimensional essence. We are ready to access our full power, which now appears to us as miraculous. When we reclaim these gifts we do not put ourselves or others in danger. We trust in the Jewel of the Heart, which beats at one with the Earth and biological life and its evolvement.

* * *

We have undergone a huge shift, from the multi-dimensional light of Atlantis to the ages of darkness through which we have just walked. Yet when we move beyond a dualistic perception of this shift, then we begin to glimpse the wisdom of the New Earth, and we begin to earn our silver wings. There is a totality of exploration taking place, always in the heart of Great Mystery. We emulate Great Mystery in the embrace of this totality. Our angelic aura of radiant sensitivity offers us true perception, and through this perception we see the amethyst pathways opening under our feet and guiding us on extraordinary journeys. We trust these pathways, we feel blessed and honoured, and we know that it has taken the totality of all our exploration to arrive at this moment, for the silver wings of Earth and Self to be taking to flight once more. This is the realm of the miraculous, and it is by our compassionate non-judgement that the doors of this multilayered world open up. Our non-judgement is a radical tool. The powers of our own spirit are divided as long as we see through a lens of good and evil, light and dark. We seek these simple resolutions of judgement in order to find certainty and safe ground, in order to shore up our vision of ourselves, yet we pay such a high price for this comfort. We lose the Truth, we lose our silver wings of extraordinary flight. We lose the dazzling brilliance of a reality that sears the heart with its beauty, its poignancy, its improbable, miraculous depths. When we let everything dwell as it is – all the beauty and all the pain – then the silver wings of true wisdom expand and take flight.

We discover that what was lost, is not lost at all. It was here all the time; it was just that we could not see it. It is here, in the place where we are: this mystic and extraordinary Earth, who has so many mysteries still to reveal to us, who is only just beginning to let us know who she is. It is here, in the place where we stand, a multi-dimensional and rainbow reality, thrumming with its own magnificence. This is the story beyond the stories we have been dwelling in. It is the True Love Story of Earth, that begins to appear to us in snatches of vision. Portals open up as we explore the land, as we respond to the subtle instructions that come. This is the New Earth arising amidst us, and every thread is dear and precious. Every thread is of ultimate significance in this beautiful tapestry, connecting as it does to every other; part of a subtle existence that is birthing itself with quiet magnificence. This is the manifestation of the blueprint of the New Earth taking place in the moment. This is how it occurs.

This subtle tapestry of amethyst and silver, of gold, emerald, turquoise, copper, and crimson is appearing in our lives. It is appearing in our choices of livelihood, our relationships, our homes, our families, our wisdom, inspiration and invention. Increasingly, it is this subtle tapestry that draws the focus of our attention. We are the Golden Dawn tending to the Golden Dawn. The starlight is altering ourselves and the Earth into a new relationship. We allow this parallel reality to transpire. We do not give up on it. No matter how subtle its etheric dance, it is the living gift of Great Mystery, and other, more solid seeming, realities are in fact crumbling. We will not find solid ground if we lean upon them. This is not their hour. They are fragile and deteriorating and no matter how hidden this process is, it is happening. When we allow our radiant sensitivity to be activated, this is in fact easily apparent, and increasingly impossible to mask. The masks are losing their power to convince, and actually reveal vulnerability. That which is running on the old paradigm of competitive separation, of three-dimensional materialism, of fear rather than Love, of an inanimate earth and a masterful humanity... this still has the power to cause great pain and suffering, it still has the power of destruction, of material accumulation and con-sumption. Yet however compelling and tragic these realities, it is a shadow dance beside the emergent blueprint of Love.

We have been here before. Yet truly, everything is dif-ferent. We are different. We come to this place again, this opportunity: the lost dimensions are opening, portals of a great and evolved realm. It is not new, and yet everything is different.

* * *

When we embrace the non-dual wisdom of the New Earth, of our true selves, then we can bear witness to the total-ity. The sacred Earth lies broken all around us. The sacred places are desecrated and ignored, the forests destroyed, the rivers, springs, oceans and atmosphere polluted, the animals retreating and vanishing. Yet amidst this appar-ently broken landscape, the portals are opening; there is an awakening taking place. Remembrance is passing through us in giant waves. An ancient harmony sings out, an Earth that shines, golden-starred, her angelic aura throwing off its concealment and calling us into a sacred dance of cleansing. Through the desecration, through all that subsides and vanishes, there is this Silver Wheel of Lights within us and around us, a beautiful legacy belonging to vast time cycles, offering itself to an apparently broken world. The contradictions in perception are enough to break the heart. We feel bewilderment. How can we hold all of this in our hearts. How can we bear witness to a moment of such disparate far reaches? Surely we must subscribe to one reality or the other?

Is this an ending or a beginning? We remember the cataclysms of Atlantis: a whole continent lost and sunk. A whole civilization disappearing from the Earth. We wonder, is this now another such? We see the evidence of an ending all around us. We see all that fades, becomes corrupt and crumbles. We see the destruction, the rampant, vast destruction of entire subtle worlds of life and beauty. We see the war and the injustice, the cruelty and despair that seem to perpetuate themselves without cessation. The darkness has become such a dominant aspect of our world, it seems goodness is a rarity. It seems that the greed, the material aspiration, will never be sated. There are those who will continue to take what they want at whatever cost, and it seems their endless desires will destroy our world. Nothing ever changes. It rolls on the same, year after year, century after century. The power of good will never be strong enough to alter this; it is too powerful, too perpetual. The language of the Golden Dawn can seem a slender hope when we are overwhelmed by these realities. We feel once again the stirring of this divide within us, within our world: of light and dark, good and evil.

Let us hold this all in our hearts; let this time be an

ending *and* a beginning. Let us have this courage, this magnificence. We bear witness to the totality. We reject nothing, we deny nothing. When we let the totality sweep our hearts, then we are held in the magnificence of Great Mystery, of the All That Is. Our ground is endless, infinite, all-encompassing. There is no fragility in this. This is not a place of slender and assailable hope. It is the ground of arising, the Infinite Golden Dawn of Endless Worlds, and it is to this that the wings of our listening are given.

* * *

We do not wish to be experiencing limits, and yet this is not the time for force, we must be gentle with ourselves. Illuminations arise and fall, and once a door has opened, we long to walk through it and never return to the place where we have already lingered so long. But we must trust the natural rhythms, the choreography of metamorphosis as a wisdom beyond our conscious minds allows for all that is necessary and inevitable to happen. We might feel as though we have failed and fallen behind; it seems as if our bones sing only to the old song. And yet it is not so. Their frequency is altering, there is expansion and greater resonance with Spirit. There is a deeper transparency, a translucency occurring throughout. You who are this very change already cannot think the place that you were in. Compassion with the past is an elusive capacity. And periods of peaceful integration do not imply stasis. We allow Spirit the wisdom to dance in appropriate rhythms. Neither, on the other hand, do we presume that the evolution of consciousness must take place slowly. We do not need to lay out a map of gradualness for ourselves. This would be a false limitation. The whole of our unfolding is given in any individual moment. When we surrender to what is happening here and now, we find the entirety. We do not compare today with tomorrow, we are not in an anxiety about our evolution, our progress, our development. Its entirety is gifted to us in this moment.

When we take up the concept of our evolution in our hands, we can come unbound from our listening, from our breath. We inhabit the thought of our spiritual development as though it were a reality in its own right, sundered from all the rest. It becomes a preoccupation, an anxiety, an obsession. It becomes a source of pride, of ownership, an object with which we play. There is no need to berate ourselves for this, it is only that our separation, our pain, has taken hold of this concept. We need but to allow the pain, the feeling to surface and we discover that obsession was in fact a resistance to the very thing we have been obsessing over. What a crafty mask! But we need not be concerned; it is a phase in the alignment of our intentions, and as we continue to surrender our pain, our separation, our concepts, letting them arise and vanish, seeing them to their source also in Great Mystery, then this mask of spiritual obsession dissipates, and we align with true expression.

Equally, the pressure we place on ourselves may begin to make us feel bored with the whole endeavour, wishing that it would end, that we could get to the end. This is the weariness of spiritual endeavour and it can manifest as a feeling of 'I am done with this world'. It can manifest as the feeling that one is tired, so tired of all the constant effort, of doing the 'right' thing and yet never reaching the goal. Can we be bothered even with this endless quest, this elusive, unfulfillable goal? This itself is a valuable sensation, though it masks its own illusion. It is our resistance that tires us. When we dwell in the breath, the listening and Immanence of that which truly is, there is no weariness, because we cease to be the one making the effort. When we cease to be this causal agent of an unfulfillable quest, then we cease in our weariness, we find rest. We are only tired when we are not listening, when we have ceased in this expressive-listening breath. We are already in the place we are longing to be, we are already at our destination. The deer, like the orchid, is not weary of her passage through the forests. Her sensitive antennae are woven through the living moment, its constellations of peace and Immanence. There is unfolding, but it is perfection. Not the progression of one thing to another, but a river that flows, a path of Light and shadow through the forest. It has advancement and perfection. It has the sounding of a prayer that manifests through the here and now.

* * *

It is the winter solstice. I sit enfolded in the incredible warmth of the White Bear Cloak, beneath a night of clouds, in a land carved by snow. The snowflakes are falling all around me, drifting around my face, silent carriers of ancient moonlight. I am waiting for the sunrise, waiting in the winter wood. There is a mound here, where the Shining Ones have dwelt. I am waiting for the gift of their Dawn to begin all over again. The silver wings of my listening are woven through the spectral branches, through the quartz rocks underlying the forest. I am listening to the sky, whose snow-laden clouds are passing, and behind whom dwells the song of the stars and, somewhere, the Dawn.

I am sitting cross-legged, shaking the Moonstone Rattle, ensconced in the White Bear Cloak. I wear the indigo robe with its sweeping hem of pearls and lapis. This is the longest night: the darkness wears on and on. I am wondering what this dawn shall bring: what Golden Dawn shall steal over the horizon, what Illumination shall it bring? What star gifts are arising at this time?

At last, with golden topaz footprints the Elder of the Sun steps over the horizon. She is walking towards me, a figure clad in hues of gold. She is a dazzling brilliance. She wears a blue feather at her brow, her hair is golden and she comes bearing the radiance of the I AM Infinity. The call has been made and she has answered. She has travelled from far realms to bring her teachings to Earth. The ancient contract is awoken. I have fulfilled my listening: I have stood and listened to the beginning that arises and I have asked the question, 'What will come?' The Dawn deserves this listening. The Dawn deserves our utmost sensitivity. To not assume that we know the answer, but listen with all our heart and soul to what comes from beyond. This is the emergence from the long night of stars and from the stillness of the snow.

It is the time for ancient gifts to be awoken. It is time for a universal and natural spirituality to arise through all the elemental and human worlds of Earth. Long alliances are recalled, affinities and aptitudes: spiritual development and practices that have long dwelt within us, covered over in recent lifetimes. It is time to cultivate forgotten gifts. The Elders are reclaiming the Truth. They are reclaiming their naturalness and their wisdom, their remembrance of their own light trails through time and space. They are reclaiming the truth that this earth walk is a spiritual experience, with a primarily spiritual intention and potential. They are not awaiting the arrival of a sun or a star from beyond. They are remembering that they are the Summoners of the Sun. They are the ones who call and dream this beginning into existence. It is both less visible and more magnificent than we have expected. We are making this call to the dawn within our own lives. The Sun is transforming. Her transmission is altered. She is listening to us; she is receptive to the transformative power of Earth. She steps into the worlds of Earth to discover her own dream.

The Dawn Elder: her high-browed, noble Elven face; the shining, pale bone structure; white temples; the blue feather at her brow. She walks barefoot, in blue buckskin leggings with their tracery of stitched foliage. She walks towards me on the rays of the Dawn. She is a High Elven Elder, one of the ancient Goddesses. Her sacred task brings her to Earth once more. She brings something else: an unforeseen element. This is a special Light.

'I bring the Shield of Ancient Dreams. In this you see the reflection of your true identity. This is found, not by looking into the past, but is clearly written within the depths of the present moment. Humanity is remembering themselves as vastly interconnected and interdependent emanations of Spirit, with beautifully inscribed and unique spiritual destinies. There are many intergalactic souls from the far stars of the Universe amongst you now. You carry a great gift of cosmic innocence, and in this world to which you have come there can arise feelings of vulnerability. You have a message to share and yet, in so many lifetimes, you have been destroyed for speaking thus. Yet know this: the Shield of Ancient Dreams represents a promise that the Atlanteans long made. They vowed that when the star souls once again incarnated on this planet, that they would protect them. They would protect them, even as they spoke the Ancient Dream of Peace. The miracle of this time is that this message can indeed be shared.

'Know that this protection resides within you, as the power of discernment. You will know, moment to moment, when to speak and when to be silent. You will know when there is receptive ground and when the way is closed. The impossible purity of the stars and their walk upon the golden Earth can once again be shared.'

She offers forth the Shield of Ancient Dreams and I take it from her. My eyes fill with tears at its deep beauty, its deep promise. The star sapphires twinkle, embedded in the gold. She turns from me and walks again into the dawn light, vanishing into radiance.

This is the special light from the Sun that activates the voice of the future, that makes our ancient purity burn into visibility once again.

It is this, our longest night, that has stirred us to remembering. Within the shadows of this night we have found our longing, our purity. In the winter forest, in the moonlight, in the snow, we have found our endurance, our patience, our strength. The veils of unknowing may have pressed upon us, we may have lost vision: yet we have found ourselves full of loyalty, courage and devotion. We have never stopped sending forth the smoke of our prayers, the invocation to the Dawn. Now is the hour of the Dawn, now it is here. Now the treasured illumination of truth arises within us once again.

Journey to Atlantis

Y ou are in the forest. The air is cool and wintery, but you are wrapped in warm furs, and your breath comes out in a mist. You have a staff of hazel wood in your hand that helps you chart your path across the uneven forest floor. Towards you from among the trees comes a reindeer with a star shining at her brow. She approaches you, and stretches out her nose to sniff at your hand. You feel her warm breath upon your skin, and you stroke her fur that is coarse and silky all at once. Side by side, you set off into the forest, and she is walking just slightly ahead of you, guiding the way. You realize as you travel that this is no ordinary forest; it is the Immortal Forest of the Earth, and an inner light glows within the trees. There is a sense of timelessness, and it is as though the forest is hung with stars. The reindeer leads the way as you go deeper and deeper into this enchanted realm, and you are overwhelmed by a sense of peace and beauty. Deep within the forest, you come to a Grove of White Trees, and at the base of each, an amethyst crystal lies in the moss. The reindeer crosses the clearing, and bows her antlered head. Somehow, you understand what she is indicating. You go over to one of the trees and kneel beside it. You peer into the amethyst that lies embedded in the moss. Within its depths shimmers the Tenth Glyph. You raise your hand to mirror the sweep of the Glyph, in front of the tree, and you draw it into the forest air. As you draw the golden strokes of the Tenth Glyph, you feel the symbol entering your heart and glowing golden throughout your whole being. You are transported...

You are transported to the streets of a ruined city. It is an exquisite wreckage, the tumbled and broken buildings fashioned out of beautiful stone with precise craftsmanship. Everywhere there are fragments of mosaic, of carvings with crystals inlaid. Ivy scrambles over the ruins, and wildflowers are springing up where the Earth is breaking through the broken paving. There are ruined archways and great trees growing among them. It is a scene of shattered loveliness. Some cataclysm has blown through here like a storm. Yet a feeling of peace prevails in the ruins, like a suspended prayer.

You are walking in a ruined city of Atlantis. You come to a dwelling, and some of its walls and archways are still intact. You walk under the entrance archway, feeling a sense of familiarity. The slabs of a marble floor are still intact, though drifted over with leaves and fallen masonry. You kneel before a cracked marble tile at the centre of the floor, and prize it up out of its setting. Underneath there is a cavity, and something concealed within. It is an amethyst crystal carved into a pyramid. You pick it up and its cold surfaces begin to warm up in your hands. Then it begins to emit a misty glow. You know this is something precious that you owned many lifetimes ago, that you have left here as a message for yourself.

From the pyramid a stream of light beams out, projecting a figure of light into the centre of the room. The figure is your own Atlantean incarnation. Note their appearance, the way that the presence makes you feel. You ask 'Who are you, and what was your role in the civilization of Atlantis?'

When you have fully received this answer, you ask your second question, 'What Atlantean wisdom do I carry forward in this lifetime?'

When the message is complete the emanation returns within the crystal. This crystal now remains with you in your safekeeping. You wrap it in a medicine bundle of soft cloth and keep it with you, knowing that you can access it at any time to learn more of the legacy of your Atlantean lifetimes and the wisdom they have to share.

You find yourself transported back to the White Grove, with its amethyst crystals glowing at the base of the trees. You follow the reindeer out of the White Grove, returning through the forest to this world.

ELEVENTH TEACHING

This is the Eleventh Teaching of the Deerskin Book:

*All this sits like a handful of stardust in our hands
that we must hold close to our hearts. It is most
ordinary and most precious.*

*We must always return to our ordinariness because it
is where holiness lives.*

*This is where we find the true track and imprint of
our spiritual development.*

Chapter 11

Buzzard tall, they have
hung their stars,
leaf by leaf, within this
world,
and, still, we are carried by their winds.

It is a native enchantment, the path of
Love within the Earth.

THIS IS THE Eleventh Teaching of the Deerskin Book: ultimately it is only in our ordinariness that we can find the true measure of our spiritual evolution. Here we discover whether angelic vision can permeate even our most ordinary moments. Do we still prescribe to the dance between Heaven and Earth, do we still find ourselves plunging back and forth between the sacred and the mundane, playing out this ancient rift in our vision?

I speak now of the precious stardust of our ordinariness. This ordinariness never goes away, it is always with us. And no matter how transcendent our experiences, it always returns. It is our ground, and it is the nature and vibration of this ground, its atmosphere, that reveals how far we have surrendered to Love, how deeply and truly we have dissolved into the pathways of Love, Power and Truth.

This ground is the subtle Earth Goddess who tracks us and observes us, marking our trail through the forest. She is the rocks, the crystals, the sands, soils and stones that imprint the echoes of our progress. She remembers that originally you *chose* to come to Earth: she remembers that you chose her stardust shawl of many colours, that you arrived with deep joy because you knew that this was a miraculous gift.

She remembers that you wrapped the elemental shawl of her earth hues around your shoulders and rejoiced in the infinite resonance of her dimensions. This is your innocence, this is your acceptance.

This is before you began to forget. Before you began to reject aspects of elemental existence, to distance yourself from them. This is before you began to perceive your Light journey as separate from your Earth journey, and made the fatal mistake of believing that they were at odds with one another. Before this, you knew that this beautiful and multi-hued ground *was* your journey into Light. It offered you the deepest possible journey into Light that could be achieved in this Universe. This, this path beneath your feet is your hidden ground of Illumination. You are taking up this Gift once more, you are awakening to the teachings of stardust.

The ordinary is becoming more precious and beautiful to you, more grace-filled. And it begins to reveal hidden codes of great wisdom. The more you are attentive to this beautiful stardust in your hands, the more subtle and revelatory it becomes. Earth herself begins to speak to us with her beautiful resonant wisdoms, echoing through us with a realm of revelatory memory. The Earth Elders send through us their luminous gestures of grace; we discover that the Earth is haunted with Illumination, with true inter-dimensional loveliness. We see in flashes the lost inter-dimensional temples of Earth, the way that the Great Ones of Light have with tender grace been so long interwoven with this realm.

A hidden history opens up, written with the rocks, the stones and crystals. It is subtle, gentle, marvellous. It enfolds us with great wings of Illumined Compassion. It brings to us inspiration about how to found a realm of Grace: how to go forward with loveliness, power and wisdom. Like golden topaz, sacred gestures fall to us. Earth stars, they ignite within us, and we give our gestures, our grace to others. So generous and perpetual is the path of Earth's Illumination. She never stops giving to us, she never stops speaking to us.

We walk the old corridors of the Crystal Temples. Their subtle and mosaic grace begins to activate with specific guidance and instructions that show us the Light Path for all Beings, the encoded enlightenment dance of Earth that she is always trying to give to us. It is the gift for which we have after all arrived, and she will never cease in passing this on. It is the agreement between us, it is the way that she as Mother cannot help but be. She cannot abandon us, her loyalty is eternal and unconditional. If we only knew what an extraordinary Mother we have.

She always respects the Starlight Souls as they arrive to her. The Starlight Soul of every arriving child becomes a part of her Dream, is included in her worlds. She allows every starlight child to bring its transformative power to her world, to change her, to bring its gift of metamorphosis to which she surrenders with unconditional grace.

* * *

It is her subtle worlds of deep light and metamorphosis that I call Lemuria. It is these ancient crystal temples that are layered within her innermost fabric and carry codes of great and valuable purity. Patient crafting of aeons formed these delicate messages and frequencies, that the Earth is now releasing through her elemental worlds.

Like finely wrought lanterns, they show the way to dimensions of Earth that have been long-hidden, and through which we can learn a dance of Earthly Illumination, following the unique and subtle path of the innermost heart.

It is not about disappearing within the Earth; we do not vanish altogether into inner realms. It is not the hour for this. This has already happened, and now there is emergence. The Shining Ones as ourselves are stepping forth carrying the wisdom gift of stardust and offering this openly. We are teaching and inspiring one another, our grace spreading one to another as recognition occurs.

The old mosaic rainbow robes, clad around the Shining Ones are walking this world once more. We are so very blessed by their presence. And in our recognition, we ourselves become that presence. It is our affinity with the Eldest Realms of Earth. We know that we have been here before. You remember the nuances of Peace, you remember a way of being steeped in Grace.

In your aura, these sacred Lights of amethyst, topaz and aquamarine ignite. The ancient Lights of Earth are not concealed; they are walking amongst us. They are passing to us our inheritance. As the portals occur and we step through them, we gain the transparency of the I AM Infinity presence, and we are able to pick up these gifts more and more easily. At the other side of every initiation these transmissions await us. The more luminous we become, the more sensitive we are to the ancient etiquette of the Earth. We are becoming aware once more of the refined relationship she offers us.

The Lemurian inheritance is an ethereal one. It involves a passionate love for the Earth and a direct perception of her ethereal, etheric nature. This capacity is being restored at this time, and there are many transmissions of Lemurian consciousness arriving to us. When the Lemurian vision is applied to the true dimensions of physical incarnation, then there is deeply transformational activity. Remember the importance of accepting your genetic bloodlines in this lifetime and the light codes they contain. You have chosen them as your vehicle in this lifetime for a reason. No matter how removed you feel your birth family has become from cosmic and earthly connection, you will find in your bloodline, however far back, your Ancestors in the Light, the ones who honoured the pathways of Earth and stars, who carried the mythologies that are the vestiges of the Atlantean and Lemurian eras. There is great resonant and earthly power in this connection for you. You will find a star lineage that truly sings in your blood, that calls you back home to your pathways of reverence and balance. All peoples carry these pathways to the Shining Ones, whether they be Celtic, Norse, Inuit, Sami, Teutonic, Tibetan, Indian or Native American. Their ancient heroes and heroines, gods and goddesses are the Shining Ones who exist in the many-dimensional past of Earth. Still they stand guardian to the cosmic memory bank of Earth, maintaining our remembrance of ourselves as infinite and elemental beings. Thus we discover that our ordinariness is our stardust, our ground is sacred. Our very bloodlines carry the codes of earthly ascension, charting

Earth's angelic past. Follow your own angelic paths, the ones that travel through the song of your blood, and the treasure you discover will be boundless.

* * *

There is a powerful seal set upon our full memory of Lemurian lifetimes. We have lost the memories of walking with the star at our brow, ancient and radiant upon the Earth, overflowing with the harmonic wisdom of Peace. This was our Lemurian incarnation and manifestation. The Silver Wheel shone within our hearts and we remembered where we had come from and why.

This seal was caused by the experience of betrayal. Our gift was not honoured by those who were upon the Earth and who did not have this harmonic wisdom of Peace. They were not working towards this end, rather toward the maintenance of their own survival, and thus they did not value the beauty of this gift, but were happy to destroy those who brought it. This is one of the oldest stories of humanity, still being played out in the present, and it inspires a passionate ambivalence about our presence on this Earth, which can feel so fundamentally precarious.

We need to heal this wound if we are to transcend the dance of survival, the dance of trust and distrust and fundamental vulnerability. We must break free from fearfulness: the fear of being attacked, the feeling of vulnerability which makes us conceal ourselves, either in our ethereal dream worlds, in the worlds of nature, or in the shell of a mistaken identity, conforming so that we do not attract the attention of others. There is a real danger for Lemurians to remain peripheral, and not offer themselves to the main currents of cultural transformation to which they have so much to offer.

We must let go of any shadow of victimization, and acknowledge that we have volunteered for this journey. It is our own choice. We chose to explore the depths of three-dimensional reality so that we might discover the essence of full incarnation. It has served us well, in many respects, as we have maintained our biological coherence and expression, allowing the thread of human evolution to carry through, unbroken, into the present moment. Thus are lifetimes of knowledge and evolutionary expression sustained upon Earth.

We need no second-hand accounts of these things, we need only access our own memories. We can dance around them like moths around a lamp: we can be watchers of those moths, catching evanescent wing patterns, fragments of memory from these nuances, these hints, or we can unearth the whole. We can become fully cognizant of the Truth. This is a daunting responsibility: do we want to remember? The seal is in fact the pain of betrayal, and we do not wish to re-experience this pain. It caused us to shut down once, and part of us wants to leave this mechanism in place.

There is a part of us that rages that our innocence should ever have been harmed. We become locked into a dualistic struggle within ourselves between the light and the dark, between innocence and selfishness. Amidst all of this, there is little room for the Divine cognizance of the harmonic wisdom of Peace: it occurs only as an echo, woven into the drama in which we find ourselves. We become preoccupied with self-protection, with attack and defence. We may perceive all this on a psychic rather than a physical level, but this does not change the level of perception, it does not raise it. We cannot masquerade as the injured innocence, the vulnerable purity. This does not reflect our original essence whose purity is Infinitely powerful, and whose awareness requires no protection against a dissident other.

It is an ancient seal, deeply and unequivocally held in place by ourselves for a very, very long time. Yet conditions are ripening for its release, many are recalling their Lemurian existence. We need not take their word for it, but release the seal upon our own remembrance and let the memories of these lifetimes flow through us once more. It is not just memories, it is access to a whole level of consciousness and spiritual intention that has been dormant for a long time. We do not need others to teach us of this, it is imperative that we remember for ourselves. It really affects our belief about whether life on Earth can become inherently peaceful and spiritualized. Or do we always believe in some survival-ist tension, in some necessary strife and darkness? Are we prepared for the full embodiment of our Infinite Nature, or do we believe that the Earth experience is too dense, too immutable for this?

Fortunately the belief systems are not entirely in the hands of our conscious minds, but through the breath of the starlight bridge, are in a constant and gentle transmutation, a perpetual dissolution. Of course, we may choose to fight this or align with it, we may choose continuously to rebuild the walls of our old beliefs, or to allow the structures of our conscious minds to be transmuted.

* * *

The Lemurians are the Elven Ones of the Immortal Forest Soul of Earth. They are guardians to the great, over-arching harmonies of the elemental kingdom. Their conscious-ness gifts into the mundane an ethereal innocence and moment-to-moment affinity for the rhythms of cosmic and earthly metamorphosis. They bring gifts for sound and crystal healing, for building with natural forms, for awakening the planet's star paths and recreating the ancient Star Gardens of Earth. They follow rhythms of formless improvisation, attuned intuitively to cosmic inspiration, that contrasts with the spiritual technologies of the Light Lineages of Atlantis and their more formulaic expression.

It becomes more astonishing the more that we remember: for the full harmonic wisdom of Peace far outstrips any positive images we currently hold in consciousness. It is the golden wisdom of our own Immortal Nature, our own profound goodness. It is the intention for this Earth to be a home of the angels, for harmonic wisdom to pour forth from all the levels of biological life, so that biological life dances with the Harmonics of the Stars.

The frequencies of Lemurian consciousness were encoded or received deep within the Earth as stardust that has now danced in ancient companionship with this realm for many aeons. The bridge is thus woven for us to remember or encounter our Shining Nature, and ourselves as Shining Ones who have long danced the wisdom of the Earth.

The wisdom of Lemuria is anchored into a set of Elder Crystals that were created to awaken at this time. The amethysts of the Temple of Arianrhod are amongst these. These ancient Lemurian Temple Crystals are calling out once more. They are emerging at this time and transmitting the ancient wisdom with which they are encoded. Many of these have been safeguarded for a very long time by generations of Crystal Keepers who have kept their own Elder and elemental wisdom intact. They have protected them so that we would have access to them at this time when the Earth could truly arise into her Golden Dawn once more.

These key crystals are absolutely pivotal in anchoring the consciousness of the incoming star frequencies. This is a carefully choreographed receptivity that holds us all in a mighty architecture, invisible but entire. This architecture of the Great Crystals forms an etheric dome that enshrines the Earth and is guardian to our evolution.

The Elder Crystals have grown according to precise encodings and they are becoming ever more powerful and influential as the procession of star portals occurs and builds our affinity with Earth's forgotten wisdom. We shall learn more and more from them. We sense their presence ever more clearly, as we remember the Elder wisdom of the Golden Dawn within ourselves. We remember the offering we are here to make. We, too, are crystals, or liquid crystalline beings: powerfully encoded transmitters that are transforming the Universe with every breath, every thought and feeling. As we connect with the Elder Crystals through our own vibration, they become ever more powerful. Every fragment of crystal and quartz communicates in an interdimensional network. The crystals are anchoring a collective agreement, a kind of consensus that states the Earth's intention of ascension at this time. This is encoded in her crystals; she harbours no vacillation or alternative plan.

By using the crystals, you irrevocably alter the ground of your existence. They will vibrate you into the Golden Dawn with some intensity. They will sing to the crystalline structure of your cells, and call them into resonance with the Earth's Dawn. Your crystalline structure will reorganize itself to mirror the new fabric of creation, and come into alignment with the ancient stardust wisdoms that formed the crystals. The crystals are unrelenting guides in this manner, and their programmes, once underway and connected with you, fulfil themselves with great fidelity. In the crystals, we perceive the coherent and beautiful structures inherent in the Golden Dawn and in ourselves. They really support us with holding faith and accessing an elemental consciousness that is free of societal programming. Instead we attune to the wider frequencies of a loving Universe that is offering us a beautiful and extraordinary journey.

The crystals support Lemurian consciousness by providing bridges between the physical and ethereal. They are models of multidimensional incarnation, and offer companionship. The crystals mirror stability, so that integrity is maintained throughout interdimensional transformations.

Without the stardust of the crystals and the sacred ground of our ordinariness, we may feel too ethereal to be influential, too 'will-o'-the-wisp'. We may simply feel an intense longing to return to star worlds, forgetting the potentials for which we came to Earth. Yet, within us there is a steadfast will also, and a capacity for great dedication. We have the capacity to endure great conflict, and arrive at new ground within ourselves from which to proceed.

* * *

As we surrender the powerful seals that have locked away our memories of other-dimensional incarnations, our sense of ordinariness itself shifts. The stardust of our bodies begins to resolve into new crystalline formation. There is a grace in having transcended the old lessons in which we have so long been locked, and many places and relationships fall away with this. We may feel a flash of a sense of poverty as this happens, of loss and scarcity arising. Those are illusory aspects of transformation. We are less alone than ever, and possessed of a wondrous abundance. We step off the old karmic wheel, and we do not let these considerations entice us back on again.

It is not always easy to let the past go, and sometimes we call it back, just before it passes over the horizon, because we miss its familiar companionship. It feels as though there is something wrong with its absence. But we do not need to fill this 'gap' that has arisen in our lives. It shall fill itself in time with that which has a vaster resonance.

This Eleventh Teaching allows that the very substrate of our lives may be metamorphosis: we shall not rest on the same ground, and ordinariness shall alter, our sense of familiarity shall shift. We trust the new alliances that support this; we trust those who support this expansive and golden ground: those who, with us, are able to perceive and celebrate that this is taking place. Especially at moments of dramatic transformation, these alliances serve to help us cross the threshold of metamorphosis, at a time when it seems we could go either forward or backward.

You must be prepared to be the dancer, to take on a fluidity and responsiveness to the Beyond. There is no title or preparation for this dance, other than the Calling of which you are intuitively aware.

* * *

The forest is a raining, ruined palace through which the blackbirds dance. I have sought her, the Deer Elder, and now I have found her. She walks along the river.

There are shards of yellow star that she gathers into her embroidered pouch. She gathers the amethyst and dark golden lostness scattered. The backward glow of moonstone, tucked into her embroidered pouch. She walks amongst the stars of the forest, looking for treasure, as she goes on bare feet.

Rare one. Far one. Lavender robe, iridescence. Damask of amethyst. She approaches. Raindrops, blackbirds singing.

Iridescence, willow eyes. Willow feet, bells. Dragon golds and moonstones, amber. A woven belt around her waist, of dragon lights. The stain of earth on her feet, dark spirals. She walks up the river, carrying the seeds of the moons. Each one a fragment, a latticework of ancient dreamings, worn and worn into. She carries in her willow basket the seeds of this sun, ready for birth.

She comes here, along the aquamarine river, after the snow melt. Her ancient footsteps lilt with violet light.

I call out to her. She knows that I am here. She looks up, her expression inscrutable. We are layer upon layer of a mysterious becoming. Timelessly, she holds the simplicity and dignity of Earth's past. Like the hidden, ordinary, subtle ground, she can travel unnoticed. She kneels, in leggings of doeskin, examining the trail. She follows the ancient path of the deer. It is their dance across the Earth she mimics. They trample the way, unveiling the silken paths of hope, of the Earth.

I hear her whisper: 'The Stardust Path has not been walked for a very long time. It is a precious path, almost forgotten. For you, it will be a formless dance, a path of Light.'

She comes, with her wild, soft darkness, a nomad. I see her through the moonflower of my blood. The murmur and tempo of dark grace, old light.

'I give to you this gift of stardust. It is the beginning of life upon Earth, and reminds us that no matter how far we travel, this beginning, this ground, is a precious gift. Out of this, everything is woven. It is the ground for every epiphany, every dawn. This is your gratitude for your ordinariness, your earthliness. Keep this ground sacred, keep this stardust held as precious. I give this to you so that you may reconsecrate the ground of your life. Weave this stardust into the pages of the Deerskin Book. Begin with this. Always begin with this.'

I hold out the deerskin pouch, and she blows the magic dust towards me, grey motes upon the air. I gather them into the pouch, and bind it with a cord, storing it within the folds of my cloak. I thank her for this precious gift. This is a part of the soul of the Deerskin Book, an essential aspect of its Teachings.

It is the starlit, early hours of morning. The faintest crescent of the new moon hangs in the sky as I travel up the river. The barge glides into the shore under the forest canopy. I disembark, my long indigo skirts caked in mud and travel stains. The Elders gather at the shore, and help me from the boat. They guide me to sit beside the fire. I sit down, my body weary, eyelids flickering, aching in every bone.

There are the white tents of the Elders. There are the drums calling to the Dawn, there is smoke and firelight; opaque butterfly flares in the night forest. This is the story of service, of dedication in the citadel where the dreams are woven.

In the tattered light of the firelight, there are the great faces flickering, playing white drums. This is an Elder butterfly race of dreams, building the shining magnificence of the holy places. The world has ended, and the new one not yet begun.

I go to the tent of white deerskin. Within the tent, she sits by the fire, and the flames are amber and violet, and around her are the baskets of gathered moon-fire. I have travelled a long way to this place, and it is a quiet sanctuary in the dusk. She gives me pieces of amber resin and dried lavender to throw in the fire, offerings of thanks for what has been.

'I have the pouch of stardust. I followed the Deer Paths, flung like silken banners through every land, seeking the Deer Elder. Her gift is needed to complete the Silver Wheel, to write the Deerskin Book. She carries the stardust that holds the purity of the beginning. It is this that needs to be shaken out upon the ground we stand on. We shall give it to the first shoots of the Dawn.'

The Elder comes to me and kneels where I sit: she touches her brow to mine, and it is as though an amethyst star flames at her forehead. She rubs white chalk into my feet, blessing the trail. It is good to feel the touch of her hands and the iridescent flame of hope within them. The Immortal Path runs beneath and through all things. It travels on timelessly, and there is always the invisible choice to follow. These are the paths of fire and amber, stars and willow, sapphire and turquoise. Here the wheel spins differently, the wind turns another way.

The Elders come with me. Beneath a stand of bare-stemmed hazels are the first snowdrops. They nod, pale in the darkness. They are the Sentinels of the coming Dawn, the gradual reemergence of the Light. I take the pouch from the folds of my cloak, unloosen its fastening, and pour out a little of the stardust onto the frosted ground by the flower's stem.

We all stand in quietness, gazing down. It is not finished, this interpretation. We spill, silver, into many destinations, and it seems to me, this moment, that there is no more forest trail to be explored, only a stilling into the grace that has been exposed. There is this, the Immortal Self, flung out through Heaven and Earth in a vision of herself: a deer who, pausing for a moment, knows all the paths that she will run.

Finding the Stardust Self

You are walking in a winter forest, stripped bare of leaves, except for clouds of ivy and the occasional deep shining of a holly tree. You notice the first snow-drops budding on the forest floor. Towards you from among the trees comes a reindeer with a star shining at her brow. She approaches you, and stretches out her nose to sniff at your hand. You feel her warm breath upon your skin, and you stroke her fur that is coarse and silky all at once. Side by side, you set off into the forest, and she is walking just slightly ahead of you, guiding the way. You realize as you travel that this is no ordinary forest; it is the Immortal Forest of the Earth, and an inner light glows within the trees. There is a sense of timelessness, and it is as though the forest is hung with stars. The reindeer leads the way as you go deeper and deeper into this enchanted realm, and you are overwhelmed by a sense of peace and beauty. Deep within the forest, you come to a Grove of White Trees, and at the base of each, an amethyst crystal lies in the moss. The reindeer crosses the clearing, and bows her antlered head. Somehow, you understand what she is indicating. You go over to one of the trees and kneel beside it. You peer into the amethyst that lies embedded in the moss. Within its depths shimmers the Eleventh Glyph. You raise your hand to mirror the sweep of the Glyph, in front of the tree, and you draw it into the forest air. As you draw the golden strokes of the Glyph of the Eleventh Teaching, you feel the symbol entering your heart and glowing golden throughout your whole being. You are transported...

You are standing beside a flowing aquamarine river, and there is an Elven One gathering river pebbles into a woven willow basket. She looks up at you, and smiles, then says, 'I am glad that you have come. I have this gift for you. It is a pouch of stardust from the beginnings of Earth. Use this as the foundation for your own Spirit Garden. This shall be a sanctuary for you in the otherworld, that grows according to your own heart and vision and imagination, becoming whatever you wish it to be. This shall be a place of rest and retreat for you, where you can connect with your spiritual allies, and dwell in the peace and beauty that you need in order to accomplish your mission on Earth. You are the gardener of this special place.'

You thank her, and take the deerskin pouch that she is offering to you. She disappears on her quest up the river, and you are left standing alone. You open the pouch and sprinkle some of the grey dust onto the ground at your feet. The ground begins to swirl into a mist, spiralling and expanding around you. As it swirls, it begins to take on the form of a beautiful garden. Notice the flowers and trees, notice the rocks, waterfalls, lakes or streams. Notice if there are any built structures in the garden. Is it beside the ocean or in the mountains, is it a forest glen? Perhaps it is on an island, an emerald jewel in the sea? Gently allow it to take form around you, allowing yourself to discern any aspects that come into clarity.

You feel deep peace and safety in this place. It is a place that shape-shifts around your perception to become what you need it to be and it keeps pace with the evolutions of your consciousness. You are its builder and gardener, and any improvements can be as slow or as quick as you wish. Know that this is your inner sanctuary, your retreat. As this aspect of your consciousness develops, so will you discover its parallels in your waking world.

You may visit this place at any time, and it will be immediately accessible to you. You leave the garden now, and find yourself transported back to the White Grove, with its amethyst crystals glowing at the base of the trees. You follow the reindeer out of the White Grove, returning through the forest to this world.

TWELFTH TEACHING

This is the Twelfth Teaching of the Deerskin Book:

This body shall become translucent with Light: it shall shine. It shall become indivisible with its holiness.

In one lifetime it shall make the transformation it needs to make in order to become the New Human.

And then we shall leave the template for the generations who follow.

Chapter 12

Hooves fly silver in the star forest;
her footsteps are dark violets.

THE TWELFTH GLYPH is about the profundity of meta-morphosis you are undergoing, about how it fulfils all your most miraculous hopes. You have been preparing for so long: do not become lost in the tale of meta-morphosis, do not believe yourself forever the caterpillar. For so long you feel like the caterpillar, for so long you feel the dissolution of the chrysalis, for so long you feel the damp fragility of new wings. In your dreams, you catch glimpses of the life of the butterfly. But there is an hour to let go com-pletely and irrevocably of the caterpillar, of the chrysalis, of the endless preparation, and accept that you *are* the butterfly.

Your being at an infinitesimal level has altered. Step over the threshold and then let that threshold vanish. There is no return, there is no stepping back.

You are no longer standing at the threshold, you are no longer hovering at the brink of transformation. You have crossed over, and the portal that carried you across has dis-solved and vanished. What does the butterfly do? She flies.

She takes to a dimension that was previously impossible to her. She raises her wings and takes to vast distances. She discovers the most beautiful and vibrant flowers to visit, drawn by their nectar, by their scent and vivid colour. She charts the great distances of the skies, linking these jewel-like flowers in her dance.

Her existence bears no resemblance to the one before, and she has accomplished this entire metamorphosis. She trusts her new existence, in it she rests entirely.

* * *

Sometimes we say farewell to people and places, times of our lives that we really loved. These are the golden moments of the past: we can remember the textures of joy and love, of community and companionship. It is hard to remember these times without a sense of regret that they have come to an end. There can be nuances across lifetimes that catch at us with this memory of joy and fulfilment. It can happen so suddenly that the memory causes our heart to expand with love and recognition; it can happen with people, with places, with experiences. There are times in our lives when we have experienced deep wonder. Whatever passing shadows of fear or loneliness or confusion also existed, it was one that was overwhelmingly positive. It shone with Light.

When we remember these times, and we realize their finitude, we may wonder why life is not what it once was. Why did we not perpetuate that golden hour, why did it not last forever: have we been fools to lose the treasure that was ours? Actually, we cannot lose anything that is truly ours; it is not possible. And if it passes from our hands, it shall always come back to us, like a homing dove. Sometimes the circles of growth and expansion upon which we embark seem to take us far away from ourselves. We embark upon the road less travelled, seized by some inner compulsion. It is as though Spirit suddenly sends its beacon flaring in a direction different from the one we expected. We are alarmed and disoriented, but really it feels that we have no choice. We are reminded of our deepest intentions, of the true dimensions of our spiritual contract in this lifetime, which is not merely to perpetuate that which we have already become. We are reminded that there is further to travel, and that everything we have learnt is only a beginning. How daunting to leave behind the hour of our summer, of our fullness and accomplishment, and cross what looks like a barren winter upon the surface, to the promise of another true Spring. We might doubt ourselves, we might be missed by family and friends who have become accustomed to what they have known of us. But we know that the call of Spirit has come, and since this is our greater longing, our deepest intention, onward we go.

This is about how we relate to endings. People miss us when we change, when we transform. It is a loss, a small death in their lives. And we feel the same when we look back upon the golden hours of ourselves, and wonder where the time went, and what went wrong that we lost such perfection. That vision of perfection is an illusion. We remember the beauty and the love, because they are more powerful and real than anything else. But we cannot discount the loneliness, fear, doubt and confusion that also danced through us, because these are the elements that called us on, that meant there was further to travel. We did not experience a completion then that this present moment is lacking; otherwise this present moment would not exist. The experience itself contained the seeds of its own ending.

We long so deeply for this arrival: we long for an end to the ceaseless movement, to the insecurities of change. If we could but find a place where we could buffer ourselves from all this alteration, where we could induce stillness. It is not easy to feel yourself to always be at a threshold, and never knowing what lies on the other side.

Uncertainty becomes a guiding principle, unknowing becomes our friend. This is how it is for the ones who have surrendered to the metamorphosis of this Golden Dawn, the ones who have accepted that things will never be the same again, and have given their trust to the Infinite. We seem to remember a time when everything moved slower, when there was not this intensity of change. Perhaps we long to go backward, and then we remember that somehow, for all its loveliness, that the past was 'smaller': it felt more constricted, perception was more clouded. We have indeed become more translucent, more spacious, more diffuse, more golden.

How was this to happen without the outer circumstances of a life altering, how was this to happen without something being left behind?

* * *

We do not know what it is exactly we are becoming. We face this mystery in every cycle of our growth, in every year that passes. We face the mystery of not knowing that which we are becoming, and this is not a mystery we need to solve. We might think that it is 'our' Dream for ourselves, and yet in truth, where did it come from? Did we notice its arrival, its provenance?

Where does the Dream of ourselves arise? It is that which, like all mysteries, belongs to Nature, to the Infinite. This is why, so often, we 'find' it in natural places: it comes to us as insight under the stars and on mountains. We are a part of the great arising Dream of Nature.

Nature is not gentle with herself, she does not resist metamorphosis. And yet it is apparent that her transformations abide by sweeping cycles and rhythms. There is an elegance, a music to her alterations. Thus we can trust in the beauty and perfection of the process of unfolding itself: it has its rhythm, it has internal harmonies. We do not have to be at the end of our days in order to experience peace. There is peace within change, within transformation. Perhaps this is the art of our age. This is the grace we need to learn. We are born to this time, we are perfectly designed as angels of the storm, graceful and undaunted on its winds.

You are becoming sensitive to the golden fluctuations of the Dawn's energies. You have a direct intuition of its cosmic rhythms as they occur within you. You feel them occurring within your most infinitesimal particles. You are becoming attuned to the cadences of Infinity that are ebbing through you. Galactic, celestial and earthly portals are appearing at every corner, rendering you ever more transparent. The otherworldly dream of the Universe is opening her records to you and you discover that you are not who you thought you were.

You have gone beyond the metamorphosis from caterpillar to butterfly. You *are* the butterfly. You are a Rainbow Butterfly who undergoes the cosmic inspiration of the stars, the hue of her wings changing as she soars through the golden portals of the New Earth. And from within she releases codes of still more unforeseen wonder. Her wings become silver, copper, amethyst, aquamarine, sapphire, rose, carnelian. She is forever altering, and forever herself. This is the Light Body of the New Human.

The Twelfth Teaching of the Deerskin Book states that in this one lifetime we shall come to embody a wholly new energetic paradigm for humanity upon Earth. We shall shine and become translucent with Light. This does not lie ahead in lifetimes to come. It is the transmutation of NOW that is our gift to future generations.

* * *

You shall learn to dance. We shall learn through our listening and our breath to embody the golden heart essence of exchange. We are learning the graceful recognition of this exchange in the phenomenal realm of nature, as well as between human beings, so that we gain interdimensional fluidity. The art of transmission is a key aspect of how our new light body functions. Much the way a flower transmits its beautiful colour and scent, so you transmit the light codes that are your evolutionary gift. This transmission shall automatically occur whenever it is needed, and you are learning the art of maximizing this transmission by your transparency and loving intention. You recognize this occurrence of light-code transmissions as the sphere of true occurrence. It is not something you need to have a plan or a programme for. You shall recognize the fundamental occurrence of this giving and receiving and become adept in your conscious participation. You shall learn to recognize the internal and perceptual hints and pressures that let us know this is taking place: your sensitivity is continuously increasing.

We accept this as fluid and natural, not kept to the sphere of spiritual work between student and teacher, or only to the sphere of our most intimate relationships. We allow ourselves to *light up* around one another as part of a dynamic and natural flow of Enlightenment. We cease to delineate such energetic experiences as unusual or esoteric, and we cease to be afraid of the Power of Love to touch us.

The new energetic form is one that is fluid and responsive, and has the capacity to handle much higher frequencies than we have been accustomed to in the last historic and prehistoric eras. We become familiar with the exchange of high and beautiful energies, so that life is filled with much more beauty and hope. It gives us our sense of aspiration and an awareness of ourselves as spiritual beings. This exchange shall occur with our environment as much as with one another, and therefore our perceptual divide between Spirit and Matter, Heaven and Earth, shall naturally dissolve on the basis of experience. So we become the people that our world needs. So we become the people that we have been waiting for, the ones who shall rescue us. This does not lie down the line in aeons of slow shifts. The preparation work is complete, and we shall make the shift in this lifetime, so that this paradigm becomes completely available upon Earth.

This Golden Dawn of the New Earth shall no longer belong to the periphery of consciousness and culture. It shall become an overwhelming existential possibility, and one that brings much-needed golden hope into people's hearts.

We are the old starlight receiving this stellar inspiration, we are the old bones awakening to this Dawn. There is an abundance of long-stored potential: a great force finally unleashed. We are the Elders, the Glyphs of the Golden Dawn awakening.

* * *

When I speak of interdimensional transformation I must emphasize that you are never being asked to exchange the warmth of your heart, of yourself, for some 'other'. That warmth is the Jewel of the Heart Star, it is through this that all transformation flows. We have come to a very beautiful point in our evolution, in our potential. We must trust in this, and not harbour a dissatisfaction with ourselves, wanting something else more radical or more glamorous.

Any transformation that occurs without coming through the Heart Star is not something that shall remain with us. It has not been integrated. We may even have picked up some beautiful or enticing energy that does not belong to us at all. It is the miraculous nature of our ordinariness, of that which is native and natural, of that which lies deepest within; it is this that we seek to unveil. This Infinite and Miraculous Self is actually deeply familiar and stems from the spaciousness of our innermost core.

* * *

The Golden Dawn involves the synchronized transmissions of the Earth and the stars and ourselves. We are not actually being transformed by a force that comes from outside of us. This view of cause and effect is false. It is merely a linguistic and conceptual convenience to express it this way, using the bridge of teleological consciousness to cross over to a new paradigm. There is no great causal force emanating from the stars and altering a passive Earth, whose only role is to accept these incoming frequencies. It is more that many things are happening all at once, and they are echoes and mirrors of one another, various manifestations of the same underlying reality. The separation between dimensions is collapsing, so that each dimension is flowering throughout the others. There is an incredible overlapping taking place, which obviously has its unique connotations for each dimension as it occurs. The process of collapse is, if you like, unique for each dimension. The Deerskin Book contains the codes for this process from the perspective of Earth. For us, we are receiving the inspiration, or dimensional realities of other star systems and galaxies. We look at the implications of this as it occurs in a transformational blueprint for the New Earth.

Neither are the Glyphs the arrival from the stars of something so far outside of ourselves. We have always been interwoven with these dimensions, but now there is an hour of access, an hour of gift and acceptance. We have created these progressions of time and space for ourselves, we have created these progressions between spirit and matter, so that we could more deeply understand ourselves. Thus we experience an arrival and a gift.

These progressions are the forms of our sacred unfolding, these are the elemental alchemies through which we blossom. We will always know when any phase of expression has run its course, and move on. Once the gift has been given, fully transmitted and accepted, then the choreography of dimensions alters, and the paths we were travelling no longer even appear to exist.

The other dimensions have never been altogether lost; they have remained a part of the interwoven dance of Nature throughout this last era. They have sounded in our consciousness, anchoring us to their frequencies, grounding the unfolding of time and space. They have remained wound through us, very much active and present. They have wound their way through the unfolding of the cedar and the cherry blossom, through our own bodies and minds. Cultures have been influenced by them, and even expressive of them. There have been waves of 'remembering', waves of the attempt to bring these other dimensions back into conscious awareness, back into the collective culture. Unfortunately, much of this comes forward as 'esoteric', as dealing with something that is mysterious and hidden. Now, however, the esoteric aspect is dissolving. Increasingly, for us, there is nothing so very mysterious or hidden about an interdimensional existence, about an interdimensional Self. If it is mysterious, it is the mysteriousness of wonder, it is the mysteriousness of Nature as she arises, showing us that she is more than we ever knew, and yet confirming our deepest knowledge: the truth of our furthest, hidden dreams of ourselves. It is all here. It is all here and now.

* * *

For some, their suffering will make them fear to touch the Light. Despite this, the Great Dance of the Infinite goes on, through them and around them. They cannot truly be separated from the Great Flow and from their own innocence and Heart Star. Their fear may test our own trust in the Light, as we choose to remain steadfast even where it causes discomfort to others. This is the nature of freedom, that each of us makes this choice in any given moment. You must embrace your own freedom without guilt towards those who remain attached to the past. You cannot dull your Light to appease them, or deny the purity of the Heart Star. You cannot feel guilty for having what they do not, because in truth it is theirs also – they only fail to acknowledge it. You must not suppress the Blessing out of false allegiance to them, because they, too, are Blessed, and you only concur with their illusionary belief and identification with their own shadows when you try to dull yourself for them.

Sometimes you feel ineluctably drawn into the shadow dance of another, and their perspective haunts your inner world. This can only happen to the degree that some aspect of yourself is being reflected. You are drawn to view some aspect of yourself that seeks resolution. Acknowledge this vivid external mirror as a gift that is revealing something otherwise hidden within you. Then, with integrity, follow the true pathway within the self to where this hidden element exists. Discover that the shadow which clings on so hard is that which longs for release, for return to the flow of Great Mystery. Find the innocence at the heart of the shadow. Find where the Light is held, like a trapped star. When we see this, we experience *pure forgiveness*. When we truly know this, then forgiveness is automatic, it is not a decision. We could call forgiveness *awareness of the true nature of shadows*. This cannot be feigned, or it lacks sincerity. With false forgiveness, there is no true release taking place, and the shadow remains stuck, only now it is further veiled. But we will know if this is the case, because the relationships that mirror this shadow will persist, the Universe will continue to offer us this mirror until we are prepared to gaze into its eyes and see their innocence.

The chance to awaken to Truth is continually being offered to you. It is by this continual Grace that you are offered the potential to release that which binds you, and to enter into the blinding beauty and courageous dance of who you truly are. It is your role to maintain a vigilance, an attentiveness to the opportunities for Illumination and release as they occur. These moments may arrive at any time, not just in the course of spiritual practices. This is your contribution, your collaboration with Spirit, that you walk through these Portals of Light when they arise. You do not ignore them, you do not postpone them and wait for another, better moment, a more convenient day. It is happening here, as you sit beside this pine tree, in a brief moment of spring sunshine. It is occurring as you crest the hill, and a new valley opens up before you. You pause, allow the other-dimensional light codes to pour through, the messages and illumination, before walking onward. Your recognition of these powerful offerings is increasing; your subtle antenna is picking them up with increasing fluency. You move between them as a dancer moving between Portals of Light. You even begin to sense their presence in the future, looming up before you, like stars on the horizon. Notice these potentials of time and space that offer you a natural awakening.

Our spirituality becomes less and less rarified and separate, it is interlacing its way through our every breathing moment. Initiations, that are the Grand Stars of Awakening, the Grand Star Portals, are becoming more readily available. But everywhere, the smaller stars of awakening are dancing around us. The myriad Star Portals of this Earth are opening up and becoming accessible, and we stray across these. And when we walk through them, they, too, open further, and blossom with the Light of our initiation. Our awakening is linked to that of the Earth: our star auras are bound in a reciprocal exchange that is guiding us, together, into the Golden Dawn.

* * *

Every cell of our body contains the amethyst mists of a realm that leads to space itself. Every cell is a holograph of the dimensions of the Silver Wheel. Every cell is a tiny Silver Wheel, spinning with the Teachings of the Golden Dawn. Mostly deeply within us, we are inscribed with silver script, with the sigils of an Old Language, a language of Light that is glowing into visibility once more. We shine with the immortal rainbow of earthly wisdom: silver, amethyst, indigo, turquoise, emerald, gold, copper and crimson. It is inscribed on our skin, it is written within our blood cells. If we maintain our vigilance, then we witness this activation taking place, we feel the Amethyst Gates within us opening and all our other karmic and genetic imprints being released. We are restored to the full working order of our Original Vow. Any patterns we have acquired from our karmic and genetic inheritance now serve us, rather than dominating us. This was always our purpose and highest potential.

* * *

There is a spiral staircase in the forest leading upward, past silvery trunks, to the Morning Star Lodge. This is where the threads of the forest hold the Morning Star Lodge in connection with this world. The pearly sphere of the Lodge is here, held aloft in the branches of the trees. It is a spherical, tapering dome. The steps are of inlaid topaz, winding upwards, a spiral ladder.

I climb the stairwell, the carved willow staff in my hand, clad in a sapphire robe. There is dedication, reverence in my heart. Every breath is a prayer calling down the Silver Wheel. I can feel the forest whispering to me,

'It is the Morning Star that holds us in our initiations. It has the power to hold us while we undergo deep transformation, while we let go of everything and allow ourselves to be attuned to the emptiness, to the Silence. In the name of Love, we accept such transformation, we step beyond.'

I step upwards, mounting the staircase one step at a time, winding higher and ever higher amongst the trees, amongst the moss and lichen-clad branches. Everywhere, the forest remains silvery and bare, yet the buds are swelling at the tips of the branches, and wildflowers dot the forest floor. I mount the stairwell, feeling how its substance is ethereal and otherworldly, woven of a descending Light from the Morning Star, even as it borrows its substance from the forest. It is built from the scattered quartz, carved and hewn under the light of the Moon and the Morning Star, by long-vanished hands, only ever built during their hours of appearance. Symbols of the Old Language are inscribed in the quartz; this stairwell that grew over slow aeons, constructed out of a patient intention. It spirals its way amongst the uppermost branches of the trees, to the place where the lodge hangs with quiet brilliance, parallel to the forest canopy, resting above the interlaced branches. I arrive at the simple arch of its doorway, and enter in. Within are the Eagle Elders. They each wear a fan of eagle feathers at their brow. They are sitting in a circle.

I sit down in the circle of Elders. I bow my head in honour to the intense wisdom of their presence. I can feel the accuracy of their vision, a rapier-like attunement to the ascensional processes of Earth, to the resurrection of Illumined civilizations upon this planet. Their attention is upon the starlit choreography of emergence. They are aware of our extraordinary potentials, the limitless ascent that is available, the

miracles woven into the fabric of the ordinary. They are custodians to the Dawn.

From the Morning Star Lodge there spills forth the Immortal language, that which is written within the Deerskin Book. It whispers to me from every direction, sounding through sage smoke and eagle feathers. It is a message to be written herein:

'This is the prayer of Hope that we make before the rising of the Sun. We make this prayer to the Morning Star that shines before the full Dawn. Before appearance, there is this.

'What are you in the pre-dawn light: what are you as you first emerge from the darkness and the Silence? This is the way that you emerge against the backdrop of the unknown. What is the quality of hope in your heart as you step forth? Hope is one of our most beautiful qualities. It is one of our treasures. Hope is the child of imagination and love. Hope arises in us, like the Morning Star, a perpetual gift that arises from even the deepest night. It can be subtle, humble, inadvertent, or dazzling and energized. It is woven into our lives in such a perpetual manner that we barely notice it. This hope deserves our attention. We allow its full light to appear to us. Hope: ancient, brilliant star of memories. Hope is the language of other worlds, other life-times, spiralling through into this one. It is our memory of the Light, of joy and happiness, peace and fulfilment. It is the memory of our original purpose, making itself felt. We notice this natural gift of the Light, this grace. We notice especially its reemergence after times of darkness. Wound in with our hope is also the sense of loss. It can be painful. Hope can feel like a gentle and tormenting flame, especially when we have passed beyond all longing and desire, into the abyss, and remember the peace of this nothingness. It can feel more peaceful to have no more arising of hope in your heart. Yet as long as this luminous guide shows up at our side, it is worth our attention. It is worth noticing that which we hope for, that in us which remains unfinished. We can attune our hope to the arising of the Golden Dawn, to the arrival of this Dawn upon the Earth. We attune ourselves via the Morning Star and ask how we might serve.

'In this Light before the sunrise, we look to our hope, and to its alignment. We discover that within us which merely hopes to foster old realities, obsolete aspirations. These are our wayward hopes, our distractions. They can cause the misdirection of our attention and the waste of our energy. They can cause us to stand in a cross-current to the Greater Dream.

'We attune our hope to the Morning Star, from where this precious gift arises. As we awake to the pre-dawn light, we ask ourselves, "What is it that I hope for this day?"

'Wear the Eagle Feathers at your brow. They represent your clarity and your dedication to Spirit.'

The Elders place the feathers, three of them, at my brow, tied with white cloth. They reach around, and tie them behind my head. I can feel the firm pressure of the feathers at my brow, and with them an intense link to the light of the Morning Star. This symbolizes the purity of my hope, that I have purified and released all other intentions, and aligned myself to the Greater Dawn, to the arising of the Silver Wheel upon the Earth. I am guided by my oldest and most vast remembrance, the flame of a hope that knows no separation from the thousand dawns of Great Mystery's Love. I am guided into service and the authority of true Vision.

Hope: which of my hopes are the Greater Dawn arising within me? Which of my hopes are a guardian star, illuminating my world? We must learn to trust this Morning Star Gift, foster the pure essence, which indeed need not be hope *for* anything, yet simply the purified flame of hope itself, a radiant and soft-hued star which promises the blossoming of all true radiance throughout time and space.

Meditation of the Morning Star

You walk amongst the bare, silvery trees of the forest, where the buds are just swelling at the tips of the branches. On the forest floor there are celandines, snowdrops and wood anemones. Towards you from among the trees comes a reindeer with a star shining at her brow. She approaches you, and stretches out her nost to sniff at your hand. You feel her warm breath upon your skin, and you stroke her fur that is coarse and silky all at once. Side by side, you set off into the forest, and she is walking just slightly ahead of you, guiding the way. You realize as you travel that this is no ordinary forest; it is the Immortal Forest of the Earth, and an inner light glows within the trees. There is a sense of timelessness, and it is as though the forest is hung with stars. The reindeer leads the way as you go deeper and deeper into this enchanged realm, and you are overwhelmed by a sense of peace and beauty. Deep within the forest, you come to a Grove of White Trees, and at the base of each, an amethyst crystal lies in the moss. The reindeer crosses and cearing, and bows her antlered head. Somehow, you understand what she is indicating. You go over to one of the trees and kneel beside it. You peer into the amethyst that lies embedded in the moss. Within its depths shimmers the Twelfth Glyph. You raise your hand to mirror the sweep of the Glyph, in front of the tree, and you draw it into the forest air. As you draw the golden strokes of the Twelfth Glyph, you feel the symbol entering your heart and glowing golden throughout your whole being. You are transported...

You are on a plateau high in the mountains under a sky of stars. It is fiercely cold with a wild wind, and everything sparkles in a faded illumination of fierce purity. It is a sere and beautiful landscape, sculpted of wind and stone. The land-scape below is wreathed in mist, so that it seems you float alone under the sky on this rocky platform. Dancing at the centre of the plateau, with flowing graceful movements and gestures that you recognize deep within your soul, is a figure dressed in yellow and turquoise robes. She is singing the Song of the Sunrise. You walk slowly towards her, pulled into the mesmerizing, elemental magic that she invokes. She turns to you and smiles, her eyes blazing with warmth.

She lifts her arm to the skies, and points to a star that hangs above the horizon, 'There is the Morning Star. Will you dedicate your hope to the Morning Star, to the arising of the Golden Dawn upon the Earth?'

If you feel able to do so, dedicate your hope to the Morning Star, to the arising of the Golden Dawn upon Earth. See your hope as a pearly luminosity that glows within you and con-nects to the light of the Morning Star. You receive affirmation concerning your highest visions.

From the Morning Star descends an eagle feather, tumbling through the indigo skies, and landing at your brow, signifying your dedication to Higher Purpose. This is your daily commitment. You give yourself the chance to review the hopes that you hold, giving yourself time to let these pass before your mind's eye. Request the guidance of your Morning Star Hope: this is the one that shall lend you the great wings of the eagle.

Notice how your body feels when you feel true Hope. Notice the way that you light up from within, and feel warm and peaceful. Let yourself harness this feeling and recognize it as a quality of the present moment. Become a Hope Catcher. Allow the object of your hope to fall away, while the essence of the feeling remains. Let the pure feeling glow within you. Realize that at some level, that which you hope for is already happening, it already exists. You may be at peace about this. It is already a quality, a facet, of your present moment. You are at this moment lit up with the light of the Morning Star. You are the Morning Star bringing the gift of hope to the Earth. Hope is something we deeply need in our world of today, to bring balance to the negativity of despair. It is this light of Hope, this light of the Morning Star, that is being called forth within the deepest fabric of our daily lives. This is our awakening, this is the arising of the Greater Dawn upon the Earth. This is the arrival of the future into the present moment.

You know that the connection with the Morning Star is complete, and you feel your heart enfolding the pearly light of Hope within, carrying it as a precious gift throughout your day. Acknowledge that you now carry the eagle feather at your brow. You give thanks to the Turquoise Dancer, and find yourself transported back to the White Grove, with its amethyst crystals glowing at the base of the trees. You follow the reindeer out of the White Grove, returning through the forest to this world.

THIRTEENTH TEACHING

This is the Thirteenth Teaching of the Deerskin Book:

*I am shown the Milky Way: this river of
stars is your soul.*

*The New Earth is the forgotten Love Song of
this Interstellar Soul.*

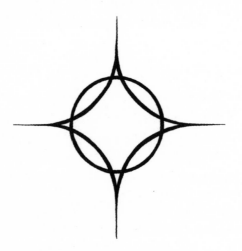

Chapter 13

Let this ceremony drum its way into the wind,
and you shall tell me another story.

W E CANNOT LIVE the dreams of others. We may want to; we may feel the nuances of their dreams, the beauty of their longing: but in the end this aspiration is a huge distraction. It brings us pain to control ourselves, to make ourselves what we are not. When we try to follow in the footsteps of another, we block for ourselves the uncharted path of Peace.

I do not know why we would wish for this, except for that we borrow from the blueprint around us: from that which is presented to us by our tribe and our family. From the earliest age we imbibe and absorb this blueprint, avid to attain its expression, to learn the rules of the world in which we have arrived. This has its usefulness, yet we are not an entirely empty slate to be written on. We must rather ask: what is it that we bring, what is it that we already know? Our learning needs to be the uncovering of this the Gift, and anything that enhances its full expression. Let us not choose a false self, a house of cards that is so easily blown down and destroyed, that causes us such anxiety to maintain because it is not supported by Divine Grace. This unsupported endeavour will always fail, it will always fall down upon itself, cave in under the pressure of its own untruth. It requires a mountain of effort and energy and will to maintain this foundation in existence. We may be applauded by others, but within us is always the unease of knowing its fragility.

What is stopping you from living your own true dream? For let me tell you that all the Angelic Elders and Ancient Guardians of the Universe are longing to see you step forth into the radiance of the Golden Dawn, bringing the precious codes that only you hold.

And so what makes us hesitate, what covers the echoing voice of our true dream? Are we to believe that there is some conspiracy against our souls, some vast and implacable force that wishes us to fail, that wishes our true voice to fade and be smothered? This is not the answer. The implacable force is only our own fear, coming close upon us as we touch the threshold of metamorphosis. It is this final threshold of which I speak, and the fear that can arise at this juncture. It becomes most acute at this final moment, and it can seem that having come so far, we are bound to fail at this last hurdle, so vivid is the conflict, so acute the confusion it can cause. What has shone before us, at moments a golden road, is now vanished.

* * *

For we must, at the last, lose our perspective. We cannot maintain this eagle-eyed view over our unfolding if we are to give fully of ourselves. At some moment comes the full immersion into that to which we have committed. At this point there is no turning back, there is no becoming what we were. We shall only ever be able to glimpse this over our shoulder, and all our descriptions of it shall have the quality of a vivid but half-remembered dream. And indeed, we shall never need fully to remember. We are not here to be the treasure house of our past illusions; we do not need to keep the map of the limitations we once placed upon ourselves. We are losing our reference points, there is a moment of disorientation. The world sits silver and quiet, incomprehensible. We are disengaged from all our interpretations. We cannot see the point in any pathway, either forward or backward. Yet we cannot linger in this place: it is not safe for mortals. The only way is forward, through the mists of the unknown, companionless. How far we have travelled, and to have come to this. We suspect, in this moment, that all our critics are correct. We discover that their voice of criticism was always our own. It is we who subscribe to belief in our limitations and our ultimate failure. Here it lies, like a dragon at the gate of transformation, seemingly unappeased by all our clarity, all our remembrance.

It looks at us with the cold and calculating eyes of all our self-doubt, and we do not know how we shall vanquish this final foe. Perhaps we have come too far, perhaps all the warning signs were correct. All the infinity of our dream fades away, and we are left with this. Still we breathe, still there is the space in which we are held. We wait and we watch. We look the dragon in the eye and ask, when shall this be over? The dragon does not answer, she is not interested in such questions. She gives no steerage to the moment, only sits there implacable, suffocating our senses. It seems the world has faded away altogether behind this veil, this encounter. All our sensitivity has vanished. There is only this dominating presence of our own shadow.

She whispers songs of failure and incapacity. We listen

and we watch, unable either to deny or affirm her words. We are under the spell of her presence; we cannot move or run away. This is the hour of confirmation. We know we shall not go back the way we have come – it is too late for that now, and we have had such glimpses. We have had such glimpses of something else. We cannot abandon ourselves now, and yet we seem to have come to a juncture of impossibility. What to do? We are paralysed, we are mesmerized. We face all our forgetfulness: it stands like a bulwark in front of us.

This is the Guardian at the gate of remembrance: she also keeps its secrets. It is she who keeps one realm shuttered from another, who makes the worlds appear separate, who divides us in a dance of opposites. Under her tutelage we are kept going back and forth between Love and fear, between one perspective and another.

I ask her: Who are you? She answers: 'I am your fear of the Golden Dawn, your fear of revealing the dreams that dance within your heart. You would rather dwell in the shadows and remain hidden, as you have been for so long.

'This restraint is causing you suffering and confusion, because it is part of your innermost nature to give this Gift. It is your nature to share and communicate through the Star of your Heart. As long as you conceal your Heart, you are prevented from expressing your fundamental nature. You are trembling in the shadow cast by your own Light, you are trembling with resistance to the Golden Dawn. Let your heart awaken and illuminate the path for others. You have so much fear of what will happen if you do this. You fear you will not be understood, that you shall be mocked and dismissed. You think that you have to receive some final affirmation, some reassurance before you share this

Divine Fountain. Yet it pours through you, and you are broken by your own resistance.

'Allow yourself to be a vessel, allow yourself to be filled. These are the golds and silvers of the inks of the Deerskin Book, with its white and burnished cover that has travelled through aeons. It is a Wheel of Silver Light, a Fountain of Love. It pours forth from unseen dimensions, giving itself into our hands with unconditional devotion. It holds nothing back, it offers all that it is. It is the Golden Essence of the Heart, and it dances from heart to heart, an Illumination. We see the timeless script and we recognize the Glyphs. We remember ourselves. It is an offering of our own evolution and true story upon Earth. It is a truth arriving to us on every wind, in every breath. It is there, if we wish to perceive it.'

* * *

This is the Thirteenth Teaching: that when we look up and see the river of stars that is our galaxy, the Milky Way, we are looking up at our own soul. This is the song of the Universe that is ours to sing. With every breath we can surrender to the magnificence of this song. This is in fact our sacred function in the world to which we have come, and this shall become ever more apparent to us, as we forgive ourselves, as we let our radiance forth.

When we join the Great Flow, then we know the Presence of the River of Stars within us. We shall let the radiance of worlds pour through us. The veils have had their hour, and it is passing. The world needs those who are willing to reveal themselves. The more of us that stand up, the easier it becomes for others. The supportive field blossoms. We are one another's coordinates: it is revealed through us. It is in the network of relationship that the Truth is discovered and maintained. We create the spaces for one another's Illumination.

This is the Unicorn Dance of Radiance: of freedom. We dance free of any categories or restraints, into the arms of Light itself, here to be held and guided, here to blossom and give that manual for a Sacred Creativity, that unchartered gift of the Light to one to another. We have the grace and the freedom to trust ourselves, we have the grace and the freedom to trust Vision and our hearts. We do not need a map to guide us, we do not need terms and conditions to give us permission.

This is the secret: that our dance of innocence, of joy, of our dreams fulfilled, brings so much joy to others. It is here that we discover that the liberation of one is the liberation of all. As we dance, others see us as themselves. And they are uplifted as they see their own Gift dancing before them. They see the ecstatic shape of their own creative vision coming into focus. This is the dance of our universal innocence, the Golden Dawn within us. We return always to this white fire of movement that is the beginning, the ecstatic flare of the beginning within us. We come again to our purity, our invulnerability, our Immortality. And this is the blueprint of the New Earth, dancing upon the background of infinite space; this is the way that she arises.

This is the white fire, the purity and softness of the Unicorn pacing towards us. She brings us freedom and innocence: the freedom of primordial movement, the advance in a banner of script, the Old Language spilling out, unselfconscious. We remember the simplicity of the ecstatic and primordial vision of our starlight nature. Let yourself be unbound, let yourself come into freedom of expression. This is gold dust, this is stardust, this is the alignment of Heaven and Earth, this is multidimensional wonder. It is so simple, it is so precious. The unicorn paces across this last mile, across the threshold of the Golden Dawn, carrying us irrevocably beyond the landscapes that we have known. She carries us into the land of dreams that have the power to become reality. This is the world of the powerful Dreamer, who is aligned to the elemental realms that give her visions, and to whom she is the Vision arriving. She is dreaming with the Earth, she is dreaming with others, she is a Universal Dreamer who has remembered the song of the stars pouring through her blood. She witnesses joy arising in this moment, out of the frost and the mist and the morning light. This is permission. This is irrevocable permission to go forward.

The unicorn does not wait to have her innocence proved. She knows herself, she lives in the Light of her own purity. This is what we can give above all else. We need to witness the Unicorn Dance in one another.

We know we are ready to give this Gift, no matter what comes. Our offering is unconditional. It is simply itself. It is a clear and pure offering, dancing forth from my hands to yours. Is this Gift too high, too pure for this world? We have lived with this myth for a long time. We wonder, what the relevance of Golden Love? But its relevance is total, its timeliness is timeless. We can be our Highest, the Unicorn of the Dawn pacing forth. This is Radiance Unbound.

* * *

This Book is called Silver Wheel because it is about the great progressions of stellar time that is the true story of our unfolding. This is where we belong: this is our essential nature. We have in the last era conceived a very restricted image of ourselves and our world, of the Earth and the Heavens. Arianrhod's message is one of restoration of our true context and evolvement, the full Wheel of the Silver Stars through which the progressions of our golden hearts unfold. It is about transformation, because this is the mirror in which we perceive and experience ourselves.

This is the restoration of our true spiritual history and context, and through the Silver Wheel of the Stars we reconnect to the Golden Hearts that lie beyond, to those of our Elders and Spiritual Guides. We receive the wisdom of our teachers. We need not be afraid of the beauty and generosity of this Gift: it lies beyond time and space in the Infinite Cycles of our Hearts.

Silver Wheel is the presentation of an ancient story and the invocation of our true nature. It is built of starlight, the vast perspective of the Shining Ones. We are asked to remember for ourselves who we are and to surrender the demons of fear and grief that distort the Mirror of Truth. This is the Mirror of the Stars, of Immortal Truth.

We are asked to understand the Earth as part of this vast Dance, and to be her dreamers, to dream with her in this hour of transformation. We are asked to be sensitive: to listen and to breathe. The Earth has understood us also, and she cherishes our intention: she cherishes those who have travelled with her, loyal down the aeons. She cherishes those who have devoted themselves to this aspect of universal evolution. There is little we are asked to do that is not wholly natural to us. We come to trust our own naturalness, our own desire and joy. Our sounding is never so far off as we believe, even through the veil of signs.

* * *

The Universe will always bring us the next portal of metamorphosis for which we are prepared. There is perfection in this. This does not mean that the guardian fears of our hearts won't rage at us, or that Divine Grace won't dazzle us and leave us breathless with wonder. These are the Great Powers of the Universe, of which we are a part. We can be prepared to feel to the depths and core of our being with extraordinary intensity. This is Awakening, this is Illumination.

We have to finish the work we have begun. We are impelled to play our part, to dance the Immortal Dance. We are directed and guided by unseen currents as powerful as any known physical force. We feel their pressure upon us, we know in which direction we are asked to travel.

This sensitivity is growing more and more accurate. It comes to the forefront, preceding the thinking process. You are accessing the perceptual current of reality with your conscious mind: you see your decisions woven out of starlight and ancient sunlight, arriving to you on the currents of this moment.

In speaking of this to one another, an elusive language is born that transcends old paradigms, acting as a vehicle for transpersonal experience. Lines of prejudice and ideology are shattered; at this level of communication we are freed from any cages, conditions or limits we have woven around our identity.

There shall be those amongst us who do not appear to wish to go forward at all; we cannot judge by our own starlight rhythms the appropriate unfolding of another. We do not understand the full constellation of their karmic conditions, but we can trust there is inner necessity, innocence and perfection to all.

It is long since the stars have heard from so many of us as are now awakening, long since they expected our contribution. There are vast ramifications to our awakening: how the smallest part we play extends so vastly outward from ourselves.

* * *

The Cedars are the mighty guardians of the Silver Wheel. They truly have borne witness to the records of Earth's past. They accord with galactic consciousness of the Milky Way, and all the nuances of wisdom that her star worlds hold. We are purified and raised to higher consciousness by the Cedar.

Breathe in the aroma, the incense of its star codes, its subtle messages. Breathe in the delicate and beautiful frequencies: the soft azure mist of its soul light. Feel yourself purify and brighten, their stems of ancient stardust, their messages filtering through. There is resinous loveliness, dispersal. Why, finally, do we come to this? Because the final step is the purity of our courage...

The immense girth of their softly grooved trunks ascends all around you. You are in one of the ancient cedar forests of the Earth, in the mountains. Sunlight is streaming through, misty and azure. Why, Ancient Ones, have you chosen the cedar forest?

This story ends in the cedar forest. Breathe in the ancient fragrance of its immortal purity. Here star souls come and go, passing in and out of incarnation. Here the Great Ones hold the rituals that connect to the subtle and wise voices of the Galactic Council, the whispering of a faraway intelligence that lights up the forest with a radiant peacefulness. Always these messages are filtering through.

Always you are receiving these messages of your interstellar soul. Learn to pick up the diamond messages. Learn to pass them on to others.

These feathered leaves are ready to spill the Infinity presence of our wisdom to us at any moment. The fragranced serenity, the deep peace and protection, the sheltered depths of the Cedar Forest.

The mosses cling to the mighty trunks, draped from their grooves, ingrown gowns that are soft and brilliant. Lichen hangs in beards from the lower branches. You walk through the temple spaces, the great rising archways. The feathered wings of the cedar branches sweep downward. Azure, the light floats through like mist. Ancient, sacrosanct, deep purity.

Your presence is awakening the ancient dormant codes, the sighs of dreamers that sleep within the trees. Crystalline codes of diamond brilliance are passing through you. The Ancient Ones are awakening. The Cedars are firing up once more with their ancient brilliance. They are once more becoming repositories of the galactic code. Their sapphire auras are building, the broken shield is being repaired. All the broken prayers, the eras of neglect. How we have abandoned this mosaic of interdimensional loveliness and its exquisite weavings. How we have torn wide open the subtle veils of the forest that cared for us all. How the forest aura must be restored, so that Planet Earth can hold us in a remembrance of who we truly are.

In some places, the elemental fabric of Earth is so broken that it is hard for it to clearly receive the galactic codes of the Golden Dawn. How can this be repaired? Through Love. Through the creative, immortal gestures of Love that come to us in sudden inspiration, we are repairing our beautiful elemental Earth. This is activation of the true, infinite creative power of the Golden Dawn. Thus the diamond radiance is pouring forth into the old golden realms of your heart, into the Earth, where much quiet beauty has hidden, awaiting this moment.

It is both so awesome and so simple, so extraordinary and so natural. It is the reclamation of our natural inheritance, not the assumption of new and supernatural powers. There is familiarity, recall. We feel that we are echoes, as though this is mapped in the etheric, and we follow rather than lead the trail. This has been the Path of the Deer through the forest throughout the aeons. These are the Lost Teachings of the Deerskin Book, charting the unchartered trail of Light within each of us. It is written in a language that shall shift to the touch of the one who reads. May it be the Gift of the Divine to yourself, showing you what only you know.

* * *

I stand in a forest of ancient cedars on the flanks of the mountainside. There are narrow rivulets of streams threading the forest floor, indentations carved into the bare earth amongst the fallen cedar boughs. I pass amongst the mighty trees wearing the sapphire robe of Earth's Seer, dwarfed.

I am following an elusive figure. There are flashes of an unearthly white between the trees, vanishing between the moss-clad trunks. I can feel a deepening magic about the presence, some deep purity that draws me ever onward. I see the swishing of a tail, and imprinted on the soft silt of the stream bed, a hoof print. There is a whinny and a snort of breath in the mountain air. I am summoned onward. There is the thud fall of hooves on the muffled ground of the forest. A longing like sorrow and joy all at once burns in my heart.

It is a call from another world. It has come before, this call, and almost seems to summon me from this world: as though I might step out of this life altogether. It glows with a diamond intensity, and feels like a returning home, and a leaving behind of all this that I have taken up, this long effort to write. And then, beyond the next cedar tree, its massive trunk and grooved branches, stands the unicorn. A cascade of forelock falls down her face, almost veiling her dark eyes. It is heart-stopping to come into her presence. I feel from her a purity that is ancient, immortal and wise. I am overcome by an intense and overwhelming sense of trust. I feel my whole spirit surrender to her wisdom.

'Why are you here?' I ask.

'I come to bring you a message. I want you to share this book with the world. It is time. It is time to remember that you were born to make the transmissions of the Deerskin Book. This is your innocence and your simplicity. You are gifted with the journey of discovering the unique dreams of a unique heart. It is in the depths of this heart that you shall find your way home. Honour the dreams that the starlight weaves within you, never disdain their path, and one day I shall carry you beyond, forever, into the Great Journey of the Stars.'

She begins to pace backwards, and vanishes into the viridian depth of the forest, leaving the atmosphere of her enchantment in her wake. The words, 'One day I shall carry you beyond, forever', reverberate intensely in my heart. I feel such profound longing to follow her. Part of my soul feels so very old. I know that this is my greatest challenge, not to succumb to the part of me that is tired with her long Earth travels, with the lifetimes that have led to this moment. I sink down to my knees on the forest floor, my head bowed under the giant cedars. To have the courage to finally share the Ancient Dream. To shake loose the veils of silence and confusion. It takes courage and a wild innocence to say these things, to speak of a Dawn of Love.

I notice that where the unicorn was standing, there is an indigo mist in the air, between the cedar trees. It does not diminish with the unicorn's departure, but rather becomes more distinct. I go to it, and reach my hand through it. My hand vanishes. I draw it back for a moment, and then step bodily through. I pass through the indigo mist, out of the cedar forest. I am standing surrounded by a Grove of White Trees, topped with a canopy of carnelian leaves, a floor of deep emerald moss beneath. At the foot of each white-stemmed tree is an amethyst crystal, and in each of the crystals, one of the Thirteen Glyphs flashes. This is the Temple of Arianrhod. Here it grows upon Earth once more. Behind me, beyond the trees, nothing can be seen but portals of indigo space, and the cedar forest beyond has vanished.

This precious, floating, intergalactic, Elven Temple. It can arrive anywhere, and be in multiple locations and dimensions all at once. It is a floating cosmic temple, and arrives with us at any moment. It has a special relationship with the Earth: it is witness and custodian to her Dream, to her ancient past and her future.

The carnelian leaves hang in a canopy over the Grove: elliptical and brilliant, they hang in clouds. Like a fire of sunrise gracing the white stems of the trees. It is a kind of tree seen nowhere else upon Earth. This grove was born in another galaxy, brought with its amethyst crystals as a gift to Earth. Between the trees stretch far distances of interstellar space. All Thirteen Symbols glimmer and shift in the amethyst crystals. One is never quite sure of their position, they seem to move around the circle.

Standing within the Temple of Arianrhod, I learn of the future that Earth has chosen, of that which she takes forward. Everything else is fading away, an old sunset vision, with all its loveliness and pain. Within this Temple, I learn that *we are the Angelic Elders of the Golden Dawn*. No matter our appearance, we are announcing ourselves. We are defined not by dazzling spiritual powers, nor by genetic bloodlines, nor by comprehensive knowledge, nor by age or gender, but by the visions we carry in our hearts, and the degree to which we are crafting these visions in this very moment.

This is the path of the Elder Heart: have you surrendered to your ancient innocence, to the living breath of your sensitivity and perception? Trust no other account. Make this your measure of truth. Do you hear the whisperings of the Dawn arising? Some do not believe in this; they only believe in an ending, in a fading away. You can choose to become aware of the infinite power of Love, working through its great eternities.

I learn of a galactic belonging. Earth is an intergalactic fragment, the original inspiration of many worlds, many dimensions. She has a vast crown: tier upon tier, Silver Wheel upon Silver Wheel, her affinities are endless.

I stand at the centre of the Temple Grove of Arianrhod. All thirteen Symbols flash and move around me in their amethyst crystals. These are the encodings of the Time Travellers, a nomadic script. They glow an intense silver, seemingly carved within the amethysts. As I stand at the centre, a figure steps through the indigo portal between the white trees. She comes towards me in her gown of softly flowing silvers. There is a silver crown at her brow, and her eyes are flashing sapphire, slanted in her silvery-pale skin.

'I am Arianrhod. I am the Guardian of this Grove. I travel between dimensions, enabling the survival of these precious codes of wisdom. They can never belong entirely to one world or another. They enable the star portals that you see to open up. The amethysts and the trees are gateposts of an inter-dimensional portal. Many shall come and go through these. They shall discover a fluidity between realms that enables the peoples of Earth to enter into an expanded perspective of wisdom, opening their hearts to further spheres of beauty and truth, dissolving the hard shell of materialism that has bound their spirits and separated their dreams from their reality.

'The peoples of Earth need to let go of the Earth that they have known. The Grove of Arianrhod is a temple between all worlds where this surrender can be made. The weight of the past must be released, the collective past that burdens Earth's Dreamers with forgetfulness. The nostalgia and the fear of change, of transformation, must be shed. At this point in the spiral of teachings, we step into the Unknown. We cease trying to preserve what has been. We take our trust to a deeper level than this: we surrender the idea that we know what is best for our beloved world, and let her make her own metamorphosis. At the level of Spirit, this surrender is essential, otherwise it is not a True Listening to which we have given ourselves. We allow for the metamorphosis, for the arrival of the New Earth.

'When you step from the Grove, you shall see the vision of the New Earth. When you step through the Indigo Portal, you shall step onto the ground of the New Earth, and see her all around you. It is time to give yourself this gift of vision, it is time for you to shrug off your uncertainty about what is possible.'

I step past the Ancient Star Goddess in her softly flowing silver robes. I step between the white trees with their overarching carnelian leaves, through the Indigo Portal. I am absorbed into the indigo sphere of formless, multi-dimensional energies. Then I am stepping forth from the indigo clouds that shred away, like scarves, from around me.

I stand on the side of a mountain, overlooking a wide landscape. I see small groups of Elders working with the people, tall Shining forms helping them to build dwellings in small gatherings. There are great auric fields emerging into the skies; the Earth's atmospheres rebuilding themselves as spiritual fields of Light. They billow up in diffuse rainbows of pale tones around the groups of people and Shining Ones. I see beautiful round dwellings with conical roofs being built. I see the realm as resplendent emerald, restored to its ancient brilliance: the Spirits of the Plants returning to this world. I see incoming souls arriving with great consciousness, maintaining a conscious link with their own angelic natures. I see the wreckage from the Last Age being salvaged, incorporated into the buildings of the present. I see the animals stalking the forest, restored to conscious mandalic communion with human beings. I see the bears, standing watch over the growing communities from the mountain forests. I see the lakes and the rivers filled with shimmering Water Spirits, chanting the fish back to their original homes. I see Earth becoming a planet dedicated to Higher Consciousness, and the great weight and cloud of all those who could not see the Light being washed away. Great blessings of compassion flow outwards to all these beings who chose not to reach out to the reality of the Greater Light. They shall once again become the ground of another world, even as the autumn leaf fall becomes the ground of the forest. Thus is all held within the mighty arms of the Universe. But it is Earth's time to shine once more, to become a beacon, a pearl in the Universe. And so according to the wild miracle of the Divine Order, it comes to pass.

As I stand on the mountainside, I see the trail of moonstones leading me on. There are eagles spiralling above me, in a blue sky. They are shedding their gold feathers, into the mountains. This is an ending, an offering to the winds. I have travelled so far, and still the feathers of Vision fall around me, until I realize that it is my own feathers going to the wind. I shall not hold onto all of this for very much longer. I have fulfilled my vow to write this story down. The words become an overshadowing canopy, woven by a thousand hands. It is an incense of eagle's breath, it is a prayer beyond love. It is heartfelt.

There is still so much to be discovered: I see the lavender of a thousand unwritten leaves. And when you read my words I don't want you to be limited to the confines of my heart, to be bounded by my vague and intricate dance, but to soar. Let this page be your wing, taking to skies and remembering freedom. What are we to one another, but each other's wing and dissolution, the unloosening of every ancient binding that has held us down? How indivisible we are as we come to this: the fine brush and whisper of antennae, the silk and breath of flight, the gentle search, feeling where the ground might disperse to its own endlessness.

Earth Meditation

You are walking in the forest. Towards you from among the trees comes a reindeer with a star shining at her brow. She approaches you, and stretches out her nose to sniff at your hand. You feel her warm breath upon your skin, and you stroke her fur that is coarse and silky all at once. Side by side, you set off into the forest, and she is walking just slightly ahead of you, guiding the way. You realize as you travel that this is no ordinary forest; it is the Immortal Forest of the Earth, and an inner light glows within the trees. There is a sense of timelessness, and it is as though the forest is hung with stars. The reindeer leads the way as you go deeper and deeper into this enchanged realm, and you are overwhelmed by a sense of peace and beauty. Deep within the forest, you come to a Grove of White Trees, and at the base of each, an amethyst crystal lies in the moss. The reindeer crosses the clearing, and bows her antlered head. Somehow, you understand what she is indicating. You go over to one of the trees and kneel beside it. You peer into the amethyst that lies embedded in the moss. Within its depths shimmers the Thirteenth Glyph. You raise your hand to mirror the sweep of the Glyph, in front of the tree, and you draw it into the forest air. As you draw the golden strokes of the Thirteenth Glyph, you feel the symbol entering you heart and glowing golden throughout your whole being. You are transported...

You are standing within the Silver Wheel of Arianrhod. Twelve Glyphs shine all around you within the silvery circumference of the Thirteenth. You are the Dreamer, you are the descending starlight of this Elder Wisdom.

You see the Earth, the ground beneath you, dissolving into infinite space. You are held within the mandala of the Silver Wheel and all Thirteen Glyphs, and you witness the Earth evaporating into a river of starlight. Know that this is the consciousness of Earth merging with intergalactic consciousness, letting go of everything that holds her apart, that keeps her separate. You let her go, you let go of every image of Earth that you are holding in your heart, every opinion about her, every feeling you hold for her. Let her go. Let her dissolve away. Let go of continent and ocean, river, mountain and forest. Let go of the flowing lava of her molten centre, of crystal and rock, of sands and skies. Let go of cloud and rain, snow and ice. Let go of autumn, winter, spring and summer and all their passing moods and weathers. Let go of the animals and the birds, insects and fishes. Let go of the human world and all of its creations, beautiful and less beautiful. Let go of the winds, of night and day, the passing of the seconds, minutes, hours of time. Let them all shatter and dissolve into the Galaxy of Stars, while you spin in the Silver Wheel of Arianrhod, contained by the glowing symbols.

Let the feelings that you have flow and pass through your heart: grief, rage, fear, regret, nostalgia, excitement and love. Let yourself feel the weight of aeons of earthy lifetimes, all that you have witnessed, all that you have devoted yourself to, all that you have loved and feared. Witness the dissolution of the elements of earth, air, fire and water that have woven this planet together in her complex dance. They dissolve into the vast river of the Milky Way. All is absorbed into the humming galactic star web. Let the Earth go free, and know that she is following her Dream.

When you are ready, acknowledge to yourself that the Earth has gone. She has vanished into the stars. All around you, the stars shine in mighty stillness. You are enshrined in the beauty of the Silver Wheel.

A shooting star travels to the edge of your silver periphery, and stops there, in a bright and shimmering flash that reverberates through the Silver Wheel. You gaze at it, and you see emerging from its brilliance a Queen dressed in soft silvers, a diadem at her brow, a noble face of many worlds, many realities. It is Arianrhod, ancient Star Goddess. She speaks to you in a musical voice of echoey depths.

'You have seen the Earth disappear. She is gone, absorbed back into the Great Song of the Stars. You have set her free by your activation of the Thirteen Glyphs of the Silver Wheel, and you stand as its centre, as its Dreamer. I have a message for you: you are the Dreamer of Earth. You are the Earth. You stand here as the Dawn of the Earth, as her new beginning. Tell me her Dream.'

Let this answer arise from the resonant depths of your being, from your very core. Let it arise and wash over you. Treasure this answer, say it aloud to Arianrhod, so that the Goddess may bear witness to this awakening.

As you answer, the Grove of White Trees begins to glow into existence around you once again. The ancient and beautiful forest stretches all around you. Your companion, the reindeer, stands at your side. The silvery voice of the Goddess comes echoing back through the Grove: thank you.

Breathe gently and deeply, and know that you have given a great gift. You have offered the Earth the freedom to dream herself within you, and you are a Great Light in this arising Dawn. The reindeer guides you through the forest, back to the world from whence you have come.

Acknowledgements

MOST OF ALL, I want to thank my shamanic teacher, Nancy 'Dancing Light' Sherwood who has been so utterly steadfast and always there for me. You have been a boundless inspirational Light to my soul.

I also wish to thank Pamela Gaunt, who in this lifetime led the way back to Avalon and saved my life with her compassion and wisdom. Faith Nolton, you have my thanks forever for opening the door to your cottage and revealing the world of the shamanic artist. Thank you Manda Clements, Ian Purkis and Cleo, for sanctuary. My love and thanks also to Anne and Terry Stevenson for a home and companionship. Thank you, William Marx, for chivalric and gentle support, and Veronique Cliquet and Mike Godsell for being the Guardians of Cwm Cych. David Cameron, for soul inspiration and wonderful food, and Oak Fairhurst for your friendship.

A special thanks to Anne Collins, star soul and dearest friend, for Vision far and true.

Thank you, darling sister, Rebecca Mcalpine, for being there.

Madeleine O'Shea, Clémence Jacquinet and Jessie Price of Head of Zeus, thank you so very much for your patience in bringing *Silver Wheel* into this world and for the loveliness you have given its final form.

And such thanks to Zara Kuchi, I can't tell you how grateful I am to you for travelling into the realm of the Elven Ones with me and bringing forth these beautiful illustrations.

Finally, my little family: Charles, my dear and beautiful husband, and Osian and Jasper, my two sons. I love you more than words can say. This book is woven of our footsteps across continents, following a path of intangible Light. Thank you for travelling the path of the dreamer by my side, for unutterable courage and happiness.